Religion in French Feminist Thought

'The French theorists discussed here, ambitious figures for many English-speaking academics, come into their own on questions of language and symbolic order, love and death, desire and political efficacy – the natural turf of the religious. This is an excellent collection of new essays on the important, but as yet under-explored, confluence of French feminist theory and religious thought.'
Janet Soskice, Reader in Philosophical Theology, University of Cambridge

Religion in French Feminist Thought: Critical Perspectives brings together in one volume some of the leading modern theological and religious responses to major French feminist writings on religion. It considers central figures such as Hélène Cixous, Julia Kristeva, Luce Irigaray and Catherine Clément, and with its focus on questions of divinity, subjectivity and ethics, provides an accessible introduction to an area of growing popularity and philosophical interest.

Illustrating the ways in which French feminist thought has become a valuable tool in feminist efforts to rethink religion, and responding to its promise as an intellectual resource for religious philosophy in the future, *Religion in French Feminist Thought* is ideal both for independent use and as a companion book to *French Feminists on Religion: A Reader* (Routledge, 2002).

Morny Joy is Professor of Religious Studies at the University of Calgary, and former President of the Canadian Society for the Study of Religion. She has published widely on feminism and religion. **Kathleen O'Grady** is a Research Associate at the Simone de Beauvoir Institute, Montréal, Québec, and the Director of Communications for t' . Canadian Women's Health Network. **Judith L. Poxon** is Lecturer in the Depart' ent of Humanities and Religious Studies at California State University, Sacramer and moderates the electronic discussion list french-feminism@lists.village.virgin' .edu on French feminist thought. Morny Joy, Kathleen O'Grady and Judith L. Poxon also co-edited the companion volume *French Feminists on Religion: A Reader*.

Religion in French Feminist Thought

Critical Perspectives

Edited by

Morny Joy, Kathleen O'Grady
and Judith L. Poxon
with an introduction by
Luce Irigaray

 Routledge
Taylor & Francis Group

LONDON AND NEW YORK

First published 2003
by Routledge
11 New Fetter Lane, London EC4P 4EE

Simultaneously published in the USA and Canada
by Routledge
29 West 35th Street, New York, NY 10001

Routledge is an imprint of the Taylor & Francis Group

Typeset in Bell Gothic and Perpetua by Graphicraft Limited, Hong Kong
Printed and bound in Great Britain by MPG Books Ltd, Bodmin

British Library Cataloguing in Publication Data
A catalogue record for this book is available from the British Library

Library of Congress Cataloging in Publication Data
Religion in French feminist thought : critical perspectives / edited by Morny Joy,
Kathleen O'Grady, and Judith L. Poxon ; introduced by Luce Irigaray.
    p. cm.
  Companion to: French feminists on religion.
  Includes bibliographical references and index.
    1. Feminism – Religious aspects. 2. Feminism – France. I. Joy, Morny.
II. O'Grady, Kathleen, 1967–   III. Poxon, Judith L., 1952–

  BL458 .R46 2003
  200'.82'0944–dc21   2002037049

ISBN 0–415–21535–8 (hbk)
ISBN 0–415–21536–6 (pbk)

Contents

Notes on Contributors

Ellen T. Armour is Associate Professor and Chair of the Religious Studies Department at Rhodes College, USA, where she currently holds the R. A. Webb Professorship in Religious Studies. She is the author of *Deconstruction, Feminist Theology, and the Problem of Difference: Subverting the Race/Gender Divide* (University of Chicago Press, 1999) and is co-editor for Theology for *Religious Studies Review*.

Charlotte A. Berkowitz is an independent scholar who received her PhD in English from the University of Houston, USA. She is currently working on a collection of essays, tentatively entitled *Torah as Maternal Relation: The Dream is One*, in which she applies the theories of Hélène Cixous and Julia Kristeva to the first five books of the Hebrew Bible.

Heidi Bostic is Assistant Professor of French at Michigan Technological University, USA. She has published articles and an interview on Luce Irigaray's thought, and is co-translator, with Stephen Pluhacek, of Irigaray's recent book *The Way of Love* (Continuum, 2002).

Sharon Gubbay Helfer has degrees in English and French literature and in Comparative Education from McGill University, Canada. She is currently teaching in the Religion Department and completing a doctorate in Judaic Studies at Concordia University, Canada.

Amy Hollywood is Professor of Religion in the Department of Religion at Dartmouth College, USA, and has written extensively on French feminism and religion. Her latest book is *Sensible Ecstasy: Mysticism, Sexual Difference, and the Demands of History* (University of Chicago Press, 2002).

Luce Irigaray is Directrice de recherche in Philosophy at the Centre National de la Recherche Scientifique, France. Her recent books include *Between East and West: From Singularity to Community* (Columbia University Press, 2002) and *The Way of Love* (Continuum, 2002), as well as an edited collection entitled *Le Souffle des femmes* (ACGF, 1996).

Grace M. Jantzen is Research Professor of Religion, Culture and Gender in the University of Manchester, UK. She is the author of many books and articles, most recently *Becoming Divine: Towards a Feminist Philosophy of Religion* (Manchester University Press, 1998) and *Power and Gender in Christian Mysticism* (Cambridge University Press, 1995). She is currently at work on a multi-volume project entitled *Death and the Displacement of Beauty.* She is a Quaker.

Morny Joy is Professor of Religious Studies at the University of Calgary, Canada. She has edited numerous collections on women and religion, including *French Feminists on Religion: A Reader* (Routledge, 2002), co-edited with Kathleen O'Grady and Judith L. Poxon. She is currently completing a book on Luce Irigaray, women and religion.

Mary L. Keller is currently an adjunct for the University of Wyoming and Northwest Community College and is based in Cody, Wyoming, USA. Her book *The Hammer and the Flute: Women, Power and Spirit Possession* (Johns Hopkins University Press, 2001) won the Best First Book in the History of Religions, 2002, from the American Academy of Religion. She is currently editing a collection of essays from a conference she organised at the University of Stirling, UK, *W. E. B. Du Bois and Frantz Fanon: Postcolonial Linkages and Trans Atlantic Receptions,* to be published by Mercer University Press.

Dawne McCance is Professor and Head of the Department of Religion at the University of Manitoba, Canada, and editor of *Mosaic: A Journal for the Interdisciplinary Study of Literature.* She has published extensively in critical theory, Continental philosophy and ethics; her most recent book is *The Hearing University: Derrida and the Institution of the Ear* (forthcoming).

Kathleen O'Grady is a Research Associate at the Simone de Beauvoir Institute, Montréal, Québec, and the Director of Communications at the Canadian Women's Health Network. She is the editor of *Sweet Secrets: Stories of Menstruation* (Sumach, 1997), with Paula Wansbrogh; *Bodies, Lives, Voices: Gender in Theology* (Sheffield Academic Press, 1998), with Ann Gilroy and Jan Gray; and *French Feminists on Religion: A Reader* (Routledge, 2002), with Morny Joy and Judith L. Poxon. Her most recent article is entitled 'The Menopause Wars', forthcoming (2003) in *Women's Studies Quarterly.*

Erika Ostrovsky is Professor Emerita of Contemporary French Literature at New York University, USA, as well as former Annual Professor of French at

NYU in Paris, France. She is author of *A Constant Journey: The Fiction of Monique Wittig* (Southern Illinois University Press, 1991), and is currently writing a study of the sacred in Nathalie Sarrautes's *Vous les entendez?*

Judith L. Poxon is Lecturer in the Department of Humanities and Religious Studies at California State University, Sacramento, USA. She is the editor of *French Feminists on Religion: A Reader* (Routledge, 2002), with Morny Joy and Kathleen O'Grady.

Martha J. Reineke is Professor of Religion in the Department of Philosophy and Religion, University of Northern Iowa, USA, and is the author of *Sacrificed Lives: Kristeva on Women and Violence* (Indiana University Press, 1997).

Sal Renshaw is Assistant Professor in the Departments of Philosophy and Gender Equality and Social Justice at Nipissing University, Canada. She is currently at work on a book on the divine in the work of Hélène Cixous.

Marie-Andrée Roy is Professor of Religious Studies in the Département des sciences religieuses, Université du Québec à Montréal, Canada. She has edited a special issue of the journal *Religiologiques* on the work of Luce Irigaray (Spring, 2000), and is the author of 'Les femmes, le féminisme et la religion', in *L'Étude de la religion au Québec. Bilan et prospective*, edited by Jean-Marc Larouche and Guy Ménard (Les Presses de l'Université Laval/Corporation canadienne des sciences religieuses, 2001).

Acknowledgements

A S WITH ANY SUCH UNDERTAKING, this book was made possible only with the co-operation and support of many people, and we would like to take this opportunity to thank those who have made this project a pleasure to complete.

We are indebted to our contributors, whose enthusiasm was matched only by their patience through the long process of bringing this book to life. Without their fine essays, this book would have been little more than a dream in the minds of its editors.

Many friends, colleagues and family members also deserve our heartfelt thanks and appreciation for their continued support.

Judith is grateful for the ongoing sustenance and appreciation of her family, including Rachel Poxon, Nancy Jim Poxon, and Terry Poxon. She has been energised throughout her work on this project by the love and enthusiasm of many friends and colleagues, including Mark David Wood, Philip C. Dimare, Janet Nelson, Patricia Warren, N. Robert Glass, David Gladstone and Robert C. Thomas. Finally, she would like to dedicate her own efforts in this endeavour to the memory of Charles E. Winquist (1944–2002), who inspired her to undertake the intellectual journey that made this work possible, and whose friendship and guidance were an invaluable part of her life.

Morny would like to thank John King for his constant encouragement and advice, and Cathy Brehaut and Marcus Pankiw for their assistance with her research. She is also grateful to the Social Sciences and Humanities Council of Canada for their support, in the form of a generous research grant.

A thousand daily kindnesses from family and friends made Kathleen's contribution possible. She is thankful for the unqualified support of her dear *conjoint*, Mebs Rehemtulla, and her loving family: Marlene O'Grady, Ron O'Grady,

Cindy Livesey and Christine O'Grady; and gracious friends: Mark Logan, Lee Tunstall, John Abraham, Meena Nallainathan, Harold Remus, Joe Artinger, Viveka von Rosen and Carolyn Saunders. Colleagues at the University of Ottawa, Institute of Women's Studies, made Kathleen's residency as 'Bank of Montréal Visiting Scholar' a pleasant and productive one; many thanks to Andrea Martinez, Naomi Goldenberg, Rubina Ramji, Margot Charbonneau and Hélène Boudreault for their generous hospitality.

We would also like to thank several individuals at Routledge for their continued support of this project, as well as for their invaluable assistance in bringing it to completion. We are grateful to Roger Thorp for his commitment to this volume during the early months of the editorial process, as well as to Julene Barnes for her help with the final stages. Clare Johnson has been a pleasure to work with throughout. We owe Liz O'Donnell a special debt of gratitude for her tireless work on our earlier project, *French Feminists on Religion: A Reader* (Routledge, 2002). We would especially like to thank Adrian Driscoll for his initial enthusiasm for this venture; without him, this book might not have come to be.

Finally, we would also like to express our special appreciation to Luce Irigaray for her regular correspondence and contribution to this project. Her continued exploration in the fields of philosophy, feminism and religious studies – controversial, but always invigorating and intrepid – is an inspiration for us all.

In Memory of Monique Wittig

Sadly, as this book was going to press, we learned of the sudden passing of Monique Wittig. Wittig died of heart failure, January 3rd, 2003, in Tucson, Arizona at the age of sixty-seven. Wittig had made Arizona her home since 1990, where she accepted the position of Professor of French, and later, Professor of Women's Studies, at the University of Arizona. Her obituary was carried by most of the leading French, Italian and English newspapers, where her significant contribution to literature, women's studies and lesbian culture was celebrated, and the loss of her person mourned. As a novelist, essayist, activist and academic, Wittig wrote of the possibility for real community between women – as true subjects and self-defined agents – and gave voice to the long-silenced vocabulary of lesbian love and desire.

Permissions

An earlier version of 'The Tower and the Chalice: Julia Kristeva and the Story of Santa Barbara', by Kathleen O'Grady, appeared in *Feminist Theology*, January

2002. It is reprinted by permission of the editors of *Feminist Theology*, and the publisher, Sheffield Academic Press, with the Continuum International Publishing Group.

Portions of 'Divining Differences: Irigaray and Religion', by Ellen T. Armour, appeared in 'Questions of Proximity: "Woman's Place" in Derrida and Irigaray', in *Hypatia*, January 1997. It is reprinted by permission of *Hypatia* and its publisher, Indiana University Press.

Editors' Introduction

SINCE THE LATE 1980s, French feminist thought has emerged as an increasingly significant interpretive tool in the theological and religious studies of the English-speaking world. In recognition of this fact, *Religion in French Feminist Thought* presents critical essays on French feminism by leading scholars in the field of religious studies. It assembles some of the most significant and provocative applications of French feminist theory to questions of religion, theology and ethics, in order to bring to the attention of a wider audience the critical reception of the religious thought of major French feminist thinkers Hélène Cixous, Luce Irigaray, Julia Kristeva, Catherine Clément and Monique Wittig.

The theoretical work of these thinkers has gained prominence across many disciplines and areas of interest within the anglophone world during the last twenty-five years. This work, informed by contemporary French philosophy and psycho-analytic theory – and thus best viewed within the context of post-structuralist and postmodernist thought – has not been without controversy. The allegiance of these theorists to feminism, and hence the attribution of the term 'French feminists' to them, has been questioned.[1] Their contribution to political forces for change has been challenged. Their implied lack of relevance for a radical realignment of religious structures and practices has led to their being neglected by many women scholars in religion. Yet they have been championed by others who see in their interrogation of the symbolic order – an order that has operated according to a male-centred modality in the Jewish and Christian West – a way to begin to introduce a viable feminine alternative. This book represents an investigation of those aspects of French feminist religious thought that have been most thoroughly attended to and developed by British, North American and Australian feminists in religion. It is both critical and constructive in assessing the impact of this work on contemporary explorations in the area of women and religion.

Luce Irigaray

Luce Irigaray has described three distinct yet related phases of her work (Hirsh and Olsen 1995). The first, beginning with *Speculum of the Other Woman* (1985a), is her critical reading of the Western philosophical and psychoanalytic traditions. The second concerns her creative explorations of alternative possibilities of subjectivity for women. The third phase is Irigaray's emphasis on a new form of ethical relationship that can exist between women and men, one that can emerge only once women have attained their own subjectivity. This 'ethics of sexual difference' is envisaged by Irigaray as based on a revised notion of gender difference between male and female, which she regards as the most important form of difference that is to be negotiated in our present age (Irigaray 1993a).

Religion has been of central significance in all these phases. In Irigaray's critical assessment of the Western metaphysical tradition, the figure of a transcendent God appears as an idealised projection of masculine identity. Irigaray regards such a superimposition as responsible for the repression of the primacy of the maternal, and for the absence of female genealogies. In contrast, she posits an alternative mode of 'becoming divine' for women. This is necessary for a gendered identity which does not subscribe to the hierarchies of the Western philosophical tradition. It is this process of becoming divine that Irigaray extends to her model of sexual difference. Here she proposes that her innovative mode of relationship of men and women can also be appreciated as divine. These 'religious' dimensions of Irigaray's work are further expanded in her more recent writings, which focus on the notions of spirit/breath as the elemental force of life. This is particularly evident in her interpretation of Eastern religious traditions, especially Hinduism.

A number of scholars have engaged with Irigaray's work from the perspective of religious studies – but often only with reference to specific books or topics that have a limited range in relation to her complete œuvre. Contemporary women scholars in religion are now taking the measure of Irigaray's work in retrospective analyses that examine the interrelationships among the different aspects of her work. They are also reflecting upon certain of her key assumptions, including sexual difference, the sensible transcendental, divinity and spirituality, in ways that are influenced by contemporary debates – such as those concerned with race and colonialism – which both engage with and put into question certain implications of Irigaray's work.

Marie-Andrée Roy introduces our consideration of Irigaray with a comprehensive overview in which she explores both the critical and the constructive movements in Irigaray's religious thought. She begins by rehearsing Irigaray's argument that women need to (re)conceive divinity in the feminine in order to found a specifically feminine subjectivity and to provide a basis for the sacralisation of female embodiment. As Roy sees it, this argument develops out of Irigaray's critique of the patriarchal legacy of Western religious and philosophical traditions, a legacy that has erased genuine sexual difference, left women divorced from their own (mother–daughter) genealogies, and produced widespread destruction of the natural world. Roy further expands upon Irigaray's well-known theorisation of sexual difference as paradigmatic of difference in itself, and, increasingly, as the privileged site of a corporeal spirituality enhanced, in Irigaray's view, by the cultivation of the breath. She is also careful to point out that Irigaray's forays into religious thought are not simply attempts to salvage a patriarchal religious past, but rest on the necessity of elaborating feminist redefinitions of key concepts and mythic elements, including virginity, chastity, the Annunciation, the Eucharist and, of course, God. Roy's essay is not, naturally, without its own critical moments. She acknowledges that Irigaray is susceptible to challenge on methodological grounds, and specifically comments on Irigaray's refusal of the conventions of scholarship; the blurring of generic boundaries in her writing; the lack of clear criteria for judgement in her valorisation of certain elements of Asian religious traditions; and the tendency to idealise 'woman'. She concludes, however, that Irigaray's revisioning of religion and spirituality provides an important resource for feminist scholars of religious studies, and one that will continue to inspire productive debate for years to come.

Ellen T. Armour's essay takes up Irigaray's notion of the sensible transcendental, an apparently oxymoronic trope that attempts to overcome the traditional Western division between transcendence (spirit or mind) and sensibility (body). Armour notes that Irigaray herself employs this trope as a means for effecting a sacralisation of material reality, and links it to her project of creating a space for women's becomings, resulting in a generally cool reading of the concept by her critics, who see it as too utopian. In contrast, Armour suggests that reading the sensible transcendental in light of Irigaray's explorations of the elements will result in a less utopian understanding, and might point a way beyond the theistic logic that Irigaray, in such key essays as 'Divine Women' (1993c: 57–72), arguably remains entrapped within. To demonstrate, Armour turns to Irigaray's reflections on the place of the element of air in the work of Heidegger. She offers a careful reading of key moments in Heidegger's thought, as taken up by Irigaray in *The Forgetting of Air in Martin Heidegger* (1999c), and argues that air provides for Irigaray a tangible example of materiality that transcends the limitations of embodiment without, for all that, being any less material. According to Armour, then, Irigaray's sensible transcendental emerges as an important resource for imagining both divine otherness and sexual difference beyond rigid separations between self and other, immanence and transcendence, human and God.

Judith L. Poxon returns to Irigaray's argument, in 'Divine Women', that women need a feminine divine to serve as the foundation for a specifically feminine subjectivity. Acknowledging the three phases of Irigaray's work (as described above), Poxon suggests that the constructive turn of Irigaray's second and third phases – as exemplified in the argument of 'Divine Women' – should provoke her readers to reconsider, with some suspicion, the deconstructive, critical moves of the first phase of her work. In Poxon's view, Irigaray's call for a specifically feminine subjectivity, grounded in and modelled on a feminine divinity, should perhaps alert us to moments in her earlier efforts in which she continues to work within the phallogocentric categories that she calls into question. Although Poxon rejects the reading of Irigaray as an essentialist, she explores Irigaray's theorisation of feminine corporeality – along with her claim that women need to give birth to a new feminine imaginary that would stand in isomorphic relation to that corporeality – in light of her recent call for a reconception of divinity in a feminine mode. She points out that Irigaray holds the body to be historically constructed in and by linguistic and social practices, and that the feminine body from which a feminine imaginary might be derived is not, for Irigaray, an empirical body, but rather an idealised construction that stands in metaphorical relation to 'real' female bodies. In light of these observations, Poxon argues that Irigaray's metaphorisation and idealisation of the female body reinvoke the phallocentric logic that she attempts to discredit. Further, according to Poxon, Irigaray's feminine metaphors can be seen, retrospectively, to foreshadow the limitation of difference that emerges in 'Divine Women' and other more recent writings. For Poxon, the question is whether Irigaray is able to articulate a theory of irreducible sexual difference *without* recuperating the multiplicity of actual differences (of race, class, or sexual preference, for example) within a logic of the Same. Moreover, it is precisely in Irigaray's religious thought that her readers must look for clues.

Morny Joy considers a more recent development in Irigaray's thought: her interest in various Asian religious traditions, particularly yoga and tantrism. After a brief discussion of Irigaray's religious thought in a Western context, Joy proceeds to evaluate Irigaray's claims about the importance of the feminine principle within Indian Hindu culture, showing how Irigaray's thinking about Hindu religious traditions is indebted to the work of scholars of myth and religion such as Mircea Eliade and Johann Bachofen, and arguing that this influence is problematically uncritical. What attracts Irigaray's attention about the traditions of yoga and tantrism, according to Joy, is the reverence for the feminine that Irigaray believes is demonstrated in those traditions, a reverence that Irigaray finds lacking in Western religious and philosophical thinking. Joy also traces Irigaray's interest in yogic exercises of breath control, noting that the cultivation of the breath represents, for Irigaray, a way of overcoming the binary oppositions – inside and outside, body and mind, sacred and profane – that plague Western thought. Joy is careful to point out, however, that Irigaray's writings on Asian religious traditions are undertaken not from a scholarly perspective, but rather from the relatively uncritical position of one who has begun to practise yoga herself. As a result, Irigaray's 'Eastern explorations' not only fail to acknowledge the readily apparent discrepancies between the elevated status of goddesses in mythic imagery and the oppression of actual women in contemporary Indian society, but also leave Irigaray vulnerable to charges of Orientalism.

In our final look at Irigaray's religious thought, Mary L. Keller returns to Irigaray's notion of the sensible transcendental in order to examine it through the lens of post-colonial theory. She argues that although the sensible transcendental can effect a productive intervention in the patriarchal legacy of the Christian West, its implicit grounding in distinctly Western understandings of religion and subjectivity renders it inapplicable to the study of other forms of religious subjectivity, including those essential to African tribal religions. After developing a 'genealogy' of Irigaray's concept by situating it in the multiple contexts from which it arises – particularly the work of de Beauvoir, Heidegger, Feuerbach and Levinas – Keller takes up the example of Nehanda, an important spiritual figure in the history of the Shona people of Africa, in order to demonstrate the limitations of a concept that, as is the case with Irigaray's sensible transcendental, relies so heavily on Western notions of autonomy and self-determination. She concludes that Irigaray's attempted undoing of the homogenous nature of Western subjectivity stops short of opening up that subjectivity to genuine otherness, as represented by the religious experiences of non-European peoples, and suggests that overcoming this failure will require moving beyond Irigaray's insistence on the priority of sexual difference as the privileged site of difference in itself.

Julia Kristeva

The body of work by Julia Kristeva is vast, spanning several decades, and covering a wide range of topics that have been of interest to feminist critics across the disciplines. Many feminist thinkers quickly embraced Kristeva's linguistic theory of 'poetic language' as a means to trace the hitherto unexamined semiotic (feminine) component of signification, as well as the inscription of the body (and its maternal origins) in all language use. Kristeva's popular theory of the subject-in-process further highlighted the illusion of mastery implicit in the normative (masculine) subject of texts and other cultural productions, and displaced this patriarchal illusion with a decentred subject of (the unconscious and bodily traces in) language. Her later focus on the relation between pre-Oedipal development and maternal abjection and maternal love brought another wave of critical appraisal, much of it searingly negative, as critics began to question her emphasis on the maternal semiotic as an inchoate and illogical dynamic posited against the logical force of the symbolic, paternal realm. However, others found this period of Kristeva's work fruitful since it provides a means for understanding the dynamics at work in the social construction of the human body – the ways in which society continues to play out on a grand scale each subject's earliest crises of separation and individuation from the body of the mother. Kristeva's work on love and abjection also provides the tools to unveil those cultural moments, frequent in religious texts and ceremonies, which attempt to efface the maternal debt in subject, linguistic and cultural creation. Her most recent writings, drawing on themes of estrangement, foreignness and exile, highlight an alterity at the base of subjectivity, granting a psychological dynamic to otherness as it is realised in ethics, politics, religion and artistic representation. Critics seem torn between situating Kristeva's work as theoretically sophisticated – unveiling primary motivations for transgression, excess and revolution in response to alterity – or as politically naïve and idealistic.

It has only been in the last decade or so, however, that scholars of religion have engaged Kristeva's writings in a thoughtful and detailed manner. This late arrival on the Kristevan scene has benefited from almost three decades of secondary source material by literary critics, psychoanalysts and linguists who have oscillated between tones of celebratory explication for Kristeva's theories (1970s and 1980s), followed by heated rejection (1980s and 1990s), and succeeded by a critical reappraisal of her corpus of work (late 1990s to the present). The latest assessment of Kristeva is the most mature and complex of the criticism to date, since critics no longer need to spend most of their time explaining the difficult and often dense passages of her theoretical texts, as did those of the first decade, and – taking into account the second decade of criticism, which brought with it charges of 'essentialism', 'Orientalism' and 'anti-feminism' – understand that there is no need to accept every aspect of her work indiscriminately.

Scholars of religion approaching Kristeva's writings in the last decade or so have been able, possibly more than other disciplines, to critically embrace Kristeva while developing their own theoretical discourse to diverse and specific ends – thanks, largely, to the difficult theoretical work completed by the literary critics before them. But religious studies scholars are, at least, a grateful bunch, and the writings on Kristeva in this volume collectively pay a warm tribute to the three decades of Kristevan criticism that have made their work possible. The essays that follow also make it clear that Kristeva's work has application for religious studies scholars with pragmatic feminist concerns (violence against women), as well as those interested in abstract theoretical construction (the creation of a feminine imaginary, the unravelling of a sacrificial discourse, the catharsis of a melancholic symbolic). If this volume is any indication, scholars of religion have only just begun to mine the depths of more than thirty-five years of Kristeva's work.

Kathleen O'Grady opens the section on Kristeva by demonstrating the tenacity with which critics outside the field of theology and religious studies refuse to engage with the religious dimensions and themes that regularly emerge in Kristeva's writings, viewing her interest in religion, primarily Catholic and Orthodox traditions, as suspect or symptomatic of a nostalgic, regressive or anti-feminist tendency in her work generally. O'Grady asserts that by truncating the religious dimension of Kristeva's writing, critics risk misunderstanding her theoretical agenda; critical neglect of these same writings on religion may also contribute to the difficulty many critics have when trying to establish Kristeva's personal relationship to both feminism and religion. O'Grady sketches Kristeva's biographical details to highlight the importance of the Orthodox faith as a potentially liberating counter-tradition in the context of the oppressively bureaucratic Communism of Kristeva's childhood in Bulgaria. O'Grady argues that although Kristeva is a self-avowed atheist, the religious texts and theological ideas of her youth nevertheless continue to exert a powerful influence on her work. To support this view, she turns to two of Kristeva's works of fiction, *The Old Man and the Wolves* (1994) and *Possessions* (1998), to highlight subtle references to a relatively obscure figure in Christian iconography, St Barbara. According to O'Grady, Kristeva's encrypted references to Barbara in her fictional works, as well as allusions in her theoretical texts, generate multiple readings: as reference to Kristeva's ambivalent but foundational relationship with her father, as emblem of the feminist struggle to forge an identity beyond that prescribed by the Law of the Father, and as fictional embodiment of Kristeva's 'subject-in-process'. Thus, O'Grady suggests, Kristeva's playful manipulation of the story of Barbara, dependent as it is on the patriarchal religious imagery of her Orthodox childhood, opens up a space within which feminine alterity might be heard.

Martha J. Reineke frames the opening of her discussion of Kristeva's work with an emphasis on pedagogy – 'Is psychoanalytic theory a constructive and helpful resource for feminism?' 'Does it lend itself to the feminist goals for social change?' 'How can we teach it?' 'Should we teach it?' – and, with the firm conviction that the psychoanalytic journey is worth taking for feminist scholars of religion, she unravels the link between Kristeva's psychoanalytic theory of sacrifice and sexually differentiated patterns of violence. However, Reineke is not content to situate herself at the level of theoretical discourse alone, and directs the Kristevan lens towards patterns of realised violence against women – specifically, violence promoted in particular sites of Jewish and Christian practice via abjection, defilement and sacrifice. She notes that detailed investigation of the sacrificial codes at the heart of these religions reveals a complex effacement of the crucial role of the maternal in subject and cultural formation – possibly even, in Kristeva's terms, a 'matricide' at the foundation of religious practice. This is not just violence at the imaginary level, as Reineke reminds us with historical examples of sixteenth- and seventeenth-century witch hunts. However, Reineke concludes her chapter by demonstrating that while Judaism and Christianity employ sacrificial logic in their texts and practices, they also offer a means to engage in 'non-sacrificial approaches to identify formation, maintenance, and transformation'. She further argues that understanding this 'other side' of religion offers promise for a feminist reappraisal of religious practice.

Grace M. Jantzen also takes up Kristeva's theory of sacrifice in order to demonstrate the extent to which Western culture is laden with symbolic structures of violence and death, with the crucified Christ as the epitome of this symbolic saturation. Jantzen notes that Kristevan theory elaborates the means by which it is women who represent death in our culture – ironically, perhaps, in light of the association between women and fecundity – permitting men to align themselves culturally with mastery over mortality. But Jantzen questions Kristeva's assertion that it is our early subject formation – our need to separate from our mothers to become individuals in the cultural realm – that initiates the logic of sacrifice and violence in the Western Symbolic. Kristeva argues that we are all founded on a 'matricide' since we must sacrifice the mother to guarantee the formation of the self. Jantzen, however, refuses this Kristevan formula: 'Not all separations are deaths; and not all deaths are murders.' Jantzen believes Kristeva's theoretical construct of the subject reinscribes the Western fixation on death and violence and contributes to its perpetuation and justification (giving it a 'natural', psychological base). Jantzen thus tackles Kristeva's theory of sacrifice in quite a different manner than Reineke, but both demonstrate its efficacy – and shortcomings – when studying the sexually differentiated patterns of violence evinced in religion. Jantzen does not disregard the importance of separation and individuation in subject formation, but she notes that this need not be understood in terms of death and violence, but as new life and nurturance. Jantzen concludes her chapter by signalling that we need to attend to the symbolic impact of birth rather than death as a strategy for creating a new imaginary construct that emphasises life and potentiality in place of violence and sacrifice.

Dawne McCance closes our consideration of Kristeva's religious thought by exploring Kristeva's work on depression and melancholia, raising the question of whether her writing, like postmodern criticism generally, engages in a kind of post-religious despair akin to the psychological phenomenon, melancholia. She studies the stylistic qualities of Kristeva's writing – her languid and lugubrious phrasing – and demonstrates how it may be aligned with Christian acedia, an ennui or ethical lethargy, a 'world-weariness'. McCance demonstrates that Kristeva's melancholic theorising is part of her larger project to practise a 'borderline writing' that opens itself up to the other of language. But this borderline writing cannot escape the religious idealisations of the West, McCance reveals; instead it perpetually revisits the grand metaphysical propositions of Western culture, but without ever reaching their promised transcendence. Kristeva, as the melancholic, pushes the boundaries of writing in such essays as 'Stabat Mater', which blends autobiography (in poetic form) with historical fact (in scholarly diction), resulting in 'an experiment in "writing-as-experience-of-limits"'. McCance notes that in this essay Kristeva provides an analysis of the maternal fantasy that undergirds Christianity – in the story of the Virgin Mary – while also incorporating the Christian drama of the Virgin into her recollections of her own childbirth experience. This is not so much an autobiographical gesture, McCance states, as a means to perform the drama through which each speaking subject comes into being as a processual subject of love. McCance situates Kristeva's dramatic re-enactment of the Virgin birth in the space of melancholia because, even while she engages with the discourse of Christianity, she nevertheless reveals the Virgin birth as a maternal fantasy that no longer provides transcendence. To make this point more forcefully, McCance turns to another important Kristevan text, 'Holbein's Dead Christ', and demonstrates that it too provides a dramatic critical moment where the transcendent properties of the Christian story collapse. With no other fantasy to replace the Christian mythos, McCance concludes, postmodern criticism attempts to write in the face of a post-Christian 'enigma or void'. Kristeva's borderline writing, then, walks the fine edge of melancholic grief, while it also opens itself to an important 'other' or 'outside of language'.

Hélène Cixous and Catherine Clément

Hélène Cixous has produced a wide variety of texts, encompassing a plurality of genres – novels, plays, essays – and of disciplines – feminist theory, philosophy, literary criticism. She is perhaps best known for her theoretical feminist works, written in the mid-1970s and translated into English during the 1980s; these include, most notably, 'The Laugh of the Medusa' (1980) and *The Newly Born Woman* (1986), co-written with Catherine Clément. Until now, however, the work of Hélène Cixous has largely been ignored by scholars of religious studies, an oversight that is especially surprising upon consideration of the frequent references to religious themes in her vast and varied œuvre. Cixous's work is unified by an abiding interest in the ways in which otherness is repressed in Western culture, and by the conviction that a certain practice of writing, *écriture féminine*, would facilitate the expression of that repressed otherness. In the context of these concerns, she makes frequent reference to a God distinct from the patriarchal God of Christianity and aligned, in her writing, with what she sees as a feminine economy, in which exchange occurs freely without thought of return.

Catherine Clément is a distinguished French writer whose work has been published in a variety of literary forms. Her work is not explicitly philosophical in nature, but she is often theoretically concerned with religious themes and practices, viewed mainly from a psychoanalytic perspective. Clément is not concerned with traditional religion and its dogmatic and repressive framework, but more with notions of the sacred – particularly as expressed in unorthodox experiences, for example, mysticism, trance, possession. She is fascinated, yet ambivalent, in her appreciation of these sacred manifestations as being at once perverse, even dangerous, yet potentially of therapeutic value.

Amy Hollywood's chapter undertakes a complex exploration of the psycho-analytically influenced investigations of mysticism in the thought of Cixous and Clément, beginning with their early elaborations in the jointly authored *The Newly Born Woman* (1986) of the relation of mysticism to hysteria and politics. Hollywood points out that Clément, although appreciative of the destructive creativity of both witches and hysterics, has reservations about the excessive desire involved and whether it can be politically efficacious. In contrast, Cixous links the mystics'/hysterics' unleashing of repressed desire with 'writing', and sees both as not only freely creative but also political. Hollywood then considers writings from the late 1980s and 1990s, where both theorists continue to be preoccupied with mysticism but now focus on death and mourning. For Cixous, in this period, 'writing' – and, by implication, mysticism – emerges as an act of mourning; that is, as a way of coming to terms with loss incurred by either death or injustice. Clément's interest in mysticism, on the other hand, now focuses on eccentric religious experiences – trance, ecstasy, states of possession – as possible modes of mourning, associated with women in many religions, that allow for a renegotiation with both loss and destructive forces, and a return to life. Hollywood concludes by suggesting that although both Cixous and Clément fail to resolve a number of crucial issues concerned with the manner in which life (desire, creativity, immortality) and death (mourning, loss, oblivion) can be integrated within a politicised understanding of mysticism, the interest of both thinkers in (w)rites of mourning points to the necessity of catharsis, particularly for women who need to mourn both religious and political losses.

Sal Renshaw focuses in her chapter on the religious thought – the 'thealogy' – of Hélène Cixous. She begins by considering Cixous's essay 'Sorties' (1986c), examining the ways in which Cixous's notions of the two economies, masculine and feminine, inform her thinking about love, and demonstrating that the feminine love envisaged by Cixous bears a startling, although perhaps unin-tended, resemblance to Christian agape. Renshaw then turns to *The Book of Promethea* – Cixous's lyrical and genre-transcending evocation of a mode of love possible between two women – to trace the development of Cixous's understanding of the relationship between human love and divinity. Here, sug-gests Renshaw, love engenders 'Paradise', seen by Cixous not as Eden but as 'subjectivity lived differently'. In this thoroughly embodied and earthly Para-dise, love approaches divinity by surrendering any desire to appropriate the other, but this is a reconfigured divinity, a divinity of 'self-dispossession' rather than self-sacrifice. Thus for Renshaw, Cixous offers not an Irigarayan call to conceive divinity in a feminine mode, but an exhortation to think divinity as an integral element of a radically new inter-subjectivity.

For Charlotte A. Berkowitz, Cixous's religious work is notable for its emphasis on the dreamlike quality of the language of biblical texts. This perspective allows Berkowitz, following Cixous, to argue for the possibility of reading the Torah in a way that gives voice to a feminine sensibility otherwise repressed by the patriarchal logic of the Hebraic Law of the Father-God. To support this claim, Berkowitz turns to Cixous's reading, in 'Sorties', of the biblical story of Eve and the apple, showing how, for Cixous, that story not only asserts but also undermines the power of divine law. Applying a dream-logic to the story, however, uncovers for Cixous and Berkowitz a metaphoric expression of the feminine economy that is based not on recuperation of otherness within the logic of the Same, but rather on an appreciation of otherness that allows for a 'liberating exchange'. Berkowitz then employs a Cixousian methodology to discover the same dream-logic in the stories of the creation of Eve and the encounter of Moses with the burning bush, showing in both cases how the patriarchal and paternal Law is underwritten and tempered by a feminine desire that 'keeps differences alive'.

Monique Wittig

It can safely be said that a long-standing tradition of self-conscious feminist criticism exists in the field of religious studies, spanning more than three decades and taking a variety of forms – not all in agreement. But this varied feminist 'canon' has largely ignored important critical works by lesbian French feminist writers who have much to offer the field. Just as French feminism has remained ghetto-ised in traditional religious studies, largely understood as a performance by women for women, so French lesbian writings have been generally cast to the sidelines by French feminist scholars of religion, and understood to have only a tangential bearing on the feminist revisioning of religious studies.

It is no coincidence, then, that it is not a scholar of religion but a literary critic, Erika Ostrovsky, who introduces us to the important religious dimensions of Monique Wittig's fictional and critical writings. As with many of her lesbian compatriots, Wittig's radical critique and reconstruction of traditional religious images, symbols, theologies and structures have gone untapped by scholars of religion. While proponents of the goddess movement of the 1980s and 1990s often cited her passage from *Les Guérillères* – 'There was a time when you were not a slave, remember that. . . . Make an effort to remember. Or failing that, invent' (1985: 89) – most religious studies scholars have largely ignored the recurrent emphasis on religious identity and subjectivity that has infused her work from the beginning. Ostrovsky provides an introductory survey and examination of the religious content and critique in several of Wittig's major works, demonstrating that these texts make a significant contribution towards a radical re-examination of Jewish and Christian religious structures by, in Wittig's own words, 'pulverising the old forms and formal conventions' to make way for the new (Wittig 1992: 69). Wittig's religious agenda is revolutionary, Ostrovsky argues, requiring a 'violent attack, subversion or overthrow of existing traditions' – albeit in textual form. Wittig mounts her radical critique of religion by adopting traditional literary genres, such as the novel, the dictionary and the epic spiritual quest, while saturating them with a highly refined literary *mélange* of fact, fantasy and theory. By shaking off the confines of genre, Wittig is then able to (re)invent a religious identity for women, by, for example, rewriting the Adam and Eve story from Genesis, or granting the Hebrew Song of Songs a lesbian inflection, or caricaturing Dante's *Divine Comedy* to her own comic advantage. Ostrovsky further demonstrates that Wittig employs a global syncretism by way of looking beyond Judaism and Christianity – drawing on a variety of goddess traditions to her own ends – as a means to create religion anew. After reading Ostrovsky's introductory foray into Wittig's work, it becomes evident that any comprehensive feminist critique of religious discourse must include the perspective of French lesbian writers, not simply as a strategy of *inclusion*, but as a means to understand fully the dynamic of *exclusion* that operates in traditional religious structures and in the study of religion itself.

Concluding comments

As these chapters demonstrate, then, French feminist thought on religion can be understood as both a critique and a (re)imagining of Western – and, to a lesser extent, non-Western – religious traditions. But it is important to reiterate that by no means has the reception of French feminist writing on religion been uniform. Scholars have varied in the ways in which they adopt French feminist writing on religion, and not all of their approaches are represented here. French feminist theory has been used as a means to defend traditional religious views, to rewrite or reform standard theologies, to reimagine the divine in radical new ways, or to reject religion outright. To make matters more confusing, some critics have also accused French feminist theory of endorsing a 'negative theology', providing a sympathetic defence of Christianity, advocating an atheistic spiritualism and vehemently repudiating orthodox theology.

What *is* clear, however, is that French feminist thinkers themselves have undertaken the tasks both of *critiquing* traditional religious structures and discourses and of *constructing* radical new modes of thinking about divinity and of the divine. Each thinker, to varying degrees, re-envisions religious structures in a process that is simultaneously *critical* (of that which has gone before) and *creative* (of what could be). Because this is the case, the combined œuvre of the major French feminists – Luce Irigaray, Julia Kristeva, Hélène Cixous, Catherine Clément and Monique Wittig – provides a rich source for feminist scholars of religious studies, including but certainly not limited to those whose essays are collected here. Thus it is the hope of the editors of this volume that these essays, in offering critical engagements with the French feminist theorists they address, will suggest new ways in which French feminist thought can become an increasingly valuable tool in feminist efforts to rethink religion and theology.

Note

1   We do not address the controversy surrounding the term 'French feminism' itself here, since it was addressed at length in our reader, *French Feminists on Religion* (Routledge, 2002), which acts as a sister publication to this anthology of critical essays (see specifically pp. 1–10 in the reader).

   We acknowledge that the thinkers assessed in this volume by no means represent the variety of thought present within feminism as it exists in the French-speaking world. The women studied in this anthology are not necessarily, as these essays suggest, 'feminist' (Cixous and Kristeva are hostile to the term, for example), nor even 'French' (Wittig was born in Germany, Kristeva is Bulgarian, Irigaray, Belgian, and Cixous has Algerian origins, though they all have resided in France and have written in French at various points in their career).

   The term 'French feminism', as used to demarcate the work of Cixous, Kristeva and Irigaray in particular, came to Anglo-academic circles in the late 1970s and 1980s, not as a part of the reality of the broad-based and varied feminist movement in France, but as a specific and concentrated brand of theoretical feminism promoted largely by the powerful Mouvement de libération des femmes (MLF). We continue to use this term here, not uncritically, to emphasise this circle of writers as they were taken up within Anglo-academic theoretical movements.

Luce Irigaray

Translated by Heidi Bostic

INTRODUCTION
On Old and New Tablets[1]

T O APPROACH THE RELIGIOUS DIMENSION requires passing from simple natural survival to a spiritual level. This supposes having energy at one's disposal and being capable of transforming it. This process always remains present, always in action, never realised. It is incumbent upon each man and woman to accomplish it. No one may carry it out for another. At times it is barely possible to open a path, to transmit an experience. But these paths or experiences may become laws or norms only at a very general level of social coexistence or a very elementary level of human being.

Is it then truly a matter of a religious sphere or of traces of a moment of the history of humanity in which religious authorities assumed the task of structuring civil society? Religious becoming, in our day, is situated on another level, it seems to me. And it is desirable that it should be so in order for the separation of the civil and the religious to allow a coexistence between cultures without hierarchy or wars between diverse traditions. Likewise, this distinction of domains is necessary in order to pursue a becoming of the human subject for whom the social, understood as a collective organisation, cannot have the last word. As indispensable as this dimension is, it is situated at a different level than the level which constantly gives rise to and supports the divine becoming of each man and woman. Let us say that this dimension would be rather, in the best of cases, an effect of a successful individual becoming.

To pursue human becoming to its divine fulfilment, such seems the spiritual task most adapted to our age. Not simply to submit to already established truths, dogmas and rites, but to search for the way of a human flourishing still to come. And to do this beyond enclosure within a single tradition that ends up making God the property of a religious community. It is the human as such, in a universal perspective, that we have to question today. How have women and men, here or elsewhere, yesterday or today, pursued their spiritual growth? Are the means that have marked out and propped up this growth still valid, now that we are discovering a panoramic view of the whole of humanity and its history? With what may we replace the religious practices of the past? And how have these practices shaped us, even without our knowing?

I To conserve and to create

Without any doubt our age corresponds to a time of cultural mutation. A simple religious regression cannot satisfy the necessities that present themselves to us, if only because of globalisation and the development of technologies. But a religious attitude requires not thoughtlessly critiquing, destroying or forgetting that which exists. Conserving, however, demands taking care of oneself, notably of one's body, particularly in moments of crisis and of mutation. The protection of life then prevails over the pursuit of more subtle tasks.

To safeguard life requires, for example, cultivating perceptions without claiming to reduce the spiritual to the mental. Listening to music – beginning with that of the voice of humans or with the song of birds – contemplating nature or a work of art, tasting flavourful foods, breathing in certain perfumes . . . can be spiritual gestures. They lead to concentration, to communication with the world, to gratitude and to beatitude. Not only do such gestures maintain life, but they make it pass imperceptibly from a natural existence to a spiritual existence, from the satisfaction of needs to the cultivation of a desire that is not satisfied with just consuming, annihilating by consuming.

To celebrate is another spiritual way of conserving: to celebrate through words, a song but also silent praise. To praise the fruits of the earth during a meal, the flowers encountered on the occasion of a walk, a beautiful landscape, is in a way a manner of praying.

To conserve becomes a spiritual gesture if it is not a matter of possessing but of respecting. To be sure, this gesture does not suffice. But constructing cannot take place to the detriment of what precedes us in nature or culture. The present and the future must not scorn what, in the past, was worthwhile.

The temporality of religious progress often appears difficult in the context of a tradition that is inclined to repeat, to submit to the already existing without elaborating a better future. But, without becoming, spiritual vitality is impossible. And, for example, it would be good to recognise in the present the positive contributions of the faithful instead of waiting for centuries to discover the gift that they have generously offered to the community.

II To become actively receptive

A behaviour that does not assure a continual passage from the objective to the subjective, a perpetual subjective becoming, cannot be considered religious. The question of the alternative between nature and grace, between activity and passivity, is, moreover, to be posed again here. The simple opposition between the two leads to an impasse. It seems rather that it is necessary to learn to be active in a way that does not prevent receptiveness to grace, to a qualitatively unpredictable gift. This can come from different sources or through diverse mediations: nature, another living being, a written document, a work of art, and so on.

The search for mediations that allow becoming between activity and passivity is vital. The same mediations do not necessarily suit each one, man or woman. It is important actively to seek those adapted to oneself: reading, music, walking in nature, collective ritual practice, silent in-gathering. . . . What counts is assuring a constant passage from an inanimate material to a living flesh, from a corporeal inertia to a body animated with intentions, from a conformity to a natural or cultural innateness or received practice to the transformation, transfiguration of these givens into means allowing natural and spiritual growth.

Each one must take charge of accomplishing the becoming of humanity, divine becoming, in oneself and for oneself, for others, for the evolution of History. Any form of conformity, of submission, of slavery is a non-religious gesture, in the sense that it paralyses becoming. For an adult human, obeying blindly does not correspond to a religious comportment except in certain moments of absolute disarray when giving up is the way to survival. In other times, the conquest of liberty linked to maturity and the autonomy that it allows are more favourable to a spiritual development. Not to venture towards them makes it difficult to measure oneself with the divine as a human dimension.

III To come back to oneself and open oneself to the other

The return to self is necessary in order to assess becoming. It is moreover indispensable for the respect of the other. And remaining dependent upon a Wholly Other, for example, does not seem a worthwhile religious ideal. In this way, I cannot consider the other as exterior to me with the goal of submitting him or her, more or less overtly, to a Wholly Other. The other, to be sure, must not merge with me, but rather participates in the elaboration of my interiority if our relation remains alive.

It is thus a matter of searching for compatibilities between personal becoming and the relation to others. Personal progress cannot be carried out to the detriment of the good of the other. But it would be good to go beyond this preoccupation, which is partly negative: not to do harm. It would be desirable that personal becoming accompany the becoming of the other. It is not for all that a question of falling back into a simply collective becoming. Becoming is rather to be sought actively in the relation with every other, while also preserving equilibrium between the active and the passive. Being able to give cannot exclude being able to receive. Progressing thanks to the concern that we have for the other presupposes that in our development we also take into account what the other brings to us. Such behaviour undoes genealogical, hierarchical rigidities: we are no longer parent or child, but in a reciprocal relation with the other. The spiritualities that we already know have not stressed this relational aspect, which is nevertheless decisive for the progress of humanity. This deficiency is partly explained by recourse to a unique vertical transcendence annulling differences between human subjectivities.

IV Vertical transcendence and horizontal transcendence

By measuring every subjectivity in relation to a Wholly Other, our tradition has underestimated the importance of the alterity of the other with whom I enter into relation every day. Respect for the other as such corresponds to an ethical task that supports my spiritual becoming.

This task is both ideal and concrete. It solicits my personal initiative on this side and beyond duties defined outside the context of their application. At each instant, it imposes the consideration of the other's transcendence, thus the acceptance of the limit of my knowledge and of my feeling in regard to what he, or she, is. This leads to the respect of a mystery that escapes my grasp without for all that belonging to the world of the beyond.

Indispensable for assisting human prematurity, bonds of genealogy do not lead the human to his or her accomplishment, except perhaps partially through a grateful attitude. But humanity is far from having reached its maturity. The instincts tied to belonging to a family or to a social group still often are close to those of the animal world. Only the assumption of a natural identity in a cultural comportment, escaping instinct – including that of domination and possession – can really be distinguished from them. How not to think here of sexuate identity serving, thanks to the difference it implies, to create thought and culture beyond any appropriation tied to instinct?

But separation from the animal world does not go without saying. And protests against the existence of an insurmountable yet fecund difference between the sexes often signify a reticence with regard to the cultural effort that this difference imposes. This effort results from the respect of a transcendence that the models inspired by the same, the similar, the identical, the equal, have neglected, models the purpose of which is to make us forget this respect. To be or to become the same, to think starting from a tautology, conceals the place where a civilisation is elaborated through taking account of difference(s). And how not to worry in the face of the current relentless denial of the key role of difference, for thought as well as in our daily behaviour towards the other, towards others.

V The religious is that which binds

The religious is the gesture that binds earth and sky, in us and outside of us. That cultivates the terrestrial so that it does not harm the celestial and that venerates the celestial in such a way that it does not destroy the terrestrial. This requires a knowledge and a cultivation of energy that allows using it with a view to the harmony of the whole and not in favour of one part to the detriment of the whole. So a technique benefiting certain aspects of life or certain living beings without regard for others infringes on the religious order. It is the same for a spirituality that harms the body.

To bind demands finding the way that supports the whole of what is, making it grow and flourish. Sacrificing the earth to the sky, the body to the spirit, does not accomplish the gesture of binding them together. It is the same way in relations between us. Any relation that does not correspond to establishing a link between the one and the other does not seem to obey the exigencies of the religious.

The most religious rapport between us is that in which the bond is reciprocal in the present, and which conserves life and promotes becoming for each one. As such, the horizontal alliance appears as a more accomplished religious gesture than the parental or filial attitude. To be sure, in so far as this attitude surmounts natural inertia or even attraction, it is already a spiritual gesture. But it does not permit reciprocity in the present. In this sense, it seems less perfect than the horizontal bond between persons.

Particularly accomplished is the gesture that succeeds in passing from – without for all that destroying – a vertical transcendence linked to genealogy, to a horizontal transcendence linked to a difference, both natural and cultural, between subjects. It is nevertheless not a question of scorning or neglecting filial duties, but of understanding that they do not represent the most accomplished relation between humans. They represent a stage of this relation, but not the most perfect one. To pass beyond this stage, without stopping there, without identifying with parental roles, including in domains other than genealogy in the strict sense, seems indispensable in order to continue human becoming.

VI To pray, yes, but how?

Prayer should be part of daily activity. Its forms may be multiple. First, it presents itself as individual or collective. It would be good to practise both each day. Personal prayer, in any case, is a daily necessity. To say it briefly, personal prayer corresponds to an active search for in-gathering. This may be a posture of the body that makes the spirit attentive, but also a reading, the writing of a text, a drawing, or even a more or less ritual chant or recitation. Each one must discover the way of praying adapted to each day. Sometimes the accent will be placed on repetition aiming to maintain faithfulness, sometimes on a creation clearing ways for becoming. To accomplish an activity with more concentration or a more spiritual intention also corresponds to a prayer.

As for collective prayer, it may consist in a particularly attentive and meditative encounter with another person. It must not be understood only with relation to a group given over to ritual activity. Prayer then serves the cohesion of a community more than an individual spiritual becoming. But this cohesion cannot be substituted for or opposed to individual becoming, nor can it impede the becoming of the singular relation between the members of the collectivity. To reduce all men and women of a community to one individual subjected to the same laws and to the same rites does not seem very religious. Except in a perspective that is more political, or even integrationist, than concerned with the spiritual becoming of humanity.

VII To pardon liberates energy

Can vengeance be a religious sentiment? It breaks bonds rather than establishing them. It turns them into darkness rather than into light of the heart, of the soul. The other is always present, in a sense, but not as a vector of a future becoming, except as the fulfilment of a vengeance. This goal preoccupies the spirit, makes it unavailable for becoming and for any form of grace. Founded upon *ressentiment* and hatred, it perhaps arouses a certain energy. But, fastened upon its objective, this energy cannot be transformed as such and it does not serve life, natural or spiritual. The more it grows, the more it becomes destructive, on the contrary.

Even for one who has suffered a harm, it is preferable to find a way that avoids vengeance and that liberates in this way energy for more fulfilling pursuits. It is not for all that a matter of falling into masochism, a bond that is satisfied with wounding, or even seeks a torturer. It is fitting rather to liberate oneself from the obsession with the evil suffered and, asking if we have some responsibility in this harm, to find out how to avoid it in the future but also how to appease in us this suffering without satisfying ourselves with hatred and vengeance.

The solution is not always easy to discover but its pursuit is certainly more positive than that for the means to avenge oneself. Detachment from the offender is already a way of distancing oneself from evil instead of revelling in it. This is not yet truly forgiveness. But at least the liberation from *ressentiment* and the preparing to grant forgiveness, in one way or another, in particular if the offender asks for it.

Granting forgiveness too quickly risks being an artificial gesture, beyond our strength, a paternalist or maternalist gesture of one who believes himself or herself superior, somehow out of reach. It is better to accept one's vulnerability, one's sufferings, to seek the means and take the time to find again one's autonomy, one's integrity. The will to avenge oneself uses up the energy indispensable for such a task. Now this task has priority for one's proper spiritual progress. Which necessitates sometimes that we ask forgiveness of ourselves for all of the mistakes that we commit and that do us harm.

VIII Become who you are: eternal life is in you[2]

The religious, in my opinion, must correspond to a way of accomplishment of the human both as a gathering of self in oneself and as a bond with the universe and the other. It seems that only two aspects of this sense of the word 'religious' have been privileged:

1   the fact that the gathering of self would result in exclusive dependence upon a Wholly Other, a God foreign to our nature: supernatural with respect to humanity. The gathering of ourselves in us is carried out also through other means and, for want of considering them, the relation to that which is designated by the name of God risks being paralysing for human becoming, while it should rather constitute an aid for this becoming in all of its stages.
2   the fact that the bond with the other is understood as a gathering in a group, a religious community or family rather than as a relation with the other as such.

The privileging of these two interpretations has paralysed becoming, notably (1) by preventing the experience of the rapport between the transcendence of the other respected in his or her difference, particularly sexual, and that of a Wholly Other supposed to be super-natural, and (2) by hindering the process of differentiation of the individual through a more or less passive belonging to a religious family or group.

So a certain conception of the religious has left human beings in a status inferior to their own nature, has deprived them of a spiritual and divine becoming of which they are capable.

Is it necessary to interpret such a paradox as the symptom of a historical evolution still to be perfected? As the fact that a religious power has substituted itself, deliberately or not, for a free development of the subject towards its accomplishment? As the effect of a permanent fossilisation of the subjective in an objective, which, imposing itself as a norm, paralyses becoming? As the difficulty in gathering oneself and entering into relation with the other starting from this synthesis, always to be achieved, of self? These hypotheses, and still others, are possible. Thus the non-consideration of the value of difference, in particular sexual difference, between us for the becoming of each man, each woman. Difference as such is unthinkable but the effects, including transcendental ones, that it produces must be taken into account for the spiritual progress of humanity. The consideration of the difference between us imposes a real conversion in the mode of thinking, of acting. But is it not to a gesture of this type that the accomplishment of the human constrains us?

The religious aspect of our becoming has not been considered enough as a way to achieve a greater perfection of our humanity. Human identity and divine identity have been artificially separated. And we generally fail to recognise that becoming divine corresponds to becoming perfectly human. Split between the one and the other, we have lost the path of the one and of the other. And we have fallen back under the control of supposedly all-knowing spiritual fathers, without making a return to ourselves in order to ask questions about what makes us progress spiritually, or prevents us from doing so. Too exclusively trusting the other, we then lose the gathering, in us and with us, which is indispensable to spiritual growth. How, in fact, to pursue this growth, if our energy is divided in two parts, human and divine, without a possible continuity between them? If we cannot transform our energy, from the most elemental natural energy to the most subtle spiritual energy, without there being strangeness, opposition, or even hostility between the two? If we cannot ourselves work to cultivate our breath, our gestures, our words in order to guide our becoming towards more wisdom, fluidity, communication with the other? If we are submitted to objective criteria of perfection controlled by others and whose benefit and positive effect we cannot value through a subjective experience?

How could we imagine, moreover, a divinity hostile to our humanity and not a model for its flourishing? What would a God opposed to the accomplishment of our flesh be? A tyrant-God who would wish us to be his stunted slaves? Would he be then anything other than a projection of our difficulties in thinking perfection and in living it? Unfortunately, this God, amputated from the completeness of the human himself, is often preached to us and has kept too many of his faithful away from a becoming of which they were capable. Fruit of an infirm and injured imagination, he led us in the direction opposite to the desirable path. For all that, to spend our existence in *ressentiment* solves nothing. It is more worth while to dare exploring new ways and to take charge ourselves of our humanity until its perfect realisation, without arrogance but with confidence and a certain audacity. These are always necessary in order to overcome past and present inertias, in order to open horizons that are still closed, in order to discover pieces of earth and sky that are still overshadowed by our failures to understand, our fears, our errors. To be sure, this cannot be accomplished in one day. And some flashes of lightning demand in the end a long patience in order to be incarnated. But how to make progress possible? Without claiming to enumerate them all, I have proposed some means useful in daily life.

Notes

1   This is also the title of the Third Part of Friedrich Nietzsche's *Thus Spoke Zarathustra*. [Tr.]
2   This section title alludes to the subtitle of Nietzsche's *Ecce Homo*, 'How One Becomes What One Is'. [Tr.]

PART ONE

On Luce Irigaray

Chapter 1

Marie-Andrée Roy

Translated by Sharon Gubbay Helfer[1]

WOMEN AND SPIRITUALITY IN THE WRITINGS OF LUCE IRIGARAY[2]

A SET OF THEMES having to do with spirituality punctuates Luce Irigaray's writings and contributes to the originality of her body of work. In what follows I review some of the elements that anchor this set of themes, starting with her major work, *Sexes et parentés*, published in 1987 (and in English in 1993, as *Sexes and Genealogies*), up to her most recent writings, *Entre Orient et Occident* (in English in 2002, as *Between East and West*) and *The Age of the Breath*, originally published in German and English in 1999.

The French philosopher and psychoanalyst has charted a singular course in the margins of the academic milieux with which she none the less carries on a lively dialogue internationally, in particular with European and North American intellectuals. This dialogue, in essence, centres on the content of Irigaray's work, which is discussed and reviewed. The scope of the debate is best appreciated in the context of the aims Irigaray has in view. These include not only to contribute to the development of feminist thought but also to 'elaborate a culture having two subjects respectful of each other's differences, a model for coexistence amidst diversity at the universal level' (Irigaray 1999b: back cover). Irigaray has undertaken to make this cultural model known and understood so as to give it the best possible exposure. In this she is pursuing a goal that is transformative and foundational for society and culture. The model emerges both from her theoretical work and from her lived experience. Her knowledge has its sources in texts and also in a reflexive turn back to the experience from which she draws her critique of contemporary culture and her vision for the future.

For the purposes of this chapter, I begin with a brief review of the question of God, as posed by Irigaray, and then turn to an investigation of two foundational elements of her thought on spirituality: her critique of the patri-archal system and her model of sexual difference. Next, I examine three ways in which the spirituality that marks out her texts is developed: the affirmation of female genealogies, the redefinition of traditional religious concepts and the development of a culture of the breath. I conclude with a few considerations suggested to me by the readership and reception of Irigaray's œuvre.

I Foundations

In her text 'Divine Women', published in *Sexes and Genealogies*, Irigaray poses the question of God. She maintains that we need a God, a mirror, a guarantor of the infinite,[3] in order to posit our gender, to become, which means 'fulfilling the wholeness of what we are capable of being' (Irigaray 1993c: 61). Man has benefited from God's help in defining his gender but women have been arrested in their divine becoming. In Christian culture, Mary becomes divine through her son. There is no *woman* God, nor a female trinity that would express the perfec-tion of female subjectivity. This has many consequences. It leaves the female becoming in gestation, without a true goal, without the possibility of attaining complete fulfilment, or it encloses 'the infinite of becoming a woman [. . .] in the role of mother through whom the *son* of God is made flesh' (Irigaray 1993c: 62). This has the further effect of hampering communication and communion among women. To counter these effects, we would need to be able to imagine a *woman* God, a God who would express the perfection of our subjectivity, who would open us up to the transfiguration of our flesh. For Irigaray, only the religious is 'fundamental enough to allow us to discover, affirm, achieve certain *ends*', to allow us definitively to love each other, to want ourselves and to lead us to freedom (Irigaray 1993c: 67). Without this we remain powerless, subject to the impositions of the (male) other, because we lack a goal for ourselves. It is essential, she argues, rereading Feuerbach, 'that we be God *for ourselves* so that we can be divine for the other, not idols, fetishes' (Irigaray 1993c: 71).

In Irigaray's view, in the beginning,[4] women's experience was different than it is today and the portrait she gives us of this period is close to being idyllic. Women had access to divine truth, transmitted from mother to daughter. The divine was rooted in the fertility of the earth and realised in its flowers and fruits. There was no disjunction between 'human and divine, body and mind, the natural and the spiritual. During those times love was respected in its corporeal manifestations, female fecundity took place both in and outside of marriage, and the public weal was the norm' (Irigaray 1994: 65). This vision of the past brings together all the components of spirituality as Irigaray understands them: transmission from mother to daughter, articulation of divinity together with the fertility of the earth, its flowers and fruits, absence of a rupture between the divine and the human, body and spirit, the corporeal dimension of love and social harmony. It is possible, Irigaray believes, to retrieve this spirituality as part of a culture where sexual difference is given due place.

If we wish to understand the feminist philosopher's thought, we can surely not neglect an examination of two of the central pillars that support it: her critique of the patriarchal system and her theory of sexual difference. These pillars are all the more important since they are solidly anchored within the whole of her intellectual project, even as they find specific applications in her thinking about spirituality and religion.

Irigaray's critique of the patriarchal system

In Irigaray's view, we are living in a patriarchal order that dominates and exploits the earth and abuses creation. The patriarchal domination of man over nature affects relationships between men and women. The 'removing of woman from herself originates in man's domination over nature – micro- or macrocosmic –, as we can read . . . in the tragedy of *Antigone* by Sophocles' (Irigaray 1999a: 11). Irigaray argues that the passage to patriarchy took place when the honouring of blood ties with the mother was outlawed, as it was when Antigone wanted to bury her brother (Irigaray 1993c: 2). Women do not belong to themselves, so they cannot construct themselves as subject. Their genealogy is constantly obscured. Even though men and women issue from two genealogies (father–son and mother–daughter), in practice they live in exclusively masculine genealogical systems. Patriarchy submits one to the other with all the alienating consequences that this entails, both for female becoming and for relations between the sexes.

Irigaray argues notably that 'the Oedipal structure . . . doesn't symbolise the woman's relation to her mother' (Irigaray 1993b: 16). Women are cut off from this type of image, even though they need it to affirm their identity. Patriarchal domination is further expressed through domination of the cosmic world by an all-powerful God the Father and Son. This obscures the ancient paired goddesses of Mother and Daughter, protectors of the earth's fertility. Male gods came to appropriate the oracle of truth, thus cutting humans off from their earthly and corporeal roots. Next followed a new logical order and the censure of women's speech. This censure became all the more efficient because, within the patriarchal linguistic order, the feminine is understood as a negative of the masculine, 'an abstract nonexistent reality' (Irigaray 1993b: 20). When they are denied by the linguistic order, women cannot easily carry on a comprehensible, coherent discourse.

Irigaray makes this point clearly on a number of occasions: because the exploitation of women is founded on sexual difference, it must be resolved through sexual difference. She therefore proposes the elaboration of a culture of the sexual, in which not equality but difference is sought. We turn now to an examination of this proposition.

Difference between the sexes

For Irigaray, the difference between man and woman is the paradigm for all other differences. Sexual difference, then, is the foundation of alterity and of spiritual experience. Each sex has a specific mode through which it constitutes its subjectivity and from which flows a different relational attitude. Let us see what Irigaray says about each of the sexes.

From birth, woman has a pronounced taste for the relational, for relationships with other subjects and with nature. Because woman is born of woman, she is in a better position to develop her own subjectivity and relationships of inter-subjectivity. She is capable of engendering difference within herself. Dialogue for her is a matter of course. She uses language to communicate. Her discourse names the concrete qualities of things and of places. It is a sexualised, experience-based discourse that leaves the conceptualisation of the world to the other because, in practice, languages do not give woman the means to organise her experience of the world. She has qualities that are particular to her (*qualités propres*), such as the 'concern for the sensible, for concrete and natural environments, for intersubjectivity, for relationships with the other gender, with the future and with being and doing together, in particular as two' (Irigaray 1996b: 197). She is called upon to preserve these particular qualities that are understood as the sites of her humanity. Woman seeks relationship to the other but in this she risks effacing herself through attraction to the other. She must learn to find her own speech and to be faithful to it. She must also learn not to renounce herself in order not to destroy the *two* that is the essential condition of relationship. She is in greater harmony with the cosmos and her consciousness is more spiritually elevated. Even though she has an 'ability to perceive the divine', she does not have access to signs that would designate a reality transcendent to her, the Other, the divine (Irigaray 1993a: 115). The uses of money can often be problematic for her and this is why Irigaray thinks that '[a]n exchange of the products of the earth, the fruits of labour, would be more appropriate to the female gender and world' (Irigaray 1996b: 194).

Man creates a world for himself using tools, laws, gods. This is often a world of the past. In male culture, the object is preferred over the relationship between subjects, the constructed over the natural. Man seeks to have others bend to his world order and uses language to conquer. The discourse of men is characterised as being fundamentally hermetic because it proceeds from rules that sever indi-viduals from their perceptions of reality, resulting in a discourse of specialists. This discourse designates the world as abstract, inanimate, unconnected to life. Caught between subjective reality and this truncated language, individuals abandon the right to a personal appreciation and fall in line with those who know.

Some of Irigaray's writings insist on female difference understood as divine and on the fact that women have a calling to become divine within their gender.

Others tend to stress the relationship of *two*, in which difference would be the most universally and radically lived out. While she argues that the character of male energy is different from that of female energy and that, as a consequence, the two genders relate differently to the sensible, Irigaray insists that male and female can teach each other this diversity, becoming alternately master and disciple. Men and women are thus invited to 'the remodelling of our culture so as to reconcile the reigns of women with patriarchal history. Only this historical synthesis . . . can reforge sexist hierarchies so as to bring about a cultural marriage between the sexes' (Irigaray 1994: 78). The difference between the sexes is so fundamental that it should entail 'a rewriting of the rights and obligations of each sex, *qua different*, in social rights and obligations' (Irigaray 1993b: 13). 'Recognition of sexual difference thus signifies . . . the possibility not only of a re-founding of the family but also of a truly democratic culture and politics in which citizens themselves would manage their relationships beyond all subjection and submission' (Irigaray 2000a: 29). Through respect for their differences, man and woman can aspire to being 'co-redeemers of the world: of their bodies, of the cosmic universe, of society and of History' (Irigaray 1996b: 187).

Irigaray's discourse on spirituality is based on the premises concerning sexual difference that I have just presented. I will now turn to an examination of how Irigaray understands spirituality and of the multiple forms it takes in her writing.

II Spirituality

Spirituality is present in a multiplicity of modes and takes different forms in Irigaray's writings, always related to sexual difference. The philosopher draws on the wellsprings of Christian and Oriental traditions, which she interprets very freely. For her, 'one achieves ethical, social and religious being by attending to the season, the time of day, the passing moment, and honouring the living order, rather than destroying it' (Irigaray 1993c: 77). The practice of harmonising with the environment leads Irigaray to question Christian tradition, in particular the practice of sacrifice that is at the heart of this tradition, and to oppose it to Oriental practice where the sacred honours nature instead of sacrificing it. 'I, woman, prefer to contemplate nature, the other, as they can be contemplated and, through contemplation, to cultivate my subjectivity, my energy, thanks to perception itself. Subjectivity, therefore, arrives at spirituality while remaining sensibility' (Irigaray 2000b: 50). Irigaray invites us to remain close to cosmic rhythms. She holds that we can train our sense perceptions by listening to beautiful sounds or contemplating beautiful colours and, in so doing, transform our physical bodies into spiritual bodies.

The body is understood as the site of the spiritual, to be cultivated, like the divine temple. The practice of breathing, of yoga, of cultivating the perceptions and of reading ancient and contemporary texts about yoga and also tantric texts, all have enabled Irigaray to understand that 'the body is the site of incarnation of the divine' (Irigaray 1999b: 83). 'The spiritual corresponds to the corporeal evolved, transmuted, transfigured. Music, colours, odours, tastes, singing, carnal love may serve to effect this transubstantiation' (Irigaray 1999b: 86). She also says that spiritual becoming entails a progressive awakening to the spiritual of the vital centres (*chakras*): the heart, speech and thought. Spiritual progress is thus separated neither from the body nor from desire, but these are trained bit by bit to renounce what harms them. Certainly it is not a case of renouncing for the sake of renouncing, but of renouncing that which thwarts our access to beatitude here on earth. Asceticism is thus not a question of privation as it has too often been in the West, it is a limitation, accepted and intended, in order to bring about progress towards happiness (Irigaray 1999b: 19).

Neither does asceticism imply an abandonment of carnal love, which is, on the contrary, presented as a spiritual path when the body is loved and respected in its difference, when there is respect for the other as transcendent to the self. In this case, the spiritual presides over a harmonisation of the genders. But woman, too often subjugated to male spirituality, has been deprived of her soul and so has not been able to provide man with this spiritual resource, which can be communicated by means of carnal love.[5]

Irigaray argues that a spiritual relationship between the sexes, understood as a relationship of energy transmission, can enable a reunification of the human and divine dimensions sundered through masculine domination. A love that can welcome difference necessarily recognises the other as transcendent to the self. This allows each partner to have access to his or her own divinisation.

Where the expression of spiritual life is concerned, Irigaray believes that some forms are more specific to women. Prayers of praise and poetry suit us better than rituals. She is also of the opinion, as far as Christian tradition is concerned, that we must dissociate two apostolic functions. Perceiving and transmitting truth and revelation would tend to be female missions. Missionary service, including the sacramental, would belong more to males (Irigaray 1989a: 15). With respect to transmission, Irigaray argues that it is sexual and that woman has a singular corporeal and spiritual experience. She does not transmit the same thing to her son and to her daughter. If we fail to take this into account, we help make the teaching process ever more ritualistic, speculative, magical, tied to the cult of the father and to the heavenly divinities that ensure society's laws. It follows that the need for transformation is urgent, in order to achieve a culture of two subjects, respectful of their differences.

I will now examine three of the focuses for spirituality in Irigaray's writings (aware that I am not exhausting the author's thought on the subject): genealogies; conceptual redefinitions; and a culture of the breath.

Genealogies

Female genealogies are defined as cultural filiations that link women with their spiritual mothers – these female figures who are so significant as references in the construction of female identity. These filiations are pathways along which to explore and root female spirituality. They also allow us to heal wounds caused by the separation between women and their daughters, a separation that has been imposed by patriarchal cultures. Irigaray insists that women need to be able to live their incarnation, the filiation to their mothers and to other women, free of contempt. They also need a divine that figures the perfection of their subjectivity. The stakes here are high. Where there are no divine representations of the mother–daughter couple, women are limited in their ability to construct their sexed identity, to provide themselves with a memory of their origins and to project themselves into the future. They end up living like asexual or neutral subjects who renounce 'their female identity and relationships with other women' (Irigaray 1993b: 21). This situation results in an impasse both for individual and for collective communication.

For Irigaray, the earth is sacred, a substrate for all that is alive, and the recognition of this reality is transmitted through female genealogies. The rupture of female genealogies entails a rupture with the earth. When humans are deprived of the spiritual relationship with the earth normally assured by women, a split is instituted between public life and private life, and relationships between men and women are affected. It then becomes more difficult for all human beings to live the carnal and spiritual covenant that is their calling.

Irigaray explores mythology and the traces of female genealogies to be found there. She evokes the myth of Demeter and Persephone in which love between mother and daughter was sacrificed to the interests of the male gods (Irigaray 1991: 110–14). Persephone is forcibly carried off by Hades and taken to the Underworld. There is no exchange of consent spoken between the spouses. Hades imposes his will through violence and ruse. The despair of Demeter, Persephone's mother, goddess of wheat, renders the earth sterile. Zeus intervenes with Hades, who agrees that Persephone should spend half the year on earth, and Demeter agrees to restore fertility to the fields. But Persephone 'is arrested in her becoming. Immortally and never more a virgin' (Irigaray 1991: 114). Henceforward she no longer belongs to herself as a woman. Irigaray also evokes Hestia, the goddess guardian of the flame of the domestic hearth, who assures its transmission from mother to daughter (Irigaray 1993b: 18–19). When a mother gives her daughter in marriage, she lights a flame at the altar of her own domestic hearth, then precedes the couple to their new dwelling and lights the first fire at the altar in her daughter's home. For Irigaray, this flame recalls the purity of woman, her faithfulness to her identity and to her female genealogy.

With a view to bringing constructive representations of female genealogy into our times, and to allow women to live out their spirituality, Irigaray proposes that images of the mother–daughter couple be present in private homes and public places. These images would also offer an alternative to the recurrent images of the mother–son couple found in abundance in the Christian religious world. In this context, representations of Anne with her daughter Mary could prove a rich source of meaning.

Redefinitions

As part of her project to critique current understandings of the religious and the spiritual and to explore new avenues, Irigaray suggests a number of redefinitions of key concepts in religions generally and the Christian tradition in particular. She has notably been interested in the notion of God, the story of the Annunciation, the concepts of chastity and virginity, the understanding of the Eucharist and the redefinition of sin and of grace. These propositions, articulated across her œuvre, take on renewed significance when they are brought together. They shed light on Irigaray's understanding of religious traditions and the orientation she wants to give her project of a culture with two subjects, respectful of their differences, a culture marked by spirituality.

In the figure of the monotheistic God, Irigaray finds a kind of idol of the spirit through which we are rendered unknown to ourselves. From the start within Christianity, she sees women being appropriated by an exclusively male God. In the absence of a divine representation of female identity, women have no means to designate and represent themselves or to communicate among themselves. To change this, Irigaray proposes that we consider that God, like the rest of humanity, is two, or that we replace the figure of God by that of an indeterminate absolute, 'a form of energy that incites us to become perfectly ourselves and to live perfectly the relationship to the other, to the others and to the world that surrounds us' (Irigaray 2000a: 18).

I take it that what is at issue in Irigaray's reading of the Annunciation is 'an engendering preceded by an exchange of breath and of words between the future lovers and parents. The angel, the bird, the ray of sunlight, the words, figure the mediations between the body of Mary and that of the Lord. . . . [These mediations] mean that a spiritual engendering cannot take place without bringing into play the breath and its mastered expression between the lovers' (Irigaray 1999b: 72). For a woman, the Annunciation would mean not accepting 'nor wishing to conceive a child without sharing speech with the lover, without preparing and receiving this sharing within the self' (Irigaray 1996b: 205).

The themes of chastity and of virginity appear frequently in the philosopher's writings, forming a sort of leitmotif. Virginity can be understood as the cornerstone of female identity, the realisation of the spiritual by women. Indeed, to be a woman means 'to freely and responsibly determine the uses of one's virginity [*disposer librement et responsablement de sa virginité*]: natural and spiritual' (Irigaray 1988: 15). Making use of Oriental concepts, Irigaray says as well that '[t]o be chaste is to keep the breath *chakra* free and alive, to keep the connection to the breath available for a relationship of interiority with oneself and for speech that communicates and exchanges with one's gender and the other gender, words of desire and not only of need' (Irigaray 1996b: 206). Irigaray's understanding of virginity does not entail the presence of a physiological hymen, but rather 'the existence of an own spiritual interiority, able to receive the speech of the other without altering it' (Irigaray 1996b: 188). She argues that 'Mary is a virgin because she was able to keep and cultivate a spiritual rapport with the breath, with the soul' (Irigaray 1999b: 105). She is the one who remains faithful to herself in love and in child-bearing.

Virginity entails a spiritual dimension that has been colonised by male culture; it 'has become the object of commerce between fathers (or brothers) and husbands, as well as a condition for the incarnation of the masculine divine. It has to be rethought as a woman's possession, a natural and spiritual possession to which she has a right and for which she holds responsibilities' (1993b: 116–17). In this sense, virginity is 'the other name for the fidelity of each gender to itself, with a respect for the other gender' (Irigaray 2000b: 111). It is also 'woman's ability to conserve and cultivate her identity in order to offer to share its qualities with man in one way or another' (Irigaray 1999b: 92). Virginity is a form of 'return to the self of the female, of the woman's spiritual interiority, able to keep itself woman and to become more and more woman', despite the existence of a male culture, despite the attraction she feels towards males, despite the motherhood she has experienced and the maternal love that animates her (Irigaray 1996b: 204). It would most definitely not be losing herself in the attraction she feels for the other, nor allowing herself to submit to the other. It would be 'giving herself a female spirit or soul, an inner dwelling place that would be not only physical but also spiritual' (Irigaray 1996b: 205).

Irigaray also questions the Christian Eucharist, the patriarchal character of which excludes and effaces women in a number of ways. When the minister 'pronounces the words of the Eucharist "This is my body, this is my blood", according to the rite that celebrates the sharing of food and that has been ours for centuries, perhaps we might remind him that he would not be there if our body and our blood had not given him life, love, spirit. And that he is also serving us up, we women-mothers, on his communion plate' (Irigaray 1993c: 21). But silence surrounds this ritual in which the sacrifice of women is masked. What is more, women are enjoined to believe in this rite that wounds and effaces them. The effacement of women is also manifest in the fact that the men who celebrate the Eucharist also appropriate to themselves the fruits of the earth, further manifestations of the female body. Finally, women are excluded from celebrating this worship service that is part of the foundation and structure of our culture.

In *Le Souffle des femmes* Irigaray develops her thought on sin and grace. Here sin is taken to be a lack of respect for the female in us, in other women and in our genealogies. It is also a lack of respect in our relationships to nature, alienation with respect to money or in the use of language or images that efface our particular qualities. Sin enters our relationships with the other when the singularity of each is reduced. Grace is the fact of being born woman, that gives us 'a privileged rapport in constituting subjectivity and intersubjectivity' (Irigaray 1996b: 200). It is also the ability to experience our virginity and to allow it to be expressed in different ways within our culture.

Even though these redefinitions taken together do not in themselves constitute a new feminist theology, the openings they provide can help us to construct one. Above all we now have new, dynamic elements for 'refounding' a female spirituality. Irigaray has freed herself from traditional, dogmatic definitions and promotes a re-centring in women's experience.

The culture of the breath

The same dynamics are at work where the culture of the breath is concerned. Irigaray reaches into different traditions to find support for thinking the breath and for proposing redefinitions as part of her cultural and spiritual project. The problematics of the breath has been present in her writings for a long time but became a central issue only with the publication in 1996 of *Le Souffle des femmes*, reaffirmed in 1999 with *Entre Orient et Occident* and *The Age of the Breath*. Irigaray argues that our contemporary culture separates the natural breath from the cultural breath, corporeal life from spiritual life, and that this has negative consequences for our relationships with ourselves, with others and with the cosmos. She has undertaken to promote a cultural model that assures circulation of the breath.

She argues that the breath is present in different ways in Christian tradition. God gives life to matter by communicating his breath to it; this is creation, the first age. Then comes the second age, the redemption, in which Jesus is born of a woman impregnated by the breath of the Spirit. The third age is in some way our responsibility. It is identified as the age of the breath: humanity is invited itself to become divine breath. This third age, of humanity's complete fulfilment, is a good time for us to connect with other traditions and to move beyond the opposition between matriarchy and patriarchy. The Oriental traditions can help us. In these traditions, sages achieve a new birth thanks to their breath-training and we too can find teachings to bring us back to the breath. Irigaray maintains that the woman who is faithful to herself 'is close to Oriental cultures, close to the Buddha, who moreover venerates the female spiritual. Woman shares her breath. She may do so by remaining at the level of the breath of life: she gives oxygen to the foetus through her blood. Or she also shares the spiritual breath, and this connects with . . . the meaning of Mary's virginity' (Irigaray 1999b: 107). But we still have not understood the mystery of the woman who shares her breath, her natural and spiritual life. We have forgotten the importance of the breath in human and divine life even though our tradition has taught it to us. It must be said that this teaching has tended to be part of dogma, rather than of gestures to be performed here and now.

For Irigaray, woman is divine from birth. She is invited to cultivate the divine in her by attending to her own breathing, her breath. Breathing is the first autonomous human gesture; 'it is not possible to be divine without being autonomous with respect to the mother and the father, to the lover, to the child and to the others in general, women and men' (Irigaray 1999a: 1). Men and women have different breaths. Women's breath is related both to the cosmos and to interiority. Women harbour a large reserve of breath within themselves. While men use their breath to construct, to create using concepts and instruments, women keep their breath within themselves to share, so that it may be made fecund. 'Woman, like God the creator, engenders with her breath. But she does it from the interior, without show. She does it invisibly and silently, before any perceptible word or gesture. Woman teaches, by her very manner of behaving [*par son faire même*], in each moment of the present and continually. . . . She does not simply give, she shares. But what she shares cannot be seen' (Irigaray 1999b: 108). So the mother shares not only blood, body, milk but also her breath, a sharing of the soul. She gives life and autonomy at the same time.

To summarise, we might say that the culture of the breath is a culture that aims to unite body and spirit, to spiritualise the body through the breath and so to accede to divinity. Spiritualisation through the breath entails a restoration of subjectivities. Inspired in this by Oriental traditions (Buddhism and Hinduism) and the practice of yoga, Irigaray proposes that individuals devote themselves to a culture of the breath that would allow them to be reborn to themselves and to harmonise with nature. To breathe consciously is to assume solitude, to take charge of one's life, to respect the lives of others. By developing a culture of the breath, women can live as spiritual beings and achieve their divinity. The breath has the power to make us spiritual beings.

III And in conclusion . . .

We can salute Luce Irigaray's dynamism and perseverance in the pursuit of her cultural and spiritual project. Her work is an important reference for many feminists and intellectuals who find in it a stimulating source for the critique of patriarchy and a significant contribution to the rethinking of women's experience and the relationships between men and women. The issue of *Religiologiques* devoted to the female and religion offers a telling example of the diversity of thought and analysis her work inspires (Roy 2000). We must also salute the fact that the philosopher and psychoanalyst took a very early interest in the question of religion and grasped its importance for the development of women's identity and a transformation of the relationship between the sexes. In this she has done pioneering work. Her intellectual and feminist project includes many rich and innovative aspects that need to be acknowledged. For me, this project also inspires a number of reservations, which I would like to detail here. In particular, I intend to comment on methodological aspects, on the type of writing, on the approach to Orientalism, on the question of sexual difference and on the content of the spiritual project.

Methodology

Where methodology is concerned, Irigaray demonstrates great freedom, a freedom that allows her to articulate her intuitions and give her creativity free rein. This freedom is essential for the distancing it enables with respect to dominant models and the critique of male paradigms of knowledge and for the openings it offers to new pathways for understanding the world. This freedom is constitutive of Irigaray's creative dynamism and her capacity for innovation. At the same time, I have been given to observe a certain methodological 'shallowness' (*légèreté*) that one might question. Several years ago, Sokal and Bricmont reproached her for critiquing a scientific discourse in which she did not understand the nature of the problems but about which she none the less formulated categorical conclusions by means of an analogical reading (Sokal and Bricmont 1997). We might express the same type of reservations about other types of discourse. Questions could be raised, notably about the solidity and rigour of Irigaray's treatment of references. Thus in *je, tu, nous: Toward a Culture of Difference* (1993), she posits the existence during another epoch (we do not know which one) of societies where women managed the social order (the societies are not named) and refers to the works of Johann Jacob Bachofen and of Mircea Eliade (without specifying which works) to support her proposition (Irigaray 1993b: 89–90). This makes for a good deal of imprecision when the intention is to support a theoretical model of the difference between the sexes. It is true that Irigaray raises the question of a female cultural order as well, in the same work, and that in that context she provides a reference to Bachofen and reminds us that she had treated the question in her *Marine Lover of Friedrich Nietzsche* (Irigaray 1993b: 17; 1991). It seems to me, none the less, that the treatment is particularly imprecise for a question as controversial as that of societies other than patriarchal, where a female cultural order existed. We find the same phenomenon reproduced in the case of the Eastern traditions that appear very inspiring to the philosopher.

In fact, it is often difficult to know precisely which traditions she is referring to or to determine from which ideas, from which schools of thought she is drawing her analyses. The lack of clarity that exists with respect to the references means that readers cannot return to the same sources, forge their own opinions and then enter into a discussion with the philosopher's œuvre. This approach to citation has a number of effects. It generates what I would call a kind of deficit in the area of democratic discussion. In the absence of pertinent information, it is not possible to truly discuss certain parts of her work. This leads us, as well, to question the validity and pertinence of her propositions, even if they otherwise appear to us, in many respects, as innovative and stimulating.

The type of writing

How should Irigaray's œuvre be considered? Is this body of work scientific, militant, poetic? The answer to these questions determines the type of reception that we will give her writings, the expectations that we can have and those we cannot have with respect to this œuvre. When we examine her publications over-all, we may observe an evolution, a transformation. The earlier, more academic writings present mainly systematic analysis and thematic studies. The later writings tend to take the form of poetic texts or pleas in favour of the institution of a cultural model. All of these literary genres are, of course, legitimate but it is important to treat each one for what it is. Part of the misunderstanding that currently exists with respect to the reception of her most recent writings, particularly in the university environment, comes from the fact that we have not adequately registered the transformation. Irigaray has shifted mainly towards writing that is engaged and poetic, linked to her personal experience, and has progressively distanced herself from academic modes of knowledge production. It is important to register this fact in order that expectations may be adjusted.

Orientalism

We must be grateful to Irigaray for interesting herself in Eastern traditions, for pointing to them as a source for spiritual renewal in the West and for having contributed to stimulating women's interest in this direction. It is important at the same time to understand that Irigaray's spirituality, even though it is marked by Orientalism, distances itself from it in a number of ways. Her understanding refuses the disappearance of the subject/object distinction which is none the less considered an end of the spiritual path in the East. She associates transcendence with the sensible/spiritual junction while Eastern spirituality seeks rather to escape from the sensible. Within the framework of spiritual development, she insists on the importance of a personal practice of yoga: 'It aspires to dispel all forms of suffering and of aging, to rediscover infancy, to be reborn' (Irigaray

2000b: 54). This objective is certainly legitimate, but it does not correspond to the traditional aims of yoga. Is it inspired by Irigaray's own experience or by recent works that offer 'contemporary' interpretations of Eastern spirituality to Westerners? It is difficult to say, since Irigaray gives us little information about her sources. We could perhaps say, using a formulation suggested to me by Julie Colpron, 'that Irigaray stresses the Eastern approach rather than its soteriological ends'.[6]

The question of sexual difference

Irigaray's writings have helped to advance current understandings of the difference between men and women. They have promoted a recognition of the value of this difference and an affirmation of its importance. They have provided a substantial critique of the patriarchal culture that obliterates female values and have brought forward propositions for a cultural transformation favouring the full expression of sexual difference. Therein lie fertile currents that have nourished feminist thought for the past two decades and that have made Irigaray a leader of the feminism of sexual difference. At the same time, the understanding that the philosopher has of sexual difference, the status that she gives it in the development of her thought, the way in which she opposes it to the concept of equality, all of these points raise serious questions that we cannot side-step.

Demands for social justice for women are often expressed in our societies in terms of equality. This causes problems for Irigaray, who believes that in order to acquire rights, to be equal subjects, women must 'become men, neutralise themselves' (Irigaray 1988: 15). Equality for her signifies becoming like, similar, identical. She opposes this and puts forward her concept of sexual difference. However, this philosophical understanding of equality is not necessarily the one advanced by the political movement for women's liberation, which has sought in practice to combat the inequalities that have been sources of a sense of inferiority and alienation for women. At the same time, we may note that many of egalitarian feminism's demands aim to recognise women's specific experience: maternity leaves, the right to contraception and to abortion, the battle against sexual harassment, and so on. None the less, there remains an ongoing lack of mutual understanding and an opposition/polarisation between equality and difference, where Irigaray has clearly taken the side of difference.

For Irigaray, male or female symbols are usually associated with a specific sex. There is practically a fusion between the symbol and the sexed subject: men exhibit symbolic male characteristics and women symbolic female characteristics. This leads to a hardening of the definition of the sexes, for woman as subject just as much as for man as subject. At the beginning of this chapter, I presented the different characteristics that Irigaray attributes to each of the sexes. When we examine the portrait that emerges, we find ourselves looking at something close to an idealised representation of women: they are naturally communicative, respectful of the earth, concerned about relations with the other, spiritually awakened, and so on. All of these qualities are clearly positive, but if we turn them into quasi-innate qualities of women do we not enclose women within an essentialist paradigm? Patriarchy long demonised women; the result would be no happier were we to construct an almost angelic portrait today, primarily because of the normative character that this portrait could have. Would women still be recognised as women, really women, if they did not fit the portrait drawn? Moreover, the portrait leaves me wondering, as there are resemblances between it and the one that Pope John Paul II drew of women in 1988 in his apostolic letter *Mulieris Dignitatem* and in the letter he addressed to the women of the world on the occasion of the 1995 Beijing World Conference on Women. In both cases, the female is exalted. In the case of Pope John Paul II, this exaltation leads to a form of ghetto-isation of women, to their marginalisation within the sphere called female and to their exclusion from the sites of power. Is this risk not equally present in Irigaray's writings, particularly when she foresees a division among religious functions according to sex (prayer through poetry for women and ritual for men; the reception and transmission of the truth by women and sacramental service for men)? All in all, do the male and female models proposed by Irigaray not serve as vehicles for traditional values, from which we have wanted to distance ourselves in order exactly to affirm the totality of our human potential?

Sexual difference structures the whole of Irigaray's discourse; for her this is the most fundamental difference. Without denying the decisive importance of sexual difference in the development of relationships between humans and cultures, may we not ask ourselves if differences of class, race, ethnic origins and so on do not also have a considerable impact? Clearly, intellectuals must have the freedom to emphasise one aspect or another of reality and so to develop and explore it. In addition, it seems to me that in Irigaray's discourse there is a quasi-absolutisation of sexual difference that may possibly generate distortions in her reading of reality.

The spiritual project

One of Irigaray's meaningful contributions is to have established that women need a representation of the divine in order to figure the perfection of their subjectivity. Further, she has demonstrated how the absence of this representation limits the development of women's sexed identity. This contribution opens the door to a renewed critique of the discourse on God and to the exploration of new understandings of the divine, understandings that are more rooted in the spiritual experience of women today and that can better express their search for meaning. Another non-negligible contribution is the opening to Eastern traditions, something that can be understood as an invitation to break out of confessional traditions, to develop a spirituality more apt to respond to the new aspirations of the human community. The invitation to respect the earth and to harmonise with it is also a part of this perspective. If the idea of knowing oneself to be an icon of the divine seems to me to be particularly fertile, the notion of being or becoming divine, the 'divine becoming', gives me pause. There might be in this a kind of narcissism or omnipotence that would be worth questioning. But that would be the subject of another article, for another occasion.

In conclusion, although we may have reservations about them, I think it is important for us to read, to appreciate and to discuss Irigaray's writings. May the debate continue!

Notes

1 Translator's note: Citations in this article are from the published English versions of Irigaray's works, where these are currently available. Where no published translations exist, I offer free translations in the hope that the benefit to readers not fluent in French will outweigh the inevitable flaws in these passages. As listed in the Bibliography, the works in question are those referenced 1988, 1989a, 1996b, 1999b and 2000a. Note that the English translation of *Entre Orient et Occident*, the work referenced here as 1999b, was published in 2002 as *Between East and West: From Singularity to Community*.

2 I would like to thank my research assistant Julie Colpron, a doctoral student in religion at UQAM, who did excellent work in preparing a large part of the literature review that I used in writing this article.

3 She refers here to Feuerbach (1957).

4 She does not offer further specifications that would locate this period.

5 Indeed, '[i]f the carnal act can appear to him as a little death, it is because he forgets what he can receive that is spiritual in drawing close to the woman's breath' (Irigaray 1999b: 115).

6 The critical commentary of Julie Colpron, who has completed a Masters thesis on Hindu philosophy, has been particularly enlightening in the rereading of Irigaray's arguments on Eastern spirituality.

Chapter 2

Ellen T. Armour

DIVINING DIFFERENCES
Irigaray and Religion

SINCE ITS ARRIVAL IN NORTH AMERICA in the early 1980s, a number of feminist scholars in religion have found in the work of Luce Irigaray important potential for exploring and reworking the connections between Western Christianity and sexual difference. On the one hand, Irigaray criticises Western Christianity because it constitutes one site of the West's primordial forgetting of women. Like Western philosophy, Western Christianity is built upon exchanges between fathers and sons (both heavenly and earthly), in which woman serves as the mere raw (maternal) material. But Irigaray also turns to religion as a site for the (im)possible recovery or discovery of sexual difference.

Irigaray's turn to religion as a site where sexual difference can register is best known through its roots in Feuerbach's claim that theology is anthropology. According to Feuerbach, God is really a projection of idealised and purified man. As such, Irigaray argues in *Sexes and Genealogies* (1993c), God functions to ground masculine subjectivity by reflecting man back to himself. She goes on to suggest that women can accomplish the same thing for themselves by seizing control of the projector and shining *their* image on its screen.

This aspect of Irigaray's work with religion has aroused considerable interest – some of it critical – from feminist scholars in philosophy and religion. Some philosophers are wary of this return of religion. They fear the resurrection of the 'good old God' in female guise. Others see Irigaray's project in instrumentalist terms: Projecting an idealised woman onto a screen gives women as a genre an infinite with which to identify, a third term through which to become a subject. Feminist philosophers of religion have taken Irigaray's suggestion as a route towards transforming the religious imaginary (Jantzen 1998a) or towards exposing the role of projection in what counts as true belief in traditional philosophy of religion (Anderson 1998). Amy Hollywood (1994: 175–6) raises a deeper question about the efficacy of a quasi-Feuerbachian project. She finds it troubling that Irigaray, who so carefully diagnoses the dynamics at work in belief within patriarchal religion, simply bypasses issues of belief in her evocation of a woman divine – completely ignoring Freud's insight that religion works only as long as its dynamics are hidden.[1] How efficacious can asserting a woman divine really be when done above the board?

In addition, I have argued elsewhere that Irigaray's evocation/invocation of a woman divine fails to take seriously the full extent of religion-as-usual's reach – even in our supposedly secularised culture (Armour 1999: 130–3). As Irigaray well knows, God-the-Father has served as guarantor of truth in a phallocentric economy of sameness where one's proximity to Truth is determined by one's proximity to the phallus. In *This Sex Which Is Not One* (1985b: 33), Irigaray warns feminism that simply replacing this standard of sameness with a female standard will keep the economy of sameness in play. The truth of her insight is, unfortunately, borne out in her failure to heed her own warning.

In my view, the strongest single contribution Irigaray brings to feminism is her insistence on grounding woman in the differences *between* women and within woman (rather than in identity and sameness). This concept offers feminism the promise of thinking and practising 'women' so that differences between women really matter, something that criticisms of feminism from women of colour suggest that feminism needs. Irigaray seems to lose sight of the radicality of that promise in these invocations of religious motifs. 'Divine Women', an essay published in *Sexes and Genealogies* (1993c: 57–72), is the fullest articulation of Irigaray's appropriation of Feuerbach. Though framed by a concern with elemental figures that promises to undercut unitary logic, its deployment of god-language in the service of female subject formation overrides this promise and threatens to return woman and the religious to a unitary horizon. It is a horizon of becoming rather than being, to be sure, but one whose invocation of diversity remains at best abstract and individual (Irigaray 1993c: 67). At worst, women's multiplicity counts here as threat rather than promise (Irigaray 1993c: 69). That this elision of difference should occur when and where Irigaray crosses into religion's terrain suggests that the power of the economy of the same remains strong. The logic of sameness that encloses Irigaray's woman divine and the women she would divinise too closely binds them to the 'good old God' and the men he divinises.[2] Simply reversing the gender of the divine will not extract the thought of divinity from its ontotheological container, which conceives of transcendence in terms of a presence that subsumes difference in an ultimate similarity.

Perpetuating the alliance between theology and anthropology is nothing new; Irigaray simply repeats the move initiated by Descartes and carried to its 'end' by Feuerbach and Freud. More efficacious feminist interventions in religion-as-usual will require thinking against the grain of the West's metaphysical economy.

Rather than simply asserting a claim to transcendence on women's behalf via projection, we need to rework the logic of immanence and transcendence itself. Transcendence and immanence form a central scaffolding for the God/man duo that Feuerbach so powerfully exposes. Deconstructing that scaffolding may provide a more effective attack on the economy of sameness.

Irigaray's work can also be mined for resources to support the project of reworking transcendence and immanence. Irigaray opens 'Divine Women' with a reference to her concern with the traditional four elements familiar from pre-Socratic thought (air, earth, fire and water). In the early pages of this essay, she identifies our culture's failure to think through our relationship to these elements as symptomatic of its disavowal of the material conditions of existence, a disavowal endemic to the economy of sexual indifference that she contests. Irigaray suggests that the elements haunt our culture in the form of mythic and fabulous tales of half-human, half-animal beings (such as Melusine or 'the Little Mermaid') who reside on the border between life and death, the visible and the invisible, the real world and the dream world. What, she asks, do these tales suggest about our culture's sense of women's present and future, about (im)possible relations between men and women, between human and divine?

I have already sketched briefly the primary route that 'Divine Women' takes in response to these questions, and raised some critical questions about its appropriation of the dynamics of projection. I want now to turn to another aspect of Irigaray's work that shadows 'Divine Women' and that other scholars connect to Irigaray's project of making space for women's subjectivity.[3] In another text, *An Ethics of Sexual Difference* (1993a), Irigaray adopts the term 'sensible transcendental', a term that, at first glance, seems self-contradictory. Its paradoxical status signals an intervention within our cultural grammar, which conceives the sensible as what is transcended rather than what transcends. Irigaray deploys this term in the service of the concerns that the myths and fables mentioned in 'Divine Women' bring to mind. What can enable genuine relations between men and women, between women and women, to take place? Again, religious motifs appear to be crucial to such projects, though through dynamics other than projection and repression. Irigaray describes us as waiting for a new god, whose coming will open up

> another epoch in history. . . . This creation would be our opportunity . . . by means of the opening of a *sensible transcendental* that ad-vents through us, of which *we would be* the mediators and bridges. Not only in mourning for the dead God of Nietzsche, not waiting passively for the god to come, but by conjuring it up among and across us, within and between us, as resurrection or transfiguration of blood, of flesh, through a language and an ethics that is ours.
>
> (1993a: 129; translation modified)

Commentators see the sensible transcendental as a counterpart to the idea of divinising women, as another ideal-yet-to-be-imagined that women can project for the sake of their own becoming and as a support for genuine relationships. The secondary literature treats it largely as an empty abstraction – necessarily empty because it lies ahead of us as future possibility, not present reality.[4]

In the space remaining to me in this chapter, I want to explore the potential of the sensible transcendental, and its limits, by linking this figure to Irigaray's interest in the elements. Her readings of the philosophical tradition frequently excavate the elements as the unacknowledged ground of philosophical reflection. I will argue that the materialities uncovered in these excavations can be productively mined as sensible transcendentals. Doing so brings the figure of the sensible transcendental out of an imagined future into a more immediate context (which is not quite here and now) and renders what remains merely abstract more concrete.

Two sites of these excavations are philosophers whose work has been important to religious thought, Plato and Heidegger. In fact, the elements that their texts assume appear most clearly where their thinking borders the religious. Irigaray's reading of Heidegger plays on religious/mystical overtones in Heidegger's thought.[5] It uncovers a metaphorical woman as the material/maternal ground of Heidegger's thinking, in the form of air as its elemental matrix. Irigaray makes a parallel move in her reading of Plato in *Speculum of the Other Woman* (1985a: 242–364). Underneath the male God *explicitly* invoked by Plato, she unearths woman/mother/matter as forgotten ground and obscured source of Plato's thought (1985a: 294–364). These elemental matrices are transcendent (in that they serve as ground) but also sensible (in that they are material). Let me illustrate how she arrives at these unearthings and what they yield through an account of her mimetic reading of Heidegger in *The Forgetting of Air in Martin Heidegger* (1999c). Her readings do not focus on any explicit invocation of woman per se in Heidegger's thinking, but on evocations of X-as-woman.

Through following out the play of gender in the French translations of Heidegger's texts, Irigaray brings to light a gendered writing and a sexual dynamic that writes itself through those texts. Many of the nominal forms of Heidegger's vocabulary are gendered female in French (and German); for example, the clearing/the opening (*la clairière, die Lichtung*),[6] language (*la langue, die Sprache*), dwelling (*la demeure, die Wohnung*), *la terre* vs. *le ciel* (*die Erde* vs. *der Himmel*) of the fourfold, and so on.[7] Irigaray's reading suggests that Heidegger himself is written by a larger 'cultural grammar', to use a term from *This Sex Which Is Not One* (1985b) – which systematically associates woman/the feminine with certain things (nature, darkness, matter, the home, the body, the earth) and man/the masculine with certain other things (spirit, form, intellect, the sky).

How does she unearth this play of sexual difference in Heidegger's writing? My use of the metaphor of terrain here (and atmosphere earlier) in describing

Irigaray's reading of Heidegger is more than fortuitous. The play of sexual difference emerges through Irigaray's *retraversée* of the metaphorical landscape on which, through which and in terms of which Heidegger thinks. The centrality of the metaphor of landscape is immediately apparent in the figure of the clearing in Heidegger's later writings, but also could be said to make itself felt as early as *Being and Time* (1962), given the importance of worldedness and situatedness to the analysis of *Dasein* ('there-being'). Thus, one could argue that Heidegger's philosophical comings and goings, turnings and/or departures, separations, longed-for reunions and so on, occur in and through this metaphorical landscape that Irigaray retraverses.

Heidegger's search for the more primordial led him from phenomenology to its ground in a fundamental ontology of the being who asks the question of being to an even more primordial connection between being and thinking. In his later work, Heidegger uncovers what is even more primordial than *Dasein*; the clearing (*la clairière, die Lichtung*) – where beings presence themselves. Heidegger's later thought focuses on evoking the clearing in order to call us back to our most primordial home (or to the home in its most primordial sense).[8] In his view, *techne*'s dominance of the modern era renders human beings deaf to the call and blind to their true home.

Through following out its gender markings, Irigaray suggests that Heidegger's nostalgia for dwelling in the clearing covers over a more primordial longing. Another central metaphor that carries Heidegger's thinking, the desire for a dwelling (*une demeure, die Wohnung*), takes up its place within a gendered landscape. Irigaray evokes worldedness, its version of the metaphor of dwelling, in *Being and Time* (the world is that into which *Dasein* comes to be as thrown/ project) as well as in the thought of the later Heidegger (where dwelling *is* the project). Underneath the desire for a proper dwelling lies a longing for a more primordial home, Irigaray suggests: 'his first "house": his dwelling in a living body' (1999c: 70). Here the shadow of the question of a *Kehre* in Heidegger's thinking makes itself felt. Rather than a dramatic change in direction, the turn to language (as the house of being) and the invocation of the fourfold (*la terre* [earth], *le ciel* [heaven], *les mortels* [mortals], *les divins* [divinities]) as a description of that home continues the trajectory begun by *Being and Time* of trying to recover the forgotten.[9] Irigaray's interrogation of Heidegger's thinking allows the return of the repressed, gives voice to the *Unheimlich* – that which has no home even in a philosophy so concerned with being at home. Underneath the longing for a reunion with being, Irigaray uncovers a more primordial longing for a reunion with the (gendered/sexed) other – as (m)other, as lover, as the divine, and so on. Thus, even as Heidegger's texts repeat the trajectory of the West's erasure of sexual difference, they also can be read in such a way that the forgotten comes to the fore. The strategy she follows here is mimicry; that is, to try to recover the place of her exploitation by discourse, without allowing herself to be simply reduced to it. It means to resubmit herself – inasmuch as she is on the side of the 'perceptible', of 'matter' – to 'ideas', in particular to ideas about herself, that are elaborated in/by a masculine logic, but so as to make 'visible', by an effect of playful repetition, what was supposed to remain invisible: the cover-up of a possible operation of the feminine in language. It also means 'to unveil' the fact, if women are such good mimics, it is because they are not simply re[ab]sorbed in this function. *They also remain elsewhere . . .*

(1985b: 76)

There are two levels to its practice here: (1) taking the place assigned to woman in Heidegger's corpus and (2) miming Heideggerian strategic moves. With Heidegger (or miming Heidegger), she asks the transcendental question of origin. What makes coming into presence possible? What grounds the togetherness of being and thinking? What grounds the clearing? What makes possible both the co-belonging of being and thinking (*l'être et la pensée*) and its own forgetting? What material condition makes possible the entry into presence? It is something impalpable, imperceptible, invisible, unintelligible and transcendent. Could it be air?

Heidegger's evocation of the metaphorical clearing (*la clairière*) emphasises coming into the light, but what makes the light possible? Irigaray reminds her readers that air is the condition of possibility for perception, for light and dark, for voice, for appearing/disappearing, for seeming/resembling/assembling, for presence or absence – for so much of what Heidegger thematises, yet it passes unnoticed in Heidegger's texts. Thus, could not air be said to constitute the proper house of being? The proper home of the being who asks the question of being? And yet this philosopher is concerned above all with finding that home passes by/through air without noticing it.

This is not to say that air leaves no mark in Heidegger's clearing. Air traces the overcoming of metaphysics and its residue in Heidegger's thought. Air's double location can be read in Heidegger's invocation of the clearing as a circle. On the one hand, Heidegger's description of the opening of the circle evokes an empty airiness that makes the circle possible and prevents its closure. On the other hand, the circle encloses, constricts, surrounds, re-forms, defines and delimits the air, which is its ground. It masters this ground and makes of it a resource for speculative reflection. Air serves as a mirror reflecting light so that beings can come into presence and slip away into absence. Thus, air is the ground of truth in its most primordial sense (as *aletheia*).

Yet what sense does it make to speak of air as ground? It is, after all, without bottom/without depth (*sans fond*) and yet not mere surface either. Again, metaphysical oppositions cannot capture it. It cannot properly be said to fill the clearing or to constitute solid support. It is the (sensible/)transcendental condition (the physical ground) for the oppositions that constitute the structure of metaphysics but, because it offers nothing to the eye, slips away, holds itself in reserve, it cannot be properly said to 'be'. Like woman, it eludes capture in metaphysical categories. Thus, air as the transcendental ground of being takes on the quality of an abyss (*l'abîme*) – an insatiable, gaping hole/mouth that threatens to swallow anything that comes its way. Air is at once necessary ground (necessary for sustaining life) and threat.

The trajectory of gendered tropes yields the mat(t)ernal sacrifice that undergirds Heidegger's text and, according to Irigaray, the whole of Western civilisation. The West's sexual economy is one of appropriation where 'she' gives and 'he' takes. His 'proper' desire is to appropriate; hers to give in to his appropriation. Indications that this economy is operative in Heidegger's philosophising are already apparent from the terrain just covered. *La clairière, la demeure, l'air, la terre,* are associated with giving – giving shelter (for truth), giving place (for beings to come into presence), giving home (for mortals). And yet, Irigaray notes, this economic structure of exchange (or, more accurately, appropriation) goes disguised under the supposedly gender-neutral construction of the '*il y a*' and the '*il (se) donne*' – the '*es gibt*'. He takes, she gives, and he forgets that she gives.

Within such an economic context, it comes as no surprise that Heidegger's corpus also exhibits the fixed positions assigned to man and woman by the economy of propriation. On the one hand, 'he' is dependent upon 'her' as the (material) ground of what is. On the other hand, she appears to him as a dangerous abyss from which he must stand out (*ek-stasis*). 'His' relation to 'her' follows a dynamic of approach/avoidance, love/hate, grief for a lost home, denial of the need for that primal dwelling in the projection of its replacement.[10] Within the confines of this economy, the only patterns for relating the one to the other (*l'un à l'autre*) are either complete separation or total fusion.

Yet this is not the end of the story. This economy does not hold absolute sway over Heidegger's corpus any more than Irigaray has shown it to hold unquestioned sway over any other moment in Western culture that has come under her scrutiny. Between the cracks of this economy, Irigaray's reading allows us to catch glimpses of another economy – one which does not divide neatly into one or two – an economy which offers a different way of relating the one to the other, the one to the one (*l'un à l'autre, l'un à l'une, l'un à l'un, l'une à l'une*). In evoking the vision of this economy, Irigaray gives us a 'something more' that we (women only?) need. But just what is this 'something more' and how is it related to the unearthing of a more primordial female 'foundation' to Heidegger's questioning of metaphysics?

One possible reading would take *The Forgetting of Air* in the direction of Irigaray's later work and associate this 'something more' and the female (groundless) ground with a project of creating or uncovering a Symbolic which can support female subjectivity as phallogocentrism supports male subjectivity.[11] Thus, Irigaray could be read as offering women the opportunity to become subjects in their own right, on their *own* terms. *The Forgetting of Air* would then be one step in a project of constructing two separate but parallel spheres – one for us (women) and one for them (men) each grounded by its own standard of sameness.[12] While there are places in *The Forgetting of Air* that might lend such a reading credence, my own reading takes a different direction, one more in accord with what I have argued earlier is Irigaray's most important contribution to feminism: thinking difference.

Two-ness – two *ek-stases* each with its own standard of sameness – does not fully capture the complex texture of the 'something more' that *The Forgetting of Air* evokes. Irigaray has unearthed femininity/female/mother at work in this economy but not, I would argue, as a new standard on which *the* female subject can take her stand. Air is neither present nor absent, neither divisible nor mixable; rather, it makes division and mingling possible. It is foundation, but as a 'groundless ground' (*le fond impensé de sa pensée*), it refuses the fixity of foundation. It holds in reserve the trace of the unsaid, which effaces itself before that which speaks itself. It is difficult to see how this groundless ground could serve as a fixed standard upon which a (finally) secure subject could rest. Indeed, the erstwhile subject herself, woman, is invoked explicitly in *The Forgetting of Air* as eluding fixation in space/time, as residing somewhere between life/death, and so on. Moreover, whatever 'woman' or 'the feminine' is in this text, it/she is multiple. She is everywhere, but never the same at any point.

An alternative 'one' running parallel to the 'one' of a masculine economy yielding a (mere) genuine binary does not describe Irigaray's woman and her economy adequately, especially as evoked in the last pages of *The Forgetting of Air*. In these provocative pages, Irigaray dreams for heterorelationality what 'When Our Lips Speak Together', in *This Sex Which Is Not One* (1985b: 205–18), conjures up for homorelationality (between women). These last pages of *The Forgetting of Air* dream a dance of *l'un et l'autre, l'un et l'une*. Irigaray never specifies the referents of these pronouns, thereby inviting the reader to imagine multiple readings kept simultaneously in play (man and woman, human and divine, father/daughter, heterosexual lovers, mother/son). This dance parallels the 'conversation' between *l'une et l'une* in 'When Our Lips Speak Together', a text that also invites simultaneous multiple readings (mother/daughter, woman-friend/woman-friend, woman-lover/woman-lover, human-woman/divine-as-woman, and more). These encounters refuse to resolve into either the union of *a* one with another one or a fusion of two *into* one. In addition to refusing to capitulate to the modes of accounting available in our current sexual economy, the 'ones' of *The Forgetting of Air* also disrupt their initial assignation as male or female. In the course of the dance, *l'un et l'une* detach themselves from the desires proper to them.

The convergence of sexual difference and religious discourse in this charged atmosphere yields something that exceeds quasi-Feuerbachian projections of a deity in female form as ground for female subjectivity. Where 'Divine Women' seems to bypass alterity, air as a sensible transcendental refuses fixation in sameness. Furthermore, it (groundlessly) grounds a sexual/symbolic economy that disturbs boundaries between one and the other, between immanence and transcendence, between sensible and intelligible, between human and divine. Following Irigaray down this path would seem to offer significant potential for a new construal of both sexual difference and divine alterity. Let me outline that potential somewhat more clearly by situating this side of Irigaray's work against the background of her critique of religion.

I noted earlier that Irigaray argues that Western Christianity, like Western philosophy, is circumscribed by an economy in which woman serves as the mere raw maternal/material sacrificed in order to fund exchanges between men. In other essays in *Sexes and Genealogies* and *An Ethics of Sexual Difference*, Irigaray takes Freud's claim, in *Totem and Taboo* (1985a), that religion originates in a prehistoric patricide one step further to expose a matricide underlying the patricide. Like the murder of the patriarch by the brothers of the primal horde, this murder of the maternal body, too, is forgotten, memorialised and repeated. The maternal body is declared off-limits as threat, even as separation from it produces unceasing mourning. Irigaray finds memorials to this sacrifice both in Greek myths (the Oresteian trilogy as well as Oedipus) and in the Christian Eucharist. In a Church where abortion, birth control, homosexuality and so on are forbidden to women, she asks, whose body and blood are *really* being sacrificed in the Eucharist (1993c: 21; see also 25–53)?

If there is to be a future for religion that can accommodate sexual difference, it will have to come from resituating ourselves in relationship to the economy of sacrifice. Repeating the religious motifs that have sustained it for so long offers only the illusion of difference, not genuine alterity. In 'Éthique de la différence sexuelle', Irigaray recalls Heidegger's famous (and highly ironic) saying: 'only a god can save us now' and asks, 'A moins d'un dieu, peut-être?' (1984: 124). The multivalence in this question is difficult to capture in translation.[13] 'At least a god, perhaps?' 'More than a god, perhaps?' 'At least ONE god, perhaps?' Taking sensible transcendentals like air as an answer to this question accords them particular resonance and relevance at this point in the history of Christian theology. Vehement reassertions of traditional theism in response to the perceived threat of nihilism continue to garner attention on the theological scene.[14] The god whose death is at issue in our epoch, Irigaray asserts, is the transcendent, self-reliant, self-contained god who exists necessarily. It is no coincidence that the question of sexual difference arises with particular resonance and resilience at the time of this god's passing away, she suggests (1993a: 140). Irigaray also reminds us that the philosophers who announced the death of god (among them Spinoza, Nietzsche and Heidegger) were not asserting that divinity had altogether passed from the scene never to return. Nor were they asserting that this god was 'truly dead, really most sincerely dead' (to borrow a phrase from *The Wizard of Oz*); in fact, according to Nietzsche, we will continue to believe in this god as long as we believe in grammar (1993a: 112).

Taking air as a sensible transcendental as one means of refiguring the religious offers an alternative to the logic of traditional theism that 'Divine Women' seems to repeat. Rather than covering over the sacrificial economy or trying to step outside it, following this figure resituates us in relationship to that economy. Thinking through air as a sensible transcendental reconfigures the mechanism or medium of our relationship to the economy of sacrifice. Rather than supplementing one belief in an ideal transcendence with another (the strategy Irigaray follows in 'Divine Women'), air as a sensible transcendental shifts our attention to a material transcendence within which we always already are and which moves through us.[15]

Reframing the religious through the figure of this sensible transcendental transgresses and transforms the sacrificial economy's identification of transcendence with escape from the conditions of finitude, embodiment and materiality. The material transcendence that funds and founds that economy invites a different calculus of embodiment than mind over matter. In *The Absent Body* (1990), phenomenologist Drew Leder describes two modes of the body's transcendence, disappearance and dysappearance. Disappearance names the conditions of embodiment that enable us to go about our daily business. In order to read, write, drive, or eat, the bodily conditions that make these activities possible (organs functioning properly, breathing occurring normally and so on) must recede from my awareness. My body necessarily eludes my conscious monitoring of it in order for me to 'be' in the world. These functions that I take for granted are called to conscious awareness when disease or injury creates dysfunction. At these times, my body dys-appears; that is, it claims my attention through disruptions in its smooth functioning. Leder's analysis helps elucidate the stakes inherent in thinking through air as a sensible transcendental. Air quite literally grounds and ungrounds our existence. Without it, without the ability to take it in and breathe it out, we die. Thus, thinking through air as sensible transcendental grounds us in finitude through bodily transcendence rather than delivering us from it.[16]

As ungrounded and ungrounding ground, air deploys materiality and ideality, transcendence and immanence, very differently and, in doing so, it opens up the possibility of (un)grounding modes of relationality that cannot be counted in our current economic system. This elusive (un)grounded (un)grounding ground takes (its) place not above or outside *l'un et l'une*, *l'une et l'autre*, *l'un et l'autre* but *entre nous*. It offers them not a solid ground for self-reflection but breathing room for new couplings and comings and goings. In what it (potentially) makes possible, it also breaks with traditional theism. Building on this potential switches our attention from issues of belief to issues of material practices (language and ethics). Whether this sensible transcendental becomes a site where differences-between can register remains to be seen. It is, after all, in large part up to us to take the risks that acknowledging our (un)groundedness involves and to develop the practices of relating that breathing room offers.[17] I use the language of risk-taking quite deliberately. Some look to religion for security from risk and a safe harbour for self-preservation. Such aims will not find satisfaction in this airy atmosphere. But religion can also be an opening towards alterity. Such openings, if genuine, put us at risk and confront us with what we might prefer not to face. Yet through such openings comes the possibility for growth and renewal.

Notes

1   For Irigaray on belief, see 'Belief Itself', in Irigaray (1993c). For discussions of this essay, see Hollywood (1998) and Armour (2001a).

2   Grosz (1993) notes anxiety on the part of other scholars about possible resurrections of the 'good old God' in Irigaray's work, but argues that this is not her intent. I agree with Grosz's assessment of Irigaray's intentions, but find the textual effects are at odds with those intentions.

3   See, for example, Deutscher (1994, 1997), Summers-Bremner (2000), Walsh (1999) and Whitford (1991b: 140–4).

4   Among the best accounts of the sensible transcendental are Deutscher (1994) and Whitford (1991b: 47–8, 93, 144, 155). Both recognise it as an alternative to the God/man duo and what surrounds it, though both see it – and arguably quite rightly, as Irigaray uses it – in instrumentalist terms.

5   An earlier version of this account of Irigaray's reading of Heidegger appears in Armour (1997).

6   In fact, Heidegger himself makes the connection between *die Lichtung* and *la clairière*. See 'The End of Philosophy and the Task of Thinking', in Heidegger (1977: 384).

7   I cite the German here, although, with the exception of *die Lichtung* (which appears untranslated only on the first page) and *der Gestell* ('frame'; the only German term to remain untranslated throughout *The Forgetting of Air*), Irigaray does not. Traditional Heideggerian scholarship is very attentive to nuances of meaning in German, and therefore often leaves important terms of Heidegger's vocabulary untranslated. Against this background, Irigaray's strategy registers as a refusal of these standard gestures of loyalty to the father. This gesture accrues interest when read against Jean-Paul Sartre's appropriation of *Being and Time*, which provoked a strong reaction from Heidegger. See Heidegger's 'Letter on Humanism', in Heidegger (1977:

189–242), and Derrida's discussion of Sartre's translation in 'The Ends of Man', in Derrida (1982: 109–36).

8   See, for example, 'Building Dwelling Thinking' and 'The End of Philosophy and the Task of Thinking', in Heidegger (1977: 319–40 and 369–92, respectively). Both of these essays figure prominently in *The Forgetting of Air*.

9   'The fourfold' is a complex idea in the thought of the later Heidegger. In addition to 'Building Dwelling Thinking' (previously cited), see also 'The Origin of the Work of Art', in Heidegger (1977: 143–88).

10 Irigaray's evocation of this dynamic recalls the fort/da game that she discusses in 'Belief Itself' (Irigaray 1993c: 25–53).

11 See, for example, essays in Irigaray (1993a and 1993c).

12 See Walsh (1999) for one such reading.

13 Indeed, Gill's translation obscures it altogether: 'Is a god what we need, then?' (1993a: 128).

14 I have in mind here a diverse range of texts, from Marion (1991) to certain proponents of radical orthodoxy (see Milbank et al. [1999] and Pickstock [1998]).

15 On the sensible transcendental as an alternative to the economy of sacrifice, see Whitford (1991b: 144–7).

16 For a particularly provocative, if occasionally problematic (especially on the topic of mysticism), consideration of the sensible transcendental's ability to help subjects negotiate with finitude and desire, see Summers-Bremner (2000).

17 Deutscher's criticism of Irigaray's lack of attention to differences between women in her later work certainly brings that point home. She attributes it to the higher priority given in Irigaray's later work to relationships between the sexes, as though that were the only salient difference in women's lives (Deutscher 1998: 179–91). For a cautionary tale about a sensible transcendental's ability to negotiate sexual and racial difference in a particular context, see Armour (2001b).

Chapter 3

Judith L. Poxon

CORPOREALITY AND DIVINITY
Irigaray and the Problem of the Ideal

R EADERS OF LUCE IRIGARAY are in general agreement that her
interest in theology has produced two distinct discourses: a critical reading
of the phallocentrism of the Western Christian tradition, found in *Speculum of the
Other Woman* (1985a) and *This Sex Which Is Not One* (1985b), and a constructive
feminist theological project that emerges in such texts as *Marine Lover of Friedrich
Nietzsche* (1991), *An Ethics of Sexual Difference* (1993a), *Sexes and Genealogies* (1993c)
and *Between East and West: From Singularity to Community* (2002).[1] Many suggest
that it is important to read the later work through the earlier. However, I
will argue in this chapter that the constructive turn of the more recent work
– particularly in the essay 'Divine Women', found in *Sexes and Genealogies* –
should alert us to moments in the earlier efforts in which Irigaray continues to
work within the phallogocentric categories that she calls into question. In other
words, her recent forays into theological thinking should prompt us to read
with renewed suspicion her early attempts to articulate an irreducible feminine
multiplicity. Specifically, this chapter will (re-)explore Irigaray's theorisation
of feminine corporeality – along with her claim that women need to give birth
to a new feminine imaginary, a new feminine morphology – in light of her call
for a reconception of divinity in a feminine mode.

This project is motivated by the realisation that the problems that arise when
one posits sexual difference as primary – as Irigaray clearly does, albeit without
succumbing to the biological essentialism of which many early critics accused
her[2] – continue to haunt feminism in spite of the articulation along lines of
race, class and sexual orientation of critiques of mainstream feminist theory.
Ellen T. Armour has argued that a close reading of Irigaray's interrogation of the
category 'woman' might help to expose and undermine the patriarchal discursive
structures that continue to mark much feminist theological thinking and

contribute to its failure to come to terms with the extent to which it remains marked by the exclusionary logic it seeks to contest (Armour 1993, 1999).[3] While I would certainly agree that the category of 'woman' needs to be challenged, I remain doubtful whether Irigaray goes far enough in her interrogations. In order to shed light on the questions that persist for me in my reading of Irigaray, I want to begin with a critical reading of 'Divine Women', and then proceed to a consideration of Irigaray's earlier theorisations of feminine corporeality, to suggest that those theorisations are marked by the same Platonic logic of idealisation that drives Irigaray's invocation of feminine divinity.

In 'Divine Women', Irigaray takes up Feuerbach's claim that God provides for humanity a mirroring of the possibility of its perfection, and in so doing guarantees the human genre, the identity of the human as distinct from the animal (Feuerbach 1957). Granted, Irigaray rejects Feuerbach's masculinist bias; that is, she argues that although the masculine and paternal God of the Jewish and Christian traditions has functioned historically to guarantee *masculine* identity (man's genre), no divinity has fulfilled that function for women. Nevertheless, she is apparently willing to adopt his premise that a conception of divinity, operating as a horizon for the constitution of subjectivity and an ideal of perfection, is an essential foundation for the possibility of freedom, autonomy and sovereignty. As she puts it, 'No human subjectivity, no human society has ever been established without the help of the divine' (Irigaray 1993c: 62). What is needed, she says, is a new conception of a specifically feminine divine – which is simultaneously a divinisation of the feminine, of women – to provide that horizon, that goal towards which women can direct their processes of infinite becoming. As women, we might reject the Father God of Judaism and Christianity, but we need our own God: 'Divinity is what we need to become free, autonomous, sovereign. . . . If women have no God, they are unable either to communicate or commune with one another. They need, we need, an infinite if they are to share *a little*' (Irigaray 1993c: 62).

In other words, rather than continuing to perform the function of underwriting masculine identity by (negatively) mirroring man – according to a Platonic logic of the same, of which Irigaray is so brilliantly critical in her earlier work (see especially Irigaray 1985a) – women must begin to claim their own subjectivity by imagining a God who guarantees feminine identity by mirroring *woman*:

> Woman has no mirror with which to become woman. Having a God and becoming one's gender go hand in hand. God is the other that we absolutely cannot be without. In order to *become*, we need some shadowy perception of achievement; not a fixed objective, not a One postulated to be immutable but rather a cohesion and a horizon that assures us the passage between past and future. . . . God alone can save us, keep us safe. The feeling or experience of a positive,

objective, glorious, existence, the feeling of subjectivity, is essential
for us. Just like a God who helps us and leads us in the path of
becoming, who keeps track of our limits and our infinite possibilities
– as women – who inspires our projects.

(Irigaray 1993c: 67)

This is a radical claim: the very possibility of feminism, it seems, is caught up
in this ability to imagine a different God – 'not [the] One postulated to be
immutable' upon which the masculine identity of Western metaphysics is
premised, but nevertheless a God who will provide 'some shadowy perception of
achievement' and thereby '[inspire] our projects'.

This appeal to a specifically feminine divinity as the ground for a specifically
feminine identity or subjectivity may seem surprising coming from a thinker
who, as Armour points out, so successfully deconstructed the identity of
'woman' in her earlier work; indeed, Serene Jones notes that it is important to
distinguish between Irigaray's earlier deconstructive project and her theological
musings if one is not to '[miscontrue] the second discourse as an essentialising
project which fails to stand up to the deconstructive criteria of the first' (Jones
1995: 47). Nevertheless, as Jones argues, it is difficult not to read 'Divine
Women' as an instance of 'the same universalising gestures she rigorously
critiques in her earlier work' (Jones 1995: 63). Jones lays the blame for this
problem at the feet of Irigaray's uncritical appropriation of Feuerbach's
argument, which seems to reproduce the specular economy of which she is so
critical in *Speculum of the Other Woman* and *This Sex Which Is Not One*. That is, if
for Irigaray the heart of the problem with the logic that establishes masculine
identity is that it requires that 'woman' be 'continually positioned as an other
who mirrors man back to himself, defining the borders of his identity and
securing the stability of his presence' (Jones 1995: 64), then why should she see
it as desirable that women should draft a newly reconceived God to play that
same role for feminine identity?

Of course, Irigaray imagines God in ways that work against the reductive force
of this logic. Most importantly, the God who operates in Irigaray's theological
discourse differs significantly from the transcendent Father God of Christianity
invoked by Feuerbach: her discourse blurs the distinction between the feminine
divine and actual women in ways that alter the form of any possible relation
between them. As Morny Joy notes in her reading of this essay, 'Irigaray does
not appear to want to make a sharp distinction between (*a*) changing the God
image to that of the feminine, and (*b*) divinising the female of the species.
She uses the two ideas interchangeably' (Joy 1990: 18). That is, Irigaray's God
lives in the bodies of women (although also, significantly, of men), but most
importantly in the relations between those bodies.[4] Irigaray does not reject
transcendence outright, but the only transcendence that marks the feminine

divine that she wants to call forth is a Levinasian transcendence that characterises the relation between irreducible others – a transcendence that, elsewhere, she locates in the 'sensible transcendental' (see especially 1993c; see also Armour, in Chapter 2 of this book).[5] Christianity, the religion of the transcendent Father God, betrays women (and men) precisely in that '[i]t has not been interpreted as the infinite that resides within us and among us, the god in us, the Other for us, becoming with and in us . . .' (Irigaray 1993c: 63).

Nevertheless, this resituating of divine transcendence within the domain of human relationships does not, for Irigaray, obviate the possibility that divinity can serve as a model for and a guarantee of identity or subjectivity. It is in this claim, I want to suggest, that she most dangerously undermines the anti-Platonic force of her early work. Irigaray clearly retains, in 'Divine Women', Feuerbach's double notion that God is *both* a 'horizon' for the constitution of subjectivity *and* an ideal of perfection, a goal towards which is directed an allegedly infinite process of becoming that is understood as the 'fulfilling [of] the wholeness of what we are capable of being' (Irigaray 1993c: 61). In her words, 'as long as woman lacks a divine made in her image she cannot establish her subjectivity or achieve a goal of her own' (Irigaray 1993c: 63). I would argue that Irigaray's use here of the notion of horizon runs counter to the Levinasian understanding of radical alterity – which is emphatically and explicitly '*not* the alterity of horizons' (Cohen 1985: 10; cited in Grosz 1989: 156)[6] – on which she relies so heavily. However, what is more disturbing to me is her insistence that divinity serve as ideal, as model of perfection – an insistence that seems reinscribed within a Platonic logic of resemblance.

For Irigaray, then, women need a feminine conception of divinity to embody specifically feminine ideals of perfection, ideals that will serve as foundation for feminine subjectivity. As she puts it,

> [t]he only diabolical thing about women is their lack of a God and the fact that, deprived of God, they are forced to comply with *models* that do not match them, that exile, double, mask them, cut them off from themselves and from one another, stripping away their ability to move forward into love, art, thought, *towards their ideal and divine fulfillment*.
>
> (Irigaray 1993c: 64; emphasis added)

Although Penelope Deutscher argues that what is significant about Irigaray's embodiment of the ideal in actual women is that it results in 'women [not being] severed from their ideal' (Deutscher 1994: 101), I would suggest that an ideal can only function *as ideal* to the extent that it *is* 'severed from' those who hold it. In other words, Irigaray's insistence that feminine divinity is properly situated within and among women, that 'we should incarnate God within us and in our sex: daughter-woman-mother' (Irigaray 1993c: 71), does not, in and of itself, adequately transform the structure of idealisation at work in her Feuerbachian argument. For Irigaray, that is, it is not the fact of having models itself that is problematic, but rather the fact that the models 'do not match' women, and thus '[strip] away their ability to move forward . . . towards their ideal and divine fulfillment' (Irigaray 1993c: 64). As Deutscher observes, if the transcendence that continues to attach itself to Irigaray's feminine divinity is embodied in relationships among actual women, then those relationships – of which '[t]he role a mother represents for her daughter could be an example' – become the divinised field of possibilities for identification and subjectification (Deutscher 1994: 103).[7]

I would argue that in invoking divinity as an idealised model for women's becoming, Irigaray has recapitulated the Platonic positing of an eternal realm of *Eidolon* (Ideas or Forms), *models* in whose essence the *copies* (objects in the material world, bodies, human thoughts and so on) participate, and to which they conform.[8] The positing of such a realm asserts the primacy of resemblance to a transcendent idea(l) as the standard by which 'truth' will be recognised. That is, an idealised image that would function as a goal for becoming cannot help but retain a normativity that dominates the process of subjectification. It is precisely this normativity, I would suggest, that provokes critiques of much feminist theology by lesbians, working-class women and women of color. Irigaray herself seems to be aware of this, and yet to accept it as a necessary element of women's accession to subjectivity *as women*. In a passage that, at least as I read it, is marked by an absence of any hint of irony, she asks:

> How is our God to be imagined? Or is it our god? Do we possess *a* quality that can reverse the predicate to the subject, as Feuerbach does for *God* and *man* . . . ? If there is no *one* quality, which of the *many* would we choose to conceive our becoming perfect women? This is not a luxury but a necessity, the need for a finalised, theoretical, and practical activity that would be both speculative and moral.
>
> (Irigaray 1993c: 67: some emphasis added)

In other words, while it may be difficult to adjudicate among the many qualities of women in order to 'choose' one (or several) that would enable 'our becoming perfect women', we have no choice but to do so if our goal is to construct a feminist practice that is 'both speculative and moral'. The question is, how do we accomplish such an adjudication? And how does our becoming as women retain any meaningful infinity if the multiplicity of our actual differences is reduced to a chosen few in order to enable us to imagine a God who would operate as idealised goal of that becoming?

I want to suggest, then, that even if Irigaray has succeeded in deconstructing the totalising transcendence of the Father God of Christianity in her linking of divine transcendence with the bodies of women, and the relations among those bodies, she has effectively foreclosed the possibility of women's infinite becoming, understood as the multiplying of actual differences among women, by re-enacting a dynamics of idealisation as the ground of subjectification. In other words, while I would agree that Irigaray's feminine divine is *not* the Father God of Christianity, it nevertheless seems to occupy the same position, and thus not only fails sufficiently to disrupt the logic of the Same that marks traditional Christian theology, but also disappoints the hope that feminist theology will imagine a non-exclusionary discursive practice. Furthermore, I would argue, Irigaray's theorisation of feminine corporeality in terms of a feminine imaginary and a feminine morphology, from *Speculum of the Other Woman* and *This Sex Which Is Not One* onward, bears the marks of the same logic that operates in 'Divine Women'.

From her earliest texts onward, Irigaray's writings on the subject of feminine corporeality have been intelligible only in the context of her desire to create 'a new *symbolic morphology* in which [women] can say: I, sexual being, woman, assert such and such' (Irigaray, quoted in Mortley 1991: 72; emphasis added). What does she mean, then, by 'symbolic morphology'? This is one way of noting that – contrary to the many readers who have labelled her an 'essentialist' – Irigaray's project to articulate a philosophy of sexual difference is motivated not by a desire to construct a positive theory of female sexuality, but by the conviction that women must intervene in the repressive phallocentrism of the Western symbolic order if they, if we, are to empower ourselves as women. Thus the body that interests Irigaray is always already thoroughly inscribed within culture, and it finds its meaning only by virtue of the social and linguistic practices in which it is enmeshed (see especially Whitford 1991a, 1991b; Grosz 1989).

In other words, for Irigaray there can be no question of a 'natural' or 'pre-linguistic' body – no question of an empirical 'anatomy' – but only of a symbolic or metaphorical body that expresses and is expressed by its culture. She approaches this metaphorical body by means of her notion of the imaginary, a concept borrowed in large part from Lacan, who posits the imaginary as the pre-symbolic phase of subjectification, in which the nascent subject misapprehends its mirror image as proof of its own wholeness.[9] What is unique to Irigaray's imaginary, of course, is the element of sexual difference. As a corrective to the implicit and explicit masculinity of Lacan's imaginary, in other words, Irigaray suggests a 'return to that repressed entity, the female imaginary', an imaginary that she describes primarily by way of the now-famous image of the two lips (Irigaray 1985b: 28, 205–18). As Whitford notes, Irigaray sees both the imaginary and the culture and discourse that grow out of it as necessarily sexed, either (morphologically) male – and thus characterised by unity and self-identity – or (morphologically) female – and thus characterised by plurality and fluidity

(Whitford 1991b: 54). Irigaray's wager, in positing a female imaginary, is that what Jane Gallop has called a 'vulvomorphic' logic might empower women, and serve as a foundation for a feminist politics based on the emergence of a feminine subjectivity (Gallop 1983: 78ff.; see also Hollywood 1999: 241).

However, in spite of the fact that Irigaray avoids the problems of biological essentialism by intervening in Western phallocentric culture on the level of the imaginary, there are still problems with this strategy. As I see it, when Irigaray attempts to undo the masculine dominance of the Lacanian imaginary by deploying a feminine imaginary, one of two outcomes is possible. First, in claiming and valorising many of those qualities traditionally ascribed to 'woman' in the Western tradition – qualities such as fluidity, non-linearity and so on – Irigaray runs the risk of allowing the feminine imaginary to be subsumed under the masculine, as its opposite and/or complement. In such a case, the gender binarisms of phallomorphic logic are left unchallenged, and sexual difference fails to emerge. Alternatively, the feminine imaginary asserts itself as a positive foundation for feminine identity, as suggested above, and – in reproducing the dynamics of Lacanian subjectification – underwrites a subjectivity that, as Irigaray has argued in *Speculum of the Other Woman*, '[is always] appropriated by the "masculine"' (1985a: 133ff.). Or, as Gallop notes, 'Vulvomorphic logic, once in place, would be no less oppressive than phallomorphic logic. Each is necessarily, like any logic, alienated from the body . . .' (Gallop 1983: 81). Again, sexual difference fails to emerge.

But I see a larger problem with Irigaray's strategic invocation of a feminine imaginary, and that problem lies precisely in the fact that such an imaginary is 'alienated from the body'. In other words, as Whitford points out, when Irigaray speaks of the 'two lips', she is clearly 'talking about an "*ideal* morphology"' (Whitford 1991b: 58). If this avoids the dilemmas of essentialism, it also effaces the multiplicity of actual bodily differences among 'women', assigning all bodies with vaginas to the same idealised category, and marking that category with only a few (albeit significant) morphological qualities. Thus Irigaray's positing, in *Speculum of the Other Woman* and *This Sex Which Is Not One*, of an idealised feminine imaginary foreshadows her invocation, in 'Divine Women', of a feminine divinity that would be imagined in terms of specifically feminine ideals of perfection. In both projects, she asserts the need for an idealised foundation for feminine subjectivity, and in so doing forecloses the possibility of the multiplying of actual differences.

What is needed, I would argue, is a (re)turn to the attempt to theorise not idealised anatomies but rather empirical bodies. The imaginary might prove to be a useful conception in this effort, but only if, as Moira Gatens suggests, we move away from the notion that there is a single feminine imaginary, and embrace the multiplicity of different imaginaries that underlie our multiple and always pro-cessual subjectivities. Gatens, invoking a Spinozist conception of embodiment, based on multiple and historically situated imaginaries, asserts the importance of 'corporeal multiplicity':

> To consider the multiplicity of body types and their specific pleasures and powers would assist in freeing up the normative dualism of two bodies, two sexes and two genders. Indeed, this multiplicity already exists: the homosexual body, the heterosexual body, the celibate body, the narcissistic body, the perverse body, the maternal body, the athletic body.
>
> (Gatens 1996: 43)

While a certain idealisation shows itself here in her use of the definite article (for example, '*the* homosexual body'), her insistence that bodies – and imaginaries – not be conceived as only masculine or feminine is, I think, an important intervention in the phallocentrism of Western culture. This insistence does not necessitate an abandoning of the notion that sexual difference is, as Irigaray claims, 'one of the major philosophical issues, if not the issue, of our age' (Irigaray 1993a: 5); rather, it holds feminist theory accountable for its failure to theorise the multiplicity of bodily differences that keep 'women' from being (simply) 'woman'. As Gatens puts it, 'It seems important . . . that feminists who are in a position of (relative) social power do not use this power to further entrench polarities that function negatively in relation to other social groups as well' (Gatens 1996: 56). I take this to mean that what Ellen T. Armour refers to as 'whitefeminist theory' (Armour 1999) cannot afford the luxury of discourses that apparently reduce all difference to sexual difference, and thereby 'further entrench [the] polarities' that characterise phallocentrism.

I do find a hopeful note in Irigaray's discourse of feminine divinity, and that is her insistence that women's becoming(s) be infinite – that, in her words, '[t]he goal that is most valuable is to go on *becoming*, infinitely' (Irigaray 1993c: 61). In this context, I find it helpful to refer to what Gilles Deleuze and Felix Guattari have to say about becoming:

> [B]ecoming is not . . . a resemblance, an imitation, or, at the limit, an identification. . . . Above all, becoming does not occur in the imagination. . . . Becoming produces nothing other than itself. . . . What is real is the becoming itself, the block of becoming, not the supposedly fixed terms through which that becoming passes. . . . Becoming is certainly not imitating, or identifying with something. . . . Becoming is a verb with a consistency all its own; it does not reduce to, or lead back to, 'appearing,' 'being,' 'equaling,' or 'producing'.
>
> (Deleuze and Guattari 1987: 237–9)

To preserve the infinity of becomings that Irigaray envisages for women, in other words, it is imperative to move beyond the oppressive and repressive founding of subjectivity in an idealisation, whether divine or imaginary. To the extent that Irigaray asks us to 'choose' from among women's many qualities one or a few that would enable us 'to conceive our becoming perfect women', and to the extent that she suggests that our goal should be 'to become *and remain* [*ourselves*]', she seems to limit the infinity that she claims to want to hold open – and in so doing limits the ways that we can conceive of ourselves as women (Irigaray 1993c: 67, 72). It is perhaps not an accident, then, but rather a mark of ways that the grounding of identity in idealisation negates and excludes an infinity of becomings that, as Serene Jones notes, 'Irigaray . . . makes no mention of race, economic class, ethnicity, or sexual orientation as contexts in which discursive and historical "others" have been exploited and repressed by the rhetoric and institutions of the dominant culture' (Jones 1993: 116–17, n. 7). It would, in other words, seem to be the case that Irigaray's conceptualisation of feminine divinity, like her evocation of a feminine imaginary, fails to provide the non-exclusionary intervention in traditional Western theological thinking that would enable mainstream feminist theology to answer to its many critics.

Notes

1   See, for example, Serene Jones (1993 and 1995), Penelope Deutscher (1994) and Morny Joy (1990). See also Margaret Whitford (1991b) and Elizabeth Grosz (1989 and 1993).

2   Irigaray asserts, for example, that '[s]exual difference is an immediate natural given and it is a real and irreducible component of the universal. The whole of human kind is composed of women and men and of nothing else. The problem of race is, in fact, a secondary problem . . .' (1996a: 47).

3   However, Armour clearly shares many of my reservations about 'Divine Women'; see her essay in Chapter 2.

4   While in 'Divine Women' the emphasis falls more heavily on the embodiment of divinity in relationships between and among women – so that the concern is explicitly 'the possibility that God might be made flesh as a woman, through the mother and the daughter, and in their relationships' (Irigaray 1993c: 71) – the essay 'Sexual Difference', in *An Ethics of Sexual Difference* (1993a), problematically locates divine transcendence in the heterosexual relationship.

5   Elizabeth Grosz (1989) writes very helpfully on the subject of Irigaray's appropriation of Levinas in *Sexual Subversions*, especially in pp. 141–6 and 155–8.

6   Cohen's point here is important: the concept of 'horizon' is meaningless outside of the frame of reference of the specular ego, and thus must operate within a logic of appropriation. Serene Jones (1993) makes what I take to be a similar point in her comparison of Irigaray and Karl Barth (whose notion of God as radically Other has been linked with Levinas's work).

7   In connection with this passage, it is telling that Graham Ward has suggested that the mother is more than a mere *example* of the kind of relation that would embody feminine divinity. He argues that Irigaray's elaboration of a feminine imaginary/morphology makes sense only in the context of a Lacanian frame, so that 'the task of women [is] to re-envision Lacan's Name of the Father in terms of a Name of the Mother' (Ward 1996: 223). While his reading of Irigaray arguably co-opts her project in the service of his neo-Orthodox theology, it is nevertheless significant, in the context of my argument, that such a reading is possible. The latter half of this chapter will develop the connection between Irigaray's feminine divinity and her feminine imaginary/morphology.

8   This critique draws heavily on Gilles Deleuze's reading of Plato's *Phaedrus*, in which he argues that, for Plato, '[m]yth, with its always circular structure, is indeed the story of a foundation. It permits the construction of a model according to which the different pretenders can be judged . . .' (Deleuze 1990: 255). It seems to me that what Irigaray is engaged in when she invokes a feminine divinity is a kind of alternative *mythopoesis*, designed to supplant the patriarchal mythology that undergirds the Western tradition. How are we to proceed, though, if myth-making itself remains bound up in Platonic logic, as my reading of 'Divine Women' seems to suggest?

9   See Whitford (1991b), especially pp. 53–7, for a much more fully developed explication of Irigaray's symbolic. She notes that Irigaray's use of the concept is influenced also by Bachelard, Castoriadis and others, and thus more richly nuanced than would be possible if Irigaray had limited herself to intervening in a strictly Lacanian discourse.

Chapter 4

Morny Joy

IRIGARAY'S EASTERN EXPLORATIONS

I Introduction

THE WORK OF IMAGINATION, in various guises, both psychoanalytical and philosophic, is at the heart of Irigaray's project. Intricately interconnected with her appreciation of women's bodies and minds as being at once constrained by patriarchal precedents, yet capable of challenge and transformation, the imagination is the agent for dynamic change. In *Speculum of the Other Woman* (1985a), the Lacanian psychoanalytic theory of the imaginary and the symbolic is not so much confronted, as undermined in ways that provide space for envisioning alternative creative configurations. From *Sexes and Genealogies* (1993c) onward, however, Irigaray adopts a more dynamic notion of the imagination, with its own generative capacity. It is this innovative notion of imagination that she invokes when proposing the idea of women becoming divine. She asks: 'This God, are we capable of imagining it as a woman?' (1993c: 63). Irigaray is here employing an act of synthetic or creative imagination, which is no longer confined to the Lacanian model. As she states, 'To remain within the limits of the senses in one's suffering or one's jouissance – both of them imaginary – is not the same as acceding to the creation of the imagination' (1993c: 161–2). Irigaray's appeal to an active imagination, while it rereads the past, also envisages new explorations or expressions of being and acting for women. Her work in this area is both provocative and suggestive of ways that women can indeed change the world, or forge a new era of history (1996a: 141).

Thus, in her most recent writings – *I Love to You* (1996a) and *Between East and West* (2002) – Irigaray does not confine herself to subversive rereadings of the myths and images of women in ancient Greek culture, such as Antigone, or even reinterpreting the Annunciation of Mary (1994b: 67–87), but turns instead towards what she terms 'Far-Eastern traditions', specifically those of India

(1996a: 140–1, 137). This chapter will be an exploration of this turn in Irigaray's work and the implications of this change, which moves beyond simply the imaginative to a more speculative and spiritual mode of writing. It will also examine Irigaray's work in the light of recent discussions of Orientalism.

II Imaginative explorations

It was in her essay 'Divine Women' that Irigaray first advocated that women begin to explore ways of becoming divine, so as to counteract centuries of a God made in the image of men (1993c: 57–72). To become divine, for a woman, implies a fulfilment of the potentialities of her being (1993b: 116–17). Ontologically, for Irigaray, this involves a mode of becoming for women that is intimately related to a distinct mode of sexual difference between men and women (1996a: 61–5). For women, this mode of sexual difference requires acknowledging a mode of god according to women's desires for identity and fulfilment.[1] This does not, however, involve a return to literal worship of goddess figures of old; rather it envisages (re-)establishing a society 'that reflects [women's] values and their fertility' (1993c: 81).

In 'Divine Women', Irigaray also posits that the only task God asks of all humanity is that it become divine. This mutual task demands of all 'to become divine men and women, to become perfectly, to refuse to allow parts of ourselves to shrivel and die that have the potential for growth and fulfillment' (1993c: 69). Thus, males have not been automatically excluded from this process, but, for Irigaray, their participation would require that they no longer assume a mode of dominance, but abide by a new mode of interaction between the sexes. This would involve a radical revision of previous forms of heterosexuality. Irigaray elaborates this new mode of relationship between men and women in *An Ethics of Sexual Difference* (1993a) and *I Love to You* (1996a). This new sexual relationship[2] requires that each person would cultivate his or her own instinctual drives and not impose them on 'the other of sexual difference'. Irigaray describes her own revised appreciation of the negotiation of the 'negative':

> [T]he negative can mean access to the other of sexual difference and thereby become happiness without being annihilating in the process. Hegel knew nothing of a negative like that. His negative is still the mastery of consciousness (historically male), over nature and human kind. The [new form of] negative in sexual difference means an acceptance of the limits of my gender and a recognition of the irreducibility of the other. It cannot be overcome, but it gives a positive access – neither instinctual nor drive-related – to the other.
> (1996a: 13)

For Irigaray, this self-reflective task of differentiation is what makes love possible. At the same time it is a spiritual task in that it brings about the divinisation of both participants. 'Love, even carnal love, is therefore cultivated and made divine. The act of love becomes the transubstantiation of the self and his or her lover into a spiritual body' (1996a: 139). Irigaray even proposes that, as a result of this development, '[t]he Third era of the West might, at least, be the era of the *couple*: of the spirit and the bride? After the coming of the Father that is inscribed in the Old Testament, after the coming of the Son in the New Testament, we would see the beginning of the era of the spirit and the bride' (1993a: 148). It needs to be noted, however, that Irigaray has not been particularly sympathetic to traditional institutional Western religions, neither Jewish nor Christian. Irigaray's 'age of spirit', as will become apparent in the course of this chapter, will involve a very different understanding of spirituality and God than current Western religious interpretations.[3]

Many of these spiritual speculations, however, have been in the abstract. Irigaray has been somewhat at a loss to provide specific images from traditional Christianity to illustrate these new forms of relationship. This is because, in Irigaray's view, Western civilisation and religion have been dominated by the image of a lone male God. Patriarchy, on Irigaray's account, has obliterated from its pantheon any traces of goddesses or a gynocratic culture (except for Mary, in her popularised version).[4] Yet, according to Irigaray, things have not always been this way. As she observes: 'A return to the [pre-Christian] origins of our culture shows that . . . there was an era in which it was the woman who initiated love. At that time woman was a goddess and not a servant, and she watched over the carnal and spiritual dimension of love' (1996a: 135).

Irigaray, however, no longer confines her imaginative explorations on this topic to Western civilisation. Since *Sexes and Genealogies*, in particular, Irigaray has continued to manifest an interest in Asian culture in general as providing exemplifications of a new form of relationship to other people and the world: 'Thus in certain Asian countries, ritual and individual prayer consists in bodily exercise that is either personal or collective: yoga, tai chi, karate, song, dance, the tea ceremony, flower arranging. There is no sacrifice of the other, and yet there is a much richer spirituality as well as a more fertile eroticism' (1993c: 77). Irigaray continues with this form of 'Oriental' idealisation in her quest for images that would be suitable for the new era of Spirit that she envisages for the West with its paucity of figures of male and female lovers that are both sexual and spiritual: 'Only certain Oriental traditions speak of the energising, aesthetic, and religious fecundity of the sexual act: the two sexes give each other the seed of life and eternity, the growing generation of and between them both' (1993a: 14).

It is India with its pantheon of gods and goddesses that has a special attraction for Irigaray. As she states, 'In India, for example, and at the beginnings of our Greek culture – for to some extent this era still exists in India – sexuality was cultural, sacred' (1994b: 11). Specifically, it is the notion of the relationship of the gods and goddesses that attracts her: 'In India, men and women are gods together, and together they create the world, including its cosmic dimension' (Irigaray 2002: 29). Irigaray intimates that there are elements of this spiritual dimension that continue today, though she is aware that they may not live up to former precedents, particularly with regard to sexual difference: 'Even the teachers of yoga trained in India forget the importance of sexual difference in the culture that they pass on' (2002: 10).

Irigaray is particularly interested in two interrelated aspects of Indian/Hindu culture and their importance for providing data on the subject of a female divine, and a divine couple. One aspect is the existence and legacy of a gynocentric society, and the other is the yogic/tantric tradition within which women are revered in the act of sexual union. These two themes interweave in her work in ways that are difficult to separate out – but for the purposes of this chapter I will begin by treating each separately, and then examine how Irigaray links them together. I would then like to evaluate these claims, particularly with reference to the writings of contemporary Indian women, within the perspective of Orientalism.

III Gynocratic cultures

In *je, tu, nous: Toward a Culture of Difference*, Irigaray refers to her understanding of gynocratic culture: 'Gynocratic traditions – which should not be restricted to matriarchy but should include eras when women reigned as women – predate patriarchy but don't go back to the time of cave living, nor to the early paleolithic period, nor to certain forms of animal behaviour as is interpreted and understood in supposedly knowledgeable circles' (1993b: 24). In *Between East and West*, Irigaray identifies her approach as being in sympathy with the pre-Aryan or indigenous elements that survive in contemporary Hinduism, which she associates with gynocentrism and which she appreciates as more feminine in their sympathies (2002: 29). Nevertheless, Irigaray does not appear to have undertaken research of textual material, and appeals to such secondary sources as J. J. Bachofen, in general, and Mircea Eliade, in particular, to support her claims for a gynocentric period and legacy in India (Irigaray 1993b: 24; 2002: 65; 1993b: 90). In *Myth, Religion and Mother Right* (1967), Bachofen, a nineteenth-century scholar, wrote a treatise on the existence of a primordial matriarchal culture. He assumed, however, that it was rightfully displaced by patriarchy – for which he is taken to task by Irigaray, who asks for his evidence (1993b: 26). She none the less accepts his matriarchal hypothesis. Eliade in turn postulates that '[m]other religion . . . once reigned over a huge Aegean-African-Asian area and from the beginning of time was the major form of devotion among India's many autochthonous populations' (1969: 178).

However, with the exception of one reference to Merlin Stone (Irigaray 1993b: 24), Irigaray does not cite the debates that Anglo-American scholars have been engaged in regarding the existence of gynocracies or matriarchies (see Eller 2000). In addition, the questioning of both Bachofen's and Eliade's approaches by women scholars – specifically concerning these male scholars' adulation of the conquering warrior tribes and their rightful suppression of the purported matriarchies – is not acknowledged in any detail (see Christ 1991). There is also no reference to any historical studies of the relevant period by prominent Indian women scholars (see, for example, Thapar 1989, Chakravarti 1989 and Roy 1995), nor to the work of post-colonial scholarship regarding the complexity involved in cultural misappropriations of traditional interpretations and cultural ideals – specifically with regard to women (see, for example, Narayan 1997 and Spivak 1990). Thus, Irigaray's work would seem to be written without reference to issues in contemporary scholarship in Anglo-American feminism, to recent historical research of early India, or to post-colonialist discussions. Instead, her interests have become more spiritual rather than theoretical in nature.

IV Yoga and tantrism

Irigaray, as does Eliade (1958: 254–67, 343–8), integrates this appreciation of gynocratic ideals with the practices of yoga and tantrism. The basic presupposition of this development is that the traces or remnants of the pre-Aryan, gynocentric cultures are at the basis of yoga and tantrism. There are indeed many scholars today who admit to the effects of indigenous influences, by way of a long undocumented process of infiltration into the Brahmanic tradition of Hinduism, and who see 'Hinduism' as a tradition that has been much more heterodox than the Brahmanically centred Western scholarship allowed. Again Irigaray, on her own admission, is not so much concerned with traditional scholarly procedures that would support her claims, as she believes they are no longer appropriate for her approach. She prefers instead to follow the ways of the masters/gurus who have instructed her in yoga, as well as her own selected reading (2002: 71).

In both *I Love to You* (1996a) and *Between East and West* (2002), Irigaray continually makes reference to yoga, which has become a personal practice for her. She relates that '[t]hrough practising breathing, through educating my perceptions, through concerning myself continually with cultivating the life of my body, through reading current and ancient texts of the yoga tradition and tantric texts, I learned what I knew: the body is the site of the incarnation of the divine and I have to treat it as such' (2002: 62). It is obvious that her practice of yoga is not just for personal well-being – it is a spiritual undertaking. This practice strongly influences Irigaray's discussion of both yoga and tantrism, which is conducted against a Hindu background. Irigaray understands yoga as intimately connected with tantrism, where the body is educated to become both spiritual and more carnal at the same time (1996a: 24). In this connection, Irigaray is influenced by Eliade's reading of yoga, and his romanticised view of women, along the lines of 'the eternal feminine' (Eliade 1969: 178–9), which is an ideal discredited by contemporary feminists beginning with Simone de Beauvoir. Eliade focuses on the divine feminine power, referred to as *shakti*,[5] but always in the context of wife or mother – never depicting woman as an initiator.[6] In contrast to Eliade, however, Irigaray acknowledges woman in her own right. Thus, while Irigaray appreciates the image of a male and female in sexual union, a symbol of enlightment in tantrism, she understands it as an exemplar of fecundity, both natural and spiritual (2002: 60). What is of central importance for Irigaray, in contrast to Eliade, is the fact that in tantrism there is a disclosure of 'the worship of a Goddess (worship of her body and her sex) by man' (Irigaray 1996a: 137).

Irigaray also recognises that the breath is of utmost importance in this yogic/ tantric discipline of spiritual transformation. The role of breath, as associated with the life source and the mother, featured in Irigaray's earlier work (1993c: 49–53). In her later works, the breath, as an element of spiritual practice, representing the generative life source, will be crucial in the movement from a simply carnal to a spiritual union. She describes the movement involved: 'Becoming spiritual amounts to transforming our elementary vital breath little by little into a more subtle breath in the service of the heart, of thought, of speech and not only in the service of physiological survival' (2002: 76). In this way the body will be changed.

> In these traditions, the body is cultivated to become both more spiritual and more carnal at the same time. A range of movements and nutritional practices, attentiveness to breath in respiration, respect for the rhythms of day, and night, for the seasons and years as the calendar of the flesh, for the world and for History, the training of the senses for accurate, rewarding and concentrated perception – all these gradually bring the body to rebirth.
>
> (1996a: 24)

In Irigaray's depiction, the male (*yogi*) and female (*yogini*), by controlling the breath and stabilising concentration, can proceed in the practice of kundalini yoga, in which a process of directing energy through the seven *chakras*[7] aids the attainment of enlightenment (*moksha*), or the realisation of Self (*jivan mukhti*), which, within Hinduism, are two of the most recognised descriptions of this ultimate state. The final product can be symbolised in various ways. Most often it is represented as the union of the god Shiva with the aspect of feminine power, *shakti* – the female or goddess form. This also represents the fact that dualities of existence which operate at the level of conditioned reality are thereby overcome. But for Irigaray, it is not necessarily this overcoming of dualities that is of primary importance, nor is it the union with *shakti*, if it remains simply a symbolic form of the feminine (2002: 63). For Irigaray, the union must be of both a spiritual and a carnal nature.

Yoga, as a discipline, does have an ancient lineage in India, with some scholars dating its history back to images found on seals at Mohenjo-daro, a third-millennium BCE site. In time it became associated with another indigenous legacy, that of tantrism, a much revered, though often exoticised, form of religious practice. Its origins, too, may well go back to pre-Vedic times and there is speculation as to the beginnings of a relationship between yoga and tantra.[8] Tantra has many different traditions or schools in both Buddhism and Hinduism, but it appears to be mainly the Hindu variety that interests Irigaray. Georges Varenne alludes to actual tantric texts in Hinduism which can be dated from about 1000 CE.

> These texts have been given the name *Tantras* (books), which is why we speak of Tantrism when referring to this branch of Hinduism. At other times the term Shaktism is referred to denote the same current of thought, because the Sanskrit word *shakti* (power, force) is the one that best evokes the goddess's true nature: Divine energy emanating from Brahman, the concrete manifestation of her power of creation.
>
> (1976: 144)

Tantra, however, has never been a unified body of knowledge, and its history is subject to many different interpretations. There have been many goddesses, many types of adepts. There have also been many schools (in Buddhism as well as Hinduism), with complex formulas and practices that are of either an externalised or an internalised nature. All of these are concerned in one way or another with the transformation of the body into a spiritual vessel.[9]

Many books on Hindu tantrism have been discreet regarding the exact function of *Shakti*, delineating her mainly as the female principle of energy, or describing her union with the god Shiva as merely a symbolic depiction of the overcoming of duality, including male/female polarity. On the other hand, there have been lurid appropriations that reduce the whole thing to erotic indulgence.

> It is . . . not surprising that so many Neo-Tantrics in the West look upon Tantra as a sexual discipline promising pleasure beyond all expectation, mostly in the form of prolonged or multiple orgasms. Neo-Tantrics seek to emulate the divine couple but typically forget that the union between Shiva and Shakti is transcendental and therefore also asexual. The fruit of their union – and hence the goal

of Tantra Yoga – is not bodily orgasm, however overwhelming, but perpetual bliss far beyond anything the human nervous system is capable of producing.

(Feuerstein 1998: 80)

In one sense, Irigaray would agree with Feuerstein, particularly in her attitude that the practice of love must be spiritual and not just sexual (2001: 59). But there is another sense where she would not agree. Again, this is because, for Irigaray, the expression of love must be both bodily and spiritual at the same time. Irigaray does not appear to be in favour of out-of-body changes of consciousness of a mystical nature. It is the affirmation of the human body itself as divine and as a means of spiritual insight that she has been seeking all along, as well as the appropriate images to portray it.

In *I Love to You* (1996a), Irigaray integrates these ideas into her own spiritual quest, which was evident, though not developed in any sustained way, in certain earlier texts. Thus it is that Irigaray departs from her radical rereadings of the Western philosophical and religious traditions to explore and envisage how a person, and the world, can be changed by this new spiritual perspective. Irigaray is now more concerned with the dynamics of personal spiritual experience, rather than simply theoretical statements with regard to 'the perfecting of our gender', as the means of fostering the integration of spirit and nature. Irigaray's perspective has changed from philosophical critique of the Western tradition to a form of confessional advocacy that basically distances itself from a philosophical or theoretical study of religion. In a sense, it has been Irigaray's aim from her earliest work to expose the objectivist illusion that she believes underlies Western conceptions of rationality – its repressions and its unconscious sexualised dichotomies. Her alternative imaginative forays have now led her to promote living according a spiritual path which respects nature and the body, and sexual difference, rather than adopting an intellectual philosophical orientation, as more conducive to achieving the changes she perceives as necessary for culture's and cosmos's survival.

It is not as if Irigaray is unaware of the difficulties involved in the alteration of her orientation, nor of the problems that she faces in this enterprise of adapting Eastern ideals and images. She does make several qualifications in the opening pages of *Between East and West* to the effect that she is aware of the complexities that preclude any simplistic adaptation of other religions (2002: 13–14). She also admits that there is far more to be learned in this area (2002: 7), and acknowledges that it is no longer simply a matter of extracting one pristine element from the living matrix of the religious ferment that comprises Hinduism, or any other Eastern religion. 'Moreover, the Eastern traditions themselves are multiple at present and the Asiatic aboriginal and Indo-European contributions live together there without real articulation between them' (2002: 15). Nonetheless, it appears that Irigaray's treatment is idiosyncratic in her imaginative interpretation of one dimension of Hinduism, that of a blend of yoga and tantrism, and its implications for a new spirituality.

Irigaray also acknowledges that she is not unaware of the atrocities that are perpetrated on women in the name of religion – a fact that was evident to her on her voyage to India (2002: 65). As a consequence, she acknowledges that there are two different strata: one where women are regarded as goddesses and one where men continue to exercise their unquestioned supremacy over women. Yet she continues this same discussion by observing that it was during this voyage to India that she heard the master T. Krishnamacharya affirm the importance of the notion of sexual difference as a part of the culture of yoga (2002: 65). Though it is not stated explicitly, the implication is that if men and women learn to respect sexual difference, this practice, where women are respected as inherently spiritual in their bodily form, will be effective in changing the current social ills. While I do believe that Irigaray means this in a sincere and profound way, it is difficult to appreciate this remark, given the number of women in India who are still living according to the traditional ideals of service to their husbands.

V India today

Perhaps a relevant question with regard to the lives of women, specifically in Hinduism, is just how many are qualified or permitted to undertake this path of tantric yoga – because it would appear that only a select number of women could today undertake, or have ever undertaken, such a discipline. The actual conditions of women in India need to be evaluated. The fact that they are regarded not just as representations of the divine, but as embodiments of it, has not been of benefit to women. For although *shakti* is honoured and feared as a divine principle, and revered in ritual, this does not seem to have a profound effect on the treatment of the vast majority of women by men, within either Buddhism or Hinduism.

Ironically, June Campbell, in *Traveller in Space: In Search of Female Identity in Tibetan Buddhism* (1996), uses the work of Irigaray as the basis of her criticism of the role of women within contemporary Tibetan Tantric Buddhism. Agreeing with Irigaray's critique of the place of women in traditional religion, as articulated in *Speculum of the Other Woman* (1985a), Campbell states:

> This seems particularly true in the Tibetan system where the potential of wholeness in the female form, quite clearly represented in some of the more archaic tantric images, is somehow never realised in the social sphere. I have argued that this is because the association of emptiness with the female links the female body to a

concept of the transcendental, which means that the female body is exploited by the male in his quest for his own typology, while she herself has no adequate means to realise her own. The transcendental therefore becomes, as Irigaray understands it, 'the arena of the (philosophical) subject split off from its ground'.

(1996: 154)

Campbell draws attention to the fact that while there is an emphasis in tantric Buddhism on the female principle, which may indeed be evidence for an earlier period in pre-Vedic India when women were honoured, the subsequent history is not so positive (1996: 153–7). The predominantly monastic movement gradually eroded the vital participation of women into more formalised meditative rituals of enlightenment.

Many Indian women scholars have discussed this puzzling anomaly. As Leela Gulati asks: 'Why does the status of women remain so low when goddesses are considered as powerful as god?' (Gulati 1995: 83). For Gulati there is no simple answer to this situation, but there is no doubt as to the social restrictions placed on most Indian women. Though there are exceptions to this rule in the history of Hinduism – such as the medieval poet saints (Gupta 1992) – and contemporary female ascetics – even of the tantric variety (Denton 1992) – who have chosen to renounce traditional marriage and householder rules, a majority of women are subject to the regulations of the *Dharma Shastras* (the sacred law codes) as propounded in the *Laws of Manu* (Bühler 1969), written somewhere between the second century BCE and the second century CE.[10] Whatever realisation of self is allowed to a woman comes to her only as a reflection of the spiritual stature of her husband. It is this wider background of women in Hinduism that Irigaray does not mention in her study.

In her book *Caste as Woman* (1995), Vrinda Nabar analyses the mythological heritage which she believes also contributes to the devaluing of women.

> We are fond, in India, of speaking of an ideal past when women were equal with men and no discrimination was visible. Such an unreal vision ignores the Sītās and Draupadīs [heroines of classic and beloved epic sagas] who are as much the postscripts of that allegedly idyllic age as are the male protagonists of our national epics. The myth denuded would reveal a pattern of unequal prescription. Both Sītā and Draupadī herald an on-going tradition of long-suffering women whose real heroism is overlaid with the message of devotion and service to their husbands, a glorification of these qualities so that martyrdom is seen, in some cases, as preferable, desirable, virtuous, and even imperative.

(Nabar 1995: 22–3)

Nabar then discusses what she believes are some of the repercussions of these attitudes in contemporary practices with regard to dowry-deaths, abortion of female foetuses, widow mistreatment, even *sati*. Though there are Indian feminists who work for change (Nabar 1995: 6–15), these societal ills seem to stem from psychologically ingrained attitudes so that even legal measures, let alone the spiritual heritage, appear insufficient as a means of redress (Narasimhan 1992: 152).

Such cultural perceptions are also being challenged today in more complex ways by post-colonialist feminist scholars, such as Chakravarti (1989), who question nationalist appeals to the glories of an Indian past and its emotional evocations of women as the guardians of the spiritual essence of the tradition (as a hedge against encroaching Westernisation). Uma Narayan is particularly concerned about this reconstructed past, much of which is actually of recent date and was the result of a collaborative effort on the part of British colonialists and Hindu nationalists, which is now being exploited by the Hindutva right-wing movement (Narayan 1997: 25).[11]

It is this form of questioning of the legitimacy of tradition and its possible use as an ideology of repression of contemporary Hindu women that Irigaray does not take into consideration. Nor does she question whether her adoption of aspects of this tradition might also have conservative significations, in that she may be reintroducing to the West another form of cultural constraints, though they are promoted as idealised figures of women. Irigaray, in her concern for the spiritual aspects of tantric Hinduism, does not question other aspects of the tradition that are less favourable for women.

Tracy Pintchman, in her essay 'Is the Hindu Goddess Tradition a Good Resource for Western Feminism?', worries about such appropriations as not necessarily being a compliment to the culture from which the borrowing is done, as they are too often for the benefit of the borrower alone (2000: 198–200). Irigaray does not take such matters into consideration, as she believes that her own experience and her vision of woman as mediator of the world of breath/ spirit is a task that has beneficial dimensions.

In her recent writings, Irigaray has thus made a distinct and somewhat surprising move – though it is now possible to read back and detect the beginnings of the change, starting with 'Divine Women' and 'Belief Itself', both in *Sexes and Genealogies* (1993c). In her early work, Irigaray's was a critical and radical voice, working to undermine entrenched Western cultural structures and practices that had been detrimental to women. Yet, in her adaptation of Indian mythology and spiritual practices, Irigaray does not subject them to the same type of critical analysis that she applied to the Christian and Western myths and values. There is also a lack of investigation of original source material, as well as of the work of contemporary Indian women scholars, particularly post-colonial ones. In addition, the unquestioning promotion of one specific mode of the

Hindu tradition at the expense of its multi-faceted and multi-layered mosaic of movements – both orthodox and heterodox – is also problematic. But these statements reflect my own approach as a scholar of religions who is concerned with certain procedures of an academic nature. Irigaray, however, makes it quite clear that she is not inclined to the traditional forms of the transmission of knowledge, which she considers as 'obsolete' (2002: 6). Her quest is of a spiritual nature, where she follows the practices of spiritual masters, and listens 'to the words and writings of those men and women who, in the last century especially, try their best to unite in themselves European traditions and those of the East' (2002: 70).

VI Post-colonialism and orientalism

In *The Age of the Breath* (1999a), Irigaray moves beyond her basic reformative model of sexual difference and its spiritualisation, to postulate that women are not only spiritual initiators but mediators between the different religious traditions. They can perform this task as, for Irigaray, women are not dependent on either dogmas or rights, nor do they need representations to approach the divine (1999a: 18). In *Between East and West*, Irigaray proposes that a woman who is 'faithful to herself' is 'close to Eastern cultures, close to the Buddha, who, moreover, venerates the feminine spiritual' (2002: 79). In addition, woman, who 'more spontaneously, keeps breath inside her', thus 'remains in greater harmony with the cosmos' (2002: 85). Woman also engenders life with breath, as does the Creator God (2002: 80). But most importantly, women are the harbingers of a new age – the age of breath/spirit:

> This passage to another epoch of the reign of spirit depends upon a cultivation of respiration, a cultivation of breathing in and by women. They are the ones who can share with the other, in particular with man, natural life and spiritual or divine life, if they are capable of transforming their vital breath into spiritual breath.
>
> (2002: 91)

Irigaray then speculates that it is these divine women (and the men with whom they cultivate their breath in the manner described by Irigaray) who will bring about a new age – the age of the spirit. It is here that Irigaray reiterates her earlier vision that '[i]n the third age of the history of Judeo-Christianity, after the age of the world's redemption, thanks to Mary and to Jesus, the task of humanity will be to become itself divine breath' (1999a: 13). The concern that arises in this connection is that Irigaray's explorations of Hinduism may have been all along in the service of her 'revisioned' ideal for Christianity and its symbolic structures. This raises a number of contentious issues – especially the charge of Orientalism, that is, appropriation of other cultures/religions, even in idealised forms. Ronald Inden, a critic of Orientalism, has been particularly censorious not only of those who do reductive Western analyses of India, but also of those who romanticise Hinduism, among whom he lists Mircea Eliade, C. G. Jung and Joseph Campbell. As he elaborates:

> The adherents of the romantic view, best exemplified academically in the discourses of Christian liberalism and analytic psychology . . . insist that India embodies a private realm of the imagination and the religious which modern, Western man lacks but needs. They . . . have a vested interest in seeing that the Orientalist view of India as 'spiritual', 'mysterious', and 'exotic' is perpetuated.
>
> (1986: 442)

Although such categories of 'Orientalist' deal in over-generalised claims and maintain a dualistic framework, it would seem, initially, from Inden's perspective, that Irigaray's recent work could certainly fall within his designation of Orientalism. Another perspective, however, can be gleaned from the work of J. J. Clarke in *Oriental Enlightenment* (1997), in which Clarke analyses Edward Said's original depiction of *Orientalism* (1978). While Clarke acknowledges that Said is correct to emphasise specifically the imperialistic and ideological elements that were intrinsic to the Western Orientalist and colonialist impulse, he believes that Said's original description remains dualistic, and does not fully acknowledge certain complexities involved in a dynamic interaction of 'East' and 'West' – terms that Clarke does not want to see as simply opposed monolithic entities. Clarke's own particular focus, in contrast to the Islamic world of Said's study, is more on South and East Asia. I will briefly examine his work, particularly with regard to Hinduism, as a foil for further discussion of Irigaray's work.

It is worth noting that Clarke's approach does not fall within the traditional rubrics of theory and method in the study of religion. His work is an historical survey of Western scholarly attitudes towards the 'East', and particularly towards Hinduism. It ranges from the Romantic enthusiasm demonstrated by Schlegel, Schopenhauer, Nietzsche and Müller, among others, to many contemporary issues involving philosophers and students of religion, including the issue of inter-religious dialogue. He covers popular elements, such as esotericism and the occult, the work of Aldous Huxley and Hermann Hesse, the Zen Buddhism of the Beat Movement, the hippie movement of the 1960s and 1970s and contemporary New Age variants. While he acknowledges that certain of these treatments of the East and its religious philosophy are not necessarily satisfactory, and may well be distortions of Hinduism or Buddhism, he does not necessarily see blatant evidence of the hegemonic tendencies of the colonialist enterprise.

Instead, he detects a subtle 'deployment of the East as a means of intellectual and cultural criticism [of the West]' (1997: 107). Clarke himself does not undertake any extensive critical evaluation of any of these movements – he seems merely content to document their development.

Central to Clarke's thesis is the fact that 'orientalism has for three centuries assumed a counter-cultural, counter-hegemonic role, and become in various ways a gadfly plaguing all kinds of orthodoxies (for example, especially traditional religion and a rationalist approach) and an energiser of radical protest, and in doing so, it has often been in the business not of reinforcing Europe's established role and identity, but rather undermining it' (1997: 27). It is in light of Clarke's thesis that a further look at Irigaray's recent work can be taken. Irigaray certainly does see her work as constituting a serious rebuke to the Jewish and Christian heritage, as well as to the cultural and religious attitudes and practices towards women. However, Irigaray does not simply criticise the Western legacy, but attempts to reform it, initially from an intellectual, now from a more spiritual orientation. Her adaptation of the spiritual symbolism of the yogic-tantric beliefs and practices is an attempt to introduce a transformative way of appreciating a new dynamic of male and female relationship. For Irigaray, this mode, in its carnal/spiritual interplay, has innovative significance for its participants and their culture. (While Clarke does not refer specifically to Irigaray, he acknowledges the present popularity of tantric yoga [1997: 99], and its contemporary secular Western adaptations.)

The question remains as to whether Clarke's discernment of these conflicting interests of appropriation and reform provides sufficient grounds to counter the legacy of imperialism and domination that has been deemed characteristic of Orientalism in its colonialist guise. Clarke himself admits that there remains a paradox at work here, where issues of 'power and interest' are still intertwined, not just in the multi-faceted interactions between cultures, but within the ambit of the 'Eurocentric' world itself and its response to these issues (1997: 111).

So where does this leave the work of Irigaray? On the one hand, Irigaray's work does disclose elements of both trends – a form of idealised recuperation at the same time as a critical attitude and a transformative intention to change Western forms of living and loving. Her work in this sense participates in the paradox that Clarke describes, ambivalent in its aims and implications. Her work will also elicit conflicting receptions. Irigaray will no doubt be faulted by scholars who will see her personalised spiritual search as just one more Orientalist episode. Other critics of Western religion will be receptive to her attempt at reform. There will also be those who will appreciate her work as one more step in a process that Irigaray herself intimates – the development of human spiritual consciousness, beyond the boundaries of religious demarcations (2002: 10, 71). These reactions are predicated on the basis of pre-existent attitudes, regarding the different orientations of religious studies as a scholarly discipline and the practice of religion as a spiritual discipline. These options have usually been regarded as mutually exclusive. Yet contemporary scholarship in religion is becoming aware, even from its predominantly Western perspective, that things are not quite that simple (as Clarke has attempted to indicate). In this connection, Irigaray's work does appear as an instance of the inevitable dilemmas, such as omissions, presuppositions and selectivity, that occur whenever attempts are made at religious integration and comparison. Does this, however, imply that 'Orientalism' is an appropriate label for Irigaray's work? The problem is that today, despite its critical impact, 'Orientalism' tends to function as a catch-all phrase, questionable in its own dualisms and caught in a narrow focus of East/ West binaries. In the coming years, there will be a need to unravel the multivalent interweavings and mutually implicated aspects of inter- and intra-cultural exchanges – especially taking into consideration contemporary post-colonial scholarship (for example, Afzal-Khan and Shesadri-Crooks 2000).

VII Conclusion

What emerges in Irigaray's recent writings is an extraordinary tale of spiritual exploration and transformation. As a result of her voyage to India, her readings, her personal practice and her imaginative recuperations, Irigaray has changed from being a scholar, radical in her critique of Western rationalism and religion, to a woman who follows a spiritual path and who is an advocate of the practice of spirituality. For Irigaray, what is important is living life as a spiritual practice – becoming fully human, or divine, as she terms it. This is a self-reflexive exercise involving an ethics of alterity that seeks to allow coexistence between cultures without hierarchy or wars between diverse traditions. As is evident from her Introduction to this book, Irigaray wishes to eschew the oppositions that she ascribes to traditional forms of Western religion and culture. Irigaray does not perceive herself trapped in a binary situation, certainly not one that posits an East/West dichotomy. Her approach is one of mediating differences by spiritual means rather than by any intellectual exercises. As a spiritual practitioner, Irigaray believes that it is this dimension that can bring about the transformation of a person, a couple and a culture. In this sense, her work continues to be at once prophetic, challenging and controversial.

Notes

1   Although Irigaray herself is not entirely consistent on this matter, for the purposes of this chapter I will spell the word 'God' with a capital 'G' to designate the (male) God of the Jewish and Christian traditions, whereas

'god', the equivalent of 'divine', and 'goddess' will be used in other contexts.

2   Irigaray, while not denying lesbian relations between women, believes that the most immediate task for the reform of the culture is that a new form of relationship between men and women, based on sexual difference, be established (1996a: 3).

3   See Joy (1998) for an exploration of Irigaray on God.

4   It needs to be observed that Irigaray does deal in generalisations regarding the nature of patriarchy and gynocracy, just as she does in her explorations of Western and Eastern cultures and religions. My analysis will thus be situated within this framework.

5   In this chapter I have chosen not to use diacritical marks when using Sanskrit terms, as Irigaray does not employ them. The exceptions to this occur in quotations and titles of books and articles.

6   Eliade has described the influence of women in tantrism accordingly: 'One must never lose sight of this primacy of the Shakti – in the final instance, the Divine Wife and Mother – in Tantrism and all the movements that derive from it. This was the road by which the great subterranean current of the autochthonous popularity emerged into Hinduism' (1969: 178–9).

7   *Chakras* are centres of energy that can be mobilised by directing the breath (*prana*) during specific meditative practices. As Feuerstein states: 'These major configurations of our "subtle anatomy" are especially responsive to mental manipulation and therefore are often made the focal point of meditation and visualisation. Many Tantric teachers speak of seven principal psychoenergetic centres, but some list five, and others name nine, ten, eleven or very many more' (Feuerstein 1998: 149).

8   See N. N. Bhattacharya (1999: 308–12). George Feuerstein explains: 'Tantra, or Tantrism, is an exceptionally ramified and complex esoteric tradition of Indic origin. It made its appearance round 500 CE, though some proponents claim a far longer history. . . . As a full-fledged movement or cultural style extending over both Hinduism and Buddhism, however, Tantra seems to have originated around the middle of the first millennium CE' (Feuerstein 1998: ix–x).

9   See the Introduction by David Gordon White to the volume *Tantra in Practice* (2000) for a comprehensive coverage of the multiple aspects of Tantra.

10 Vasudha Narayanan states that the *Dharma Shastras* 'were not well known and utilized in many parts of India' (1999: 34). She allows that it was more custom and habit, rather than these specific legal texts, that maintained the low status of women, and the impression of its prevalence was due to British colonial emphasis on the Brahmanic tradition.

11   It needs to be observed in this context that, while the counter-tactics of the Hindu right – Hindutva – are diverse and multi-faceted, one obvious fact cannot be ignored – a predominant agenda has been to essentialise the definition of Hindu womanhood. In its appeals to the Vedas and the Manusmrti as normative texts, a single idealised vision of womanhood is constructed, ignoring the divergences of caste/class/regional/historical variants during a long history. Ironically, this standardisation has obvious parallels to the British artificial acclamation and promotion of the Brahmanical tradition as the defining element of Hinduism. See Roy (1995) and Joy (2000).

Chapter 5

Mary L. Keller

DIVINE WOMEN AND THE
NEHANDA *MHONDORO*
Strengths and Limitations of the Sensible
Transcendental in a Post-Colonial World of
Religious Women

For building bridges between different traditions, women are privileged
mediatrices.

(Irigaray 1999a: 18)

IN HER RECENT REFLECTIONS, Luce Irigaray has continued to write
boldly about women's religious lives in ways that are likely to inspire and
outrage. I aim to deliver a post-colonial critique following the lines of qualified
engagement made by Armour (1997, 1999), Bloodsworth (1999) and Cheah and
Grosz (1998), focusing on the sensible transcendental and her notion of divinity.
The sensible transcendental can be thought of as the epistemological machine
through which Irigaray has produced a feminist philosophy of sexual difference.
Using this machine, Irigaray has reconfigured divinity, and for this reason her
work has been very important for feminist philosophers of religion. As epitomised
in her 1984 lecture 'Divine Women' (published in English as part of *Sexes and
Genealogies* [1993c]), Irigaray employs the sensible transcendental to collapse the
transcendent/immanent dichotomy that distinguishes the God of the Christian
tradition (1993c). However, her reconfiguration of Christian notions of religious
subjectivity retains a Eurocentric sense. That is, to the extent that religious subjectivity is thought: (1) to be an individual's experience, (2) to consist of beliefs
that exist in consciousness, (3) to be a matter of choice and/or invention, and
(4) to promote one's autonomy, one is seeing a modern, European conception
of religious subjectivity. This conception is a product of the Enlightenment and
creates an image of religious subjectivity as being either more sophisticated
(progressive) or less sophisticated (backward or fundamentalist) according to the

extent to which one has reflexively cultivated one's relationship to the social symbolic. Irigaray's vision of the future of religious bodies is a Eurocentric future and, to paraphrase Frantz Fanon, the future is white (Fanon 1986).[1]

There are important resources within post-colonial theories that destabilise the potential neo-colonialism of Irigaray's 'divine women'. In order to deliver this critique I have constructed two genealogies using two figures that I call religious women: Irigaray's 'divine women' on the one hand, and on the other hand, taken from my research into women and spirit possession, Nehanda, an important figure in Zimbabwe's struggle for independence. The comparison is an odd juxtaposition in that Irigaray's 'divine women' is a philosophical construct, a utopian proposal, while Nehanda was an actual woman. Indeed, I am creating a comparison between two religious women who belong to different registers, and I will present different kinds of information about each. To construct a genealogy of divine women I will trace the philosophical roots of the sensible transcendental, whereas I will describe Nehanda's life and tradition as I construct her genealogy. The difference between the two figures highlights one of the perceived underlying differences that keeps French feminist theory from engaging significantly with feminist post-colonial theorisations (as evidenced in Spivak's 1999 text *A Critique of Postcolonial Reason*, in which she briefly mentions and critiques Kristeva and Cixous but does not even reference Irigaray). French feminism, and especially Irigaray's prioritisation of sexual difference over race as a model of difference, is considered to be abstract, reflecting its 'whiteness' (it has no stake in exploring the fact of blackness, to borrow from Fanon), while post-colonial theory carries with it the weight and terror of colonial history.

I create this juxtaposition in order to challenge it and to identify the most important aspects of the two registers. Each register infers a model of religious subjectivity that I will contrast with the other. While Irigaray's sensible transcendental is a strategic response to a particularly modern and Christian problem with the figuration of women's religious lives, there are other important models of women's religious subjectivity found in the world's religions, models that it has taken post-colonial theories to identify. The difference between these models of religious subjectivity hinges on the question of autonomy and how agency is evaluated differently in the two registers. This difference has major ramifications for how religious subjectivity is constructed and evaluated, which will be of great importance for those scholars of religion concerned with representing and evaluating women's religiousness in the contemporary world.

I A genealogy of divine women

Until recently, post-structuralist thought had been fairly unanimous in its treatment of religion, following the Enlightenment trajectory of equating religiousness with beliefs. The word 'religion' conjured up the association 'beliefs', and beliefs were interpreted to be ideological symbols. Post-structuralism dethroned the repressive ideological force of transcendental abstracts (God, King, Heaven, Divinity). Theology was approached as an ideology of oppression, the long arm of religiousness. Hence Derrida's early statement that deconstruction 'blocks every relationship to theology' (Derrida 1981: 40). Religiousness was, in general, viewed as an anachronistic space occupied by bodies that had not yet achieved a level of critical consciousness or autonomy.[2]

In many ways, Irigaray delivered one of the most profound and early challenges to post-structuralist engagements with religion when she instigated her discussion of the divine. More recently, Derrida himself (1998 [with G. Vattimo] and 2002) and feminist philosophers such as Carol Wayne White (2000) have articulated new approaches to the value and valuations of religiousness.[3] In part due to Irigaray's influence, not only is religion *not* dead, but 'becoming divine' is the future. One of the roots of this contemporary revaluation of religion is found in the sensible transcendental, because with this machine she was able to reconfigure religious subjectivity in a way that was compelling for scholars as diverse as neo-Marxists and feminist theologians. Grace Jantzen argues that the sensible transcendental is the foundation for a pantheistic, feminist philosophy of religion that 'enables the recognition of alterities, especially gender, "race", age and ability' (Jantzen 1997: 282). It is the cross-cultural applicability of the sensible transcendental that concerns me.

Irigaray's 'sensible transcendental' is a classic post-structuralist effort to deconstruct the binary opposition between transcendental and sensible, de-throning divinity by paradoxically re-assigning it to both an abstract and an embodied realm. The sensible transcendental is 'that which confuses the opposition between immanence and transcendence' (Irigaray 1989b: 44). By 'classic post-structuralist' I mean that she has identified a dualism and she is strategically subverting the dualism by noting the dependence of the primary term on the repression of the secondary term; in this case, the sensible becomes prioritised.[4] Three philosophers with whom Irigaray is engaging in using the term 'sensible transcendental' are de Beauvoir, Heidegger and Levinas, the relation to each of whom I will discuss briefly.

The sensible transcendental is a reaction to de Beauvoir's positive valuation of the transcendent (Chanter 1995: 47–80; Jantzen 1997: 275–6). According to Chanter, de Beauvoir's question was, '[G]iven that all human relations are fundamentally conflictual, why is it that women, rather than men, have been systematically oppressed?' (Chanter 1995: 75). De Beauvoir's answer was that men take the leap into transcendence, risking death in an existentialist version of the master/slave dialectic, but women remain safely in the realm of the immanent, living for the other as the second sex. In de Beauvoir's framework, women should aspire to transcendence, just like men. Irigaray challenges de

Beauvoir on this point, arguing that if one maintains a supervaluation of transcendence, one will perpetuate the devaluation of the second term. Philosophy that maintains a hierarchical distinction between transcendence and immanence will perpetuate logocentrism, which is driven by a logic of the same. For Irigaray the male philosophers did not risk death as much as they denied their debt to the maternal in proposing a gender-neutral subjectivity. Acknowledging bodies (immanence) in the processes of thinking (transcendence) alters the horizon of philosophy such that male and female bodies, in their sexuate differences, are recognised as the matter of thought, the pre-condition of any and all necessarily vested abstractions. The sensible transcendental creates a new ground upon which male and female philosophers might meet and identify themselves within an ethics of sexual difference.

As a critique of the metaphysical tradition, the sensible transcendental is informed by Heidegger's critique of the metaphysics of presence. Claire Colebrook evaluates Heidegger's influence as follows: for Heidegger, the metaphysical tradition in the West was based on a mistake and it was philosophy's task to recognise that mistake and reorient the philosopher in relation to being. The mistake was to overvalue representational thinking; by re-presenting being as Being, philosophy was forgetting the being and becoming of beings. Philosophy needed instead to think the difference between difference and identity so as not to build abstracts that forgot their lively roots. Openings, dwellings and jugs were metaphors intended to prioritise receptivity and attentiveness to alterity in Heidegger's philosophy (Colebrook 1997).

The debt to Heidegger is obvious not only in the critique of transcendentals, but also in the prioritisation of differences. If we say that Heidegger identified the problem of the hermeneutical circle, then Heidegger's goal was to create a philosophy that was always attendant and receptive to differences that might continually broaden the horizons of the circle. However, Irigaray argues that it is the feminine that is forgotten in Heidegger. Heidegger's openings, dwellings and jugs assume gender neutrality, and by so doing deny philosophy's other, the feminine, upon which philosophy is dependent. Irigaray's strategic alternative is the sensible transcendental, which recognises sexual difference as the constitutive ground of all representation.

Finally, the sensible transcendental marks an engagement with Levinas. According to Chanter, the sensible transcendental echoes Levinas's strategy to combine the insights of idealism with materialism. Levinas conflates freedom or autonomy (an abstract ideal) with responsibility to the other, which is the product of a face-to-face encounter (material sensibility), because the very possibility of being itself is only realisable in the encounter with an other. This paradoxical conflation of ideal and material is vital because it is the new ground of ethics in a world where ontotheological foundations (such as God) have been called into question (Chanter 1995: 180–224). Irigaray adopts this paradoxical ground. Greatly indebted to Levinas, she nevertheless finds in his narrative a tendency to keep the sensible and the transcendental apart in metaphors that infer masculine subjectivity as a norm and feminine subjectivity as the passive other whose purpose is to bring masculine subjectivity to its awareness.

The sensible transcendental therefore begins not with the other as the ground that precedes philosophy (Levinas's position), but with the *sexuate* other as the ground that precedes philosophy. Sexual difference is the paradigmatic model of the otherness of the other. In light of these influences, the purpose of the sensible transcendental is philosophical and political. Until we can think difference we cannot imagine the legal and social parameters that will allow for the sexuate becoming of female and male subjects.

Divinity and the reconfiguration of the religious subject in Irigaray's work

Divinity is one of the most important tropes in Irigaray's work (Martin 1995), and might be pictured as one of the excessive gifts produced by the machinations of the sensible transcendental – Irigaray's Pandora's box. Three of her discussions of divinity demonstrate how the sensible transcendental reconfigures divinity. In her early work, she reconfigures Platonic divinity in Diotoma's speech in Plato's *Symposium*. Deconstructing Platonic idealism, she refigures beauty as the possible, personal attainment of experiencing divinity within one's corporeality. The sublime experience described by Diotoma is the attainment of an individual's potential. 'This person would have then attained what I shall call a sensible transcendental, the material texture of beauty' (Irigaray 1993a: 32).

In 'Divine Women' Irigaray adopts a Feuerbachian and Lacanian analysis of 'Good Old God' as a masculine projection of an ideal that guarantees masculine gender. She argues that *a* horizon is indispensable for the development of identity – we need an ideal towards which our becoming is directed and by which our ethics is governed. Becoming divine women is the process and praxis of realising a sexuate genre for women and men (Irigaray 1993a: 57–72). She argues that the Trinity is attributed with the power of creativity and is dependent on the oppression of female subjectivity either as asexual (mother of God, Mary) or as evil sexuality (Eve). In contrast, with a God appropriate to the feminine, divine women are sexual, require exchange with males and are capable of relating to other women as sister-subjects.

Most recently, divinity is being figured as a practice and an ideal – breathing and the breath – as in her text *The Age of the Breath*:

> To cultivate the divine in herself, the woman, in my opinion, has to attend to her own breathing, her own breath, more even than to

love. Breathing, in fact, corresponds to the first autonomous gesture
of human living, and it is not possible to be divine without being
autonomous with respect to the mother and the father, to the lover,
to the child and to the others in general, women and men.

(Irigaray 1999a: 1)

Autonomy figures as a primary ideal in this meditation upon the breath, and is
considered of primary importance for ethical relationships. We will see a very
different configuration of breath in Part II.

For my purposes, the sensible transcendental has produced a space where
religious subjectivity has been revalued. Taking God and divinity seriously,
Irigaray becomes a partner for critically analysing religious traditions. Because
religions have been and continue to be singularly powerful in their contributions
to the social symbolic, the sensible transcendental becomes the ground for
activist engagements with religious traditions. God is not thrown out as a
concept but rather is refigured as the ideal potential of sexuate becoming. The
sensible transcendental is a tool, a conceptual grid that can be used as a utopian,
feminist vision for evaluating religious practice and theology, to borrow from
Carol Wayne White (2000). As a grid, the sensible transcendental prioritises
sexual difference as the ultimate model of difference, leading Irigaray to argue that
differences such as race are secondary to sexual difference in their importance
(Irigaray 1996a: 47). Scholars concerned with the interactions of race, class and
gender have interrogated Irigaray's argument that sexual difference is the primary
model of difference (Armour 1997: 75; Cheah and Grosz 1998; Bloodsworth
1999). It is a formal argument: 'Between man and woman, there really is otherness: biological, morphological, relational' (Irigaray 1996a: 61). Race is not
primary, because differently raced bodies, male and female, can copulate. The
essential difference required for futurity, on the other hand, is sexual difference.
In this way, an ethics of 'being-two' is different from and more fundamental than
any claims to multiplicity, pluralism, or diversity (Cheah and Grosz 1998: 7).
Irigaray argues, 'Sexual difference is, as it were, the most powerful motor of
a dialectic without masters or slaves' (Irigaray 1996a: 51). The question for me
is whether such a goal denies the historical momentum of the North–South
dialectic from which white women have benefited as mistresses to the masters.

To recap this register, the model of religious subjectivity that comes from the
Irigarayan sensible transcendental is the model of an autonomous body. Male and
female, the religious subject would breathe and remember that male and female
sexuate identities are necessary for the futurity of a life that facilitates the full
potential becoming of all subjects. Difference of any sort will be respected
because difference itself is the ground of ethics. This reconfiguration of religious
subjectivity has moved the religious subject out of the old association (a religious subject is one who believes in all-powerful, patriarchal and oppressive

transcendentals) and towards a feminist ideal of sacralised bodies that navigate between the necessary horizon of divine ideals and a social system that sustains the ethics of sexual difference. Moving to the story of Nehanda, however, the question of agency resides in a different register.

II A genealogy of Nehanda

Nehanda is one of the most powerful and important religious women of the past century, yet her story is little known outside of Zimbabwe. Perhaps this is in part because the pervasive devaluations of lingering colonialist constructions render this woman, possessed by her ancestors, a curiosity. Possession, which is an important element of the vast majority of religious traditions that are dominated by women (Sered 1994), is an excellent example of the problems that are raised when autonomy is the standard for evaluating women's religious practices. Nehanda was the daughter of an important chief in early Shona history.[5] Upon her death she became breath, *mweya*, a spirit. Because she was a powerful woman, her spirit is a powerful ancestor, a *mhondoro*, who can commandeer the body of a woman in order to speak through that body and advise her people. When she possesses a woman, the woman is renamed Nehanda because the woman is wholly overcome, transformed. A woman possessed by Nehanda will be tested rigorously to determine whether or not she has really been overcome (is really not consciously present) and whether or not she has access to knowledge that illustrates Nehanda's presence. Paradoxically powerful, the possessed woman embodies the power of spirit, a power greater than human power, but is herself considered *homwe*, a pocket or little bag; she is unimportant and insignificant as an individual (Lan 1985: 49). Ancestors will only choose women once they have quit menstruating because the dryness of the breath should not mingle with the wetness of menstruation. The possessed woman gains social status but only because her consciousness and identity have been overcome; she is a powerful figure of radical non-autonomy.

Nehanda was speaking through an old woman at the time when Cecil Rhodes and the British South Africa Company began to colonise the region we now call Zimbabwe. When Rhodes moved in with the Pioneer Column of 1890, in the largest deployment of white power to enter Eastern and Central Africa (Ranger 1967: 46), an awful confrontation occurred between the *mhondoro* and the British because '[t]he single most important duty of the spirit mediums is to protect the land. From the grave, from the depths of the forest, from the body of a lion or of their mediums, the *mhondoro* control in perpetuity the land they conquered during their lives' (Lan 1985: 148). Nehanda was consulted by her people and she counselled them to fight against the British South Africa Company, which was violently overtaking the land. Her counsel contributed to the first of two *chimurenga* (battles for indigenous independence) that the Shona would wage, the first occurring in the 1890s and the second in the 1960s to the 1970s.

Nehanda and a male medium, Kagubi, were perceived by the British forces to be the inspiration behind indigenous resistance, so they were captured and brought to trial. Her religious subjectivity was an impossible and intolerable subjectivity for the British. She was perceived to be both a witch and a dangerous rebel. She was sentenced to death by hanging. The following account of Nehanda's death, written by the mission priest Reverend Father Francis Richartz, became an important part of the legacy of Nehanda.

> To Neanda [Nehanda] I did not speak until evening, in order to avoid a scene, though I had a long quiet talk with her, which made me feel hopeful. However, when in the evening about 6 o'clock I saw her again [and] I told her that she had to die next morning, she began to behave like a mad woman. She took her blankets and wished to leave the cell, and when told to remain and keep quiet, she refused and said she never would endure to be locked up. When I saw that nothing could be done with her I went away . . . and Neanda began to dance, to laugh and talk, so that the warders were obliged to tie her hands and watch her continually, as she threatened to kill herself. On Wednesday April 27th I again made an attempt to speak to Neanda and bring her to a better frame of mind, but she refused, called for her people and wanted to go back to her own country, the Mazoe – and die there, and behaved as she had done the night before. When I saw that nothing could be done with her, the time for execution having arrived, I left Neanda and went to Kakubi (Kagubi) who received me in good disposition. Whilst I was conversing with him, Neanda was taken out to the scaffold. Her cries and resistance when she was taken up the ladder, the screaming and yelling on the scaffold disturbed my conversation with Kakubi very much, until the noisy opening of the trap-door upon which she stood followed by the heavy thud of her body as it fell, made an end to the interruption.
>
> (Weiss 1986: 38–40)

According to tradition, while she was incarcerated she prophesied that 'my bones will rise again'. The British crushed the revolt.[6]

It was not until the Pan-African movement of the middle of the twentieth century that large-scale revolt was again mounted. During the second *chimurenga*, in the 1960s to the 1970s, songs were sung to Nehanda by the Marxist guerrilla forces that successfully fought against Ian Smith's white government. Her image was used atop the flags that portrayed Robert Mugabe as the new president of Zimbabwe, confirming the prophecy that her bones would rise again.

How might a feminist evaluate the power of this woman? I want to emphasise the following key features of Nehanda as a religious woman. (1) Her conscious-ness was overcome and she was a pocket for the ancestor Nehanda. (2) Her religious authority was tied to the authority to govern the land. (3) She did not choose to be possessed, but once the possession was identified and verified by her community she had to lead a highly disciplined and austere existence. (4) She was radically non-autonomous and served as the instrumental agency for Nehanda (Keller 2001). Together these factors suggest that a feminist and post-colonial hermeneutic will be a critical element in the remembering of Zimbabwe's history. In the current battles over land in Zimbabwe, Mugabe appears to have forgotten Nehanda and it will likely be feminist genealogies that will remember her. My goal is to develop a hermeneutic that would allow 'us' to become subject to the meanings and agencies of Nehanda's life, to paraphrase Lawrence Sullivan, with a horizon that is different from that of the sensible transcendental (Sullivan 1988: 3).

Power and the reconfiguration of religious subjectivity in post-colonial theory

Where Irigaray's problem was with the hyper-valuation of transcendentals and masculinity, the problem the post-colonial register faces is that Nehanda is likely to be perceived with the devalued terms of colonialist dualisms: primitive, super-stitious, backward, simple. The post-colonial register begins to challenge this perception by approaching Nehanda as a historically specific model of religious subjectivity. There will be unique philosophical concepts within the Shona tradition to be translated, there were unique geographical elements that impacted upon life on the Zambezi plateau, and the force of contact and exchange between the Shona and their colonisers was specific to this encounter. By approaching Nehanda's story in its specificity, one engages in the project of remembering and preserving the differences that marked Shona culture at the turn of the century. Nehanda is neither 'woman' nor a representative of all African women.

In addition to the requirement of specificity is the need to reconfigure the relationship of religion and politics. Talal Asad argues that anthropologists have been exporting a modern, Christian notion of religiousness that is built on the dichotomy religion/politics (Asad 1993). That which distinguishes religion from politics is that religion is belief where politics is real power. Asad surmises that this dichotomy produces an understanding of religion that is similar to Marx's description of religion as 'a mode of consciousness which is other than consciousness of reality, external to the relations of production, producing no knowledge, but expressing at once the anguish of the oppressed and a spurious consolation' (Asad 1993: 46). The connection between religious lives and 'real' forms of power, such as guardianship of the land, has been severed, which prevents us from understanding why religious lives are so often embroiled in real battles for territory. We will understand this persistent relationship better if we alter our understanding of religious subjectivity. Asad argues that the academic understanding of religion reflects a model of subjectivity and agency that is based on an individual who chooses identities. Agency, in this model, is the extent to which one has critical consciousness and can exercise choice. Proper religiousness, from this perspective, should be a reasonable matter that one can choose to believe in. When the scholar sees a veiled Muslim woman, for instance, suspicions are raised that this individual is not being given a choice about her identity. In contrast Asad argues that religious subjectivity is better understood as the lifelong and embodied practices of building moral selves. These practices are not individualistic, but rather negotiate between one's desires, one's traditions, the power to name divine authority, and the power to govern land.

In a related vein, agency is reconfigured in several important post-colonial texts that argue that women's agency in India, Africa, and other post-colonial countries cannot be understood adequately using the Western feminist grid that presupposes individual, democratic and autonomous agency as an ideal (see Nair 1994, O'Hanlon 1988, Spivak 1999, Trinh 1989). It is significant that womanist theologians have argued the same point, as have other feminist theorists of race (see Cannon 1988, hooks 1982, Collins 1991). Bulbeck also emphasises this issue in her discussion of 'Agency and "Customary Practices"' (Bulbeck 1998: 70–93). Was Nehanda a powerful Shona woman? The name Shona is itself a product of the Western imagination, indicating that autonomy (that is, the power to name oneself) is not even a possibility. Rather, a more complex notion of agency is required that recognises multiple axes of power (race, wealth, gender) and multiple networks of support that also can constrain (kinship, extended family, creative responses within the community, tradition, maintaining links to historical memory).

Following from these arguments, religious subjectivity is understood in the post-colonial register to be the negotiations one pursues with the embodied practices of one's traditions. A religious subject is more like a soldier or dancer than a 'believer'. It is as foolish to ask whether Nehanda believed in her ancestors as to ask a yogi if she really believes her handstands are going to make her stronger and more flexible. If we shift from the Western habit of thought and consider religiousness to be practices that have been developed to negotiate with power, then the question about whether or not religiousness is 'real' disappears. The religious body engages with ritualising practices that make it stronger in order to deal with external forces that have greater power than does the individual. The ancestors of Zimbabwe are not beliefs that float about; they are forces with which people must contend and negotiate. Women's agency is understood to reside in the systems and networks in which women live their lives: economic, kinship and cultural systems that include religious traditions. Rather than de-value the 'third-world woman' as oppressed, one recognises the complex interrelated systems of power with which she must negotiate. Shifting the evaluation of agency from the domain of an individual's conscious choices to recognition of the interrelated systems of power with which a woman must negotiate is one of the key contributions made by post-colonial theorists and is a corrective, I would argue, to the hypervaluation of autonomy found in many examples of Western, feminist theory.

III Concluding comparison and contrast

The point of tension between divine women and Nehanda, as I have constructed this comparison, is that the Irigarayan model proposes autonomy, albeit the autonomy of sexuate becoming, as the standard by which religious subjectivity is evaluated. Any negotiations that are undertaken in the Irigarayan sensible transcendental are negotiations that promote autonomy. The autonomy Irigaray proposes is not rigid. In *The Age of the Breath*, Irigaray describes the interplay of receptivity and activity required in the practice of breathing:

> [T]he woman can receive the other in her soul, and not only in her body, as it is too often believed. But this place of woman's hospitality and spiritual generation is hardly known, even by herself. In order to give being to it, the woman cannot remain solely passive, as asked of her for centuries: she must accept active responsibility for her spiritual life, for her soul. She must become a creatress of humanity, generate it spiritually, and not only naturally.
>
> (Irigaray 1999a: 9–10)

Further expanding on the kinds of receptivity and activity that mark the divine woman, she writes, 'The path which goes from nature to grace requires the woman to be attentive, available and receptive to a sort of energy, of light, of comfort which cannot be mastered' (Irigaray 1999a: 11). The autonomy of two-ness is different from an individual's autonomy. It is based on the non-hierarchical interdependence that can be attained only through the autonomy of each, an autonomy that is developed in relation to a divine that is appropriate to one's genre. This combination of interdependence (male and female) and autonomy (sexuate divinity) is Irigaray's unique gesture in reconfiguring religious subjectivity.

In contrast to Irigaray's model of harmony, cultural harmony for the Shona is dependent upon maintaining the connection to the ancestors so that the community is thriving. Dziva notes that it might sound romantic, but ethnographic substantiation shows that in most of the African societies, good health, harmony, order, integrity and continuity are all key words which summarise the African beliefs in a life-affirming and life-sustaining religious society. Thus, 'salvation' in African traditional religions is perceived to be an ongoing process which starts in this world when people are still alive. The present community is a religious arena for human and divine interaction, an arena where punishment, justice, reconciliation, forgiveness and reward are executed.

(Dziva 1996: 6)

Where Irigaray argues that a dialectic of difference between autonomous sexuate humans is the motor for the ethics of sexual difference, it is the dialectic between ancestors and humans that promotes cultural harmony within the Shona horizon. '[I]t is believed that the spiritual beings expect ritual sacrifices from their descendants and, in return, the Shona expect material prosperity and well-being in their society' (Dziva 1996: 20).

Possession is the link, the embodied practice of making that connection between ancestors and mortals. Possession produces a non-autonomous model of human subjectivity, in contrast to the autonomy produced by the sensible transcendental. Possessions are diagnosed after a period of illness that cannot be cured by other means. While it is recognised that possession is a hardship on the person who is possessed, the possessing spirits are not blamed for their interventions. Rather the spirits are appeased with offerings of beer, sacrifice and remembrance. '[S]uch spirits have a right to be honoured in this way and they have no way of making their wishes known except through mild illness in the community' (Bourdillon 1987: 183). Where possession is experienced as a hardship and communities are required to perform rituals, Irigaray envisions a third age without rites, dogma, or troubles.

For them [women], neither dogmas nor rites, and even not representations are indispensable to approach the divine. The contemplation of the universe, as well as the contemplation of the other, the respect for that which exists outside of oneself, is often more appropriate to their becoming spiritual, to a culture of interiority adequate to them. The divine gives energy for such gestures, and the divine rises from them as well. Divine is the love for the other as other, divine is the praise of nature as nature. But the divine does not necessarily signify for woman that an entity called God exists. The relation of the woman with God seems both subtler and more incarnated, less reduced to an object, even sent beyond our world. Women's God does not appear as a hypostasis of another

world we have to believe in. That is to say, a God appropriate to
the feminine may not paralyze the fluidity of the breath or of the
grace through a fixed identity or fixed commandments, on pain of
depriving the woman of the relation within her soul.

(Irigaray 1999a: 18–19)

She proposes a divine appropriate to woman, which raises the question 'Which
woman?' As an exemplary description of her post-structuralist engagement with
religion, 'women's God does not appear as a hypostasis of another world we
have to believe in'. The old patriarchal transcendentals are being replaced by
the sensible transcendental, 'subtler and more incarnated'. However, as Irigaray
expands upon the reason women are the privileged mediatrices for cross-cultural
engagements, the diaphanous, white veil of a Eurocentric notion of religion is
drawn across the differences between women's religious bodies. What would it
mean for Nehanda's life to be evaluated with reference to a 'God appropriate to
the feminine'? From the post-colonial perspective it appears that the sensible
transcendental is tilting at windmills.

Conclusion

If one attempted to take the sensible transcendental out in the world as a feminist
tool for studying gender in different religious traditions, one would need to
counter the neo-colonial propensity of the register by historicising the notion of
religious subjectivity Irigaray proposes and broadening theories of agency,
especially by drawing from the arguments made by post-colonial theorists and
race theorists. If one were pragmatically trying to build bridges between women
of different traditions, a goal that Irigaray herself proposes, then one would need
to drop Irigaray's formal argument regarding the priority of gender. Beginning
with Marilyn Frye's analysis of the whiteness of white feminism in which she
noted that 'white women are *almost* white men', and more recently in Armour's
discussion of why whitefeminist theory and theology has failed to maintain the
analysis of race, I think the suspicion has been well established that white
feminists prefer to inhabit the space of the underdog (women are oppressed
by patriarchy) and are uncomfortable with their role as co-beneficiaries of racial-
ised and classist forms of domination (Frye 1983: 121; Armour 1999: 19–44).
Irigaray's formal argument is detrimental to the project of building coalitions
because it produces a less pragmatic recognition of power.

To dismiss religious subjectivity as anachronistic, as does much critical theory,
is to dismiss much that continues to be constitutive of women's identity globally.
Irigaray walks an interesting line between remembering women and remembering and forgetting God, a line that makes her work very important for the
project of thinking subjectivity in light of post-colonial valuations of indigenous

memories and the importance of traditional practices. Unlike Jantzen, I remain concerned with the cross-cultural engagements of Irigaray's machine (see Jantzen 1997: 282). While de-throning 'Good Old God' makes for good sport, something very different is at stake from a post-colonial perspective in terms of negotiating one's relationship to traditions that are always already impacted by colonialism. While Irigaray has been very important for thinking the un-thought in Western Christianity – divine women – there is for me a whole new set of un-thought differences to be found in the study of other traditions. It is the radical differences in models of subjectivity that are of primary importance, and following from them are the distinctive power relations that can be variously tracked along gender lines (Amadiume 1987). Without such attention to historical and regional specificities, Nehanda will not stand as one of the most powerful and important religious women of the past century. If she is evaluated according to whether or not she was autonomous, her role as the pocket for the ancestor would always be found to be lacking. The divine appropriate to women? In the spirit of producing feminist genealogies I would argue that Nehanda's power was tied to her aged black body, the fight for indigenous control of the land, and her receptivity to a breath that overcame her. The 'Age of the Breath' is linked to Mugabe's desperate and amnesiac struggle. If we remember Nehanda's power, her radical non-autonomy, perhaps her bones can rise yet again in the service of Zimbabwe's people, and in this way feminist scholars of religion might contribute to the task of building bridges in Zimbabwe.

Notes

1   In his classic text, *Black Skin, White Masks* (1986), Fanon writes: 'However painful it may be for me to accept this conclusion, I am obliged to state it: For the black man there is only one destiny. And it is white.' I am unaware of any text in which Irigaray engages with Fanon, though his response to Sartre and Lacan suggests that he would be an important conversation partner. His first chapter, 'The Negro and Language', anticipates much of Irigaray's argument. Irigaray ignores what Fanon called 'the fact of blackness'.

2   Anne McClintock develops the phrase 'anachronistic space' in *Imperial Leather* (London: Routledge, 1994). In *The Hammer and the Flute*, I argue that religious bodies occupy anachronistic space in the imagination of critical consciousness (Keller 2001).

3   Feminists from socialist and post-communist contexts are also reconsidering religion and divinity. For a discussion of contemporary Italian feminist explorations of the divine see Andrea Günter (2001).

4   It is because the sensible transcendental is a classic post-structuralist move that Rosi Braidotti has identified a shared trajectory of thought between

Irigaray and Gilles Deleuze. Braidotti argues that the concept of 'becoming' is central to both Irigaray's and Deleuze's philosophical concerns because it relates immanence to transcendence (Braidotti 1994).

5   Nehanda's story is famous throughout Zimbabwe and can be read in Chenjerai Hove's novel *Bones* (1990), Charles Samupindi's novel *Death Throes: The Trial of Mbuya Nehanda* (1990) and Yvonne Vera's *Nehanda* (1993), a text which has received critical attention as an important example of post-colonial feminist writing.

6   One could analyse Nehanda's behaviour in her cell prior to her death as a parallel experience to that which Irigaray calls the 'mystical madness of women inside the patriarchal culture' (Irigaray 1999a: 8). However, to do so is to miss the important differences between Shona traditional religion and mystical madness. Mystics retain memory and can recount their experiences when their visions are over. Though impacted by their visions they do not become empty bags for the will of the intervening agency. Where mystical madness suggests a consciousness-based religious experience, the *mhondoro* represents a very different model of subjectivity in which the self is gone and an ancestor takes over.

PART TWO

On Julia Kristeva

Chapter 6

Kathleen O'Grady

THE TOWER AND THE CHALICE
Julia Kristeva and the Story of
Santa Barbara

But we are, I know not how, double within ourselves.

(Michel de Montaigne, quoted in Kristeva 1991: 120)

I We feminists '*don't* need Gods or Goddesses'

IN FOOTNOTES WE CAN FIND some of the most fascinating examples of what an age of critics does not fully comprehend about the philosophy the critics claim to explicate. A footnote is often a deliberate method of marginalising that aspect of a philosopher's work that cannot be comfortably assimilated into the schema of the commentator. In the case of Julia Kristeva, a glance at the footnotes of her readers will demonstrate that many seem bewildered by her focus on religious and theological concerns. While it is true that critics from the fields of divinity, theology and religious studies have long included these writings in their discussions of Kristeva, they often employ Kristevan philosophy to buttress their own religious beliefs or theological systems. Commentators outside of departments of religious studies, however, have been quick to disregard the religious element of Kristeva's work, and instead have focused on the semiotic, psychoanalytic and feminist dimensions of her texts. Topics such as maternity, abjection, love and melancholia have been covered extensively by readers of Kristeva, yet most neglect to forge a connection between Kristevan theory and her religious, primarily Catholic, examples, choosing to view these theologically inspired illustrations as merely incidental to her theory. And those readers who have addressed the religious component of Kristeva's work, most notably feminist commentators, have dismissed it, labelling it 'regressive', 'sentimental', 'nostalgic' and 'troubling', and have consigned these observations only to the occasional footnote or aside (Doane and Hodges 1992: 73; Oliver 1993: 129).

Teresa Brennan's compelling *History after Lacan* (1993) provides an excellent example of the discomfort that feminists feel towards the theological component that appears in the writings of Kristeva, as well as in the writings of her contemporary, Luce Irigaray. After an exhaustive examination of Kristeva and Irigaray's feminist and psychoanalytic project, Brennan places the following into a footnote:

> The question of divinity and more generally spirituality is returning in some of the feminist writing I have already mentioned. . . . The difficulty with these writings is less with the writings as such than with the commentators' attempts to deal with the *embarrassment* of having an otherwise admired thinker apparently endorsing God.
> (Brennan 1993: 109; my emphasis)[1]

Demonstrating Brennan's observation, Cynthia Chase understands Kristeva's theoretical project of late to have taken 'the *disquieting* form of an attempt to provide a psychoanalytic explanation for the possibility of religious experience' (1989: 77; my emphasis).[2] Chase ridicules what she calls the 'incipient theological character' of Kristeva's project, and in a related essay, adds that Kristevan theory 'seems tantamount to accepting the real existence of God' (1987: 224). Teresa de Lauretis has stated that Kristeva 'assumes and glorifies' certain aspects of Freudian theory, 'as only a Christian can' (1989: 269). Janice Doane and Devon Hodges echo this viewpoint when they declare that Kristevan theory offers up a 'Christian orthodoxy' in place of a psychoanalysis (1992: 64). Miglena Nikolchina asserts that Kristeva's texts 'veer' towards metaphysics and risk 'toppling over' (1991: 232). Edith Kurzweil, too, in the midst of a close reading of Kristeva and Irigaray, states rather abruptly: 'I am bypassing the neoreligious dimension of [the writing] not only because I consider it pie-in-the-sky and fantasy but because I am concerned *only with feminism and psychoanalysis*' (1995: 133; my emphasis). These comments are not isolated examples. There are countless more, and they often come from the most respected critics and commentators, who, otherwise, provide a comprehensive account of Kristeva's project.

What seems implicit in these examples, which openly display the confusion, shame, hostility and lightly cloaked fear that many feminist commentators feel towards the theological element of feminist texts generally, is that divinity in any form is anathema to a feminist agenda. It is as if even the faintest trace of interest in religion is enough to cause feminism itself to come toppling down. Penelope Magee calls this the 'feminist flight' from the interrogation of 'the sacred' and suggests: 'Maybe this is because the "religious/mystical/spiritual" is understood as being absolutely Hellenic-Christian, or absolutely patriarchal, or if feminist, absolutely soft-minded and anti-theoretical' (1995: 105–6). A number of questions emerge: Why must any reference to theology be excluded from an analysis of feminism? Is it not conceivable that one may reflect on theological texts and religious experience and still practise a theoretically rigorous feminism? And, on what grounds do critics appoint themselves judges of the scope of feminist theory anyway?

Valerie Raoul, in her comical and contradictory checklist of ingredients necessary for 'cooking up a feminism', makes clear the current feminist position on religion. In her list of feminist criteria, which she has culled from assorted contemporary feminist texts, she includes the following guideline – or is it a warning?: 'We [feminists] *don't* need Gods or Goddesses!' (1995).

As Morny Joy has indicated, this flat rejection of religion is symptomatic of feminist theory generally, where 'secular feminists are either indifferent or hostile to religion' and the common consensus is that 'no woman in her right mind would have anything to do with religion' (1996: 601–19). But such an a priori rejection of reflection on religion or theology risks overlooking the impact that religious structures have had on other social and cultural phenomena (including feminism itself), and the epistemic values inherited from theological thought. The truncation of important aspects of cultural formation, of which religion has been an essential part, necessarily risks making any feminist analysis incomplete. A facile division between sacred and secular structures needs to be abandoned in all aspects of feminist thinking. As Grace Jantzen has stated,

> Is it [not] time for feminists to rethink religion rather than either to dismiss it or defend it? . . . Whether we are personally religious or not, whether we deplore it or not, all women in modern western cities are affected [by it]. . . . If feminists ignore it, that does not make it go away.
>
> (1998b: 72)

It is precisely this necessary connection between religious structures and other cultural formations – art, literature, philosophy and even the operations of subjectivity itself – that theoretical works by Kristeva illuminate, and which feminists most need to take note of.

None of the critics that I have listed above takes the time to examine the link between Kristeva's use of theology and her psychoanalytic or feminist work; all reject the theological component of her writing as necessarily conservative and anti-feminist. They make painstaking detours to leave behind the theologically sullied texts, as a means – a kind of methodology even – to study specific topics, like psychoanalysis or feminism, within the writings themselves. But this technique of breaking a philosophy down into single component parts to the exclusion of the rest of the work is a bit like trying to ride a bicycle on only one wheel. It can be done, but it is more than just a little bit precarious. And the problem is intensified with a theory where 'ethics', 'psychoanalysis', 'politics' and even 'theology' are often inextricably linked together in a complex mosaic.

What I would like to suggest is that, in the case of Julia Kristeva, much of the confusion concerning her relationship to feminism – as well as the all-too-common charges of essentialism, sexism and conservatism that are regularly made against her – arises directly out of the exclusion of Kristeva's theological writings from an examination of her other works. What has ensued has been a proliferation of false information concerning both Kristeva herself and her theoretical work, and a number of misplaced criticisms have followed. By truncating the religious dimension of Kristeva's philosophy, feminist readers have risked misunderstanding the import and scope of her entire project.

It must be said that just as critics have had difficulty establishing Kristeva's relationship to feminism, so her attitude towards religion is difficult to categorise, but a look at her biographical details may help to clarify her position. For many Western feminists, religious discourse in any form can only signify the narrow-minded intolerance that comes from a dogmatic system of beliefs. But we must remember that Kristeva was not raised in the West, but in communist Bulgaria, where religious discourse demonstrated a rebellious vivacity and richness that could survive, like very little else, the strictures, rigid regulations and homogenising rigour of a communist regime. So, though religions have failed many in the West, Kristeva has witnessed the ability of religious discourse and rituals to support the individual in times of great personal and cultural distress. Kristeva comprehends the many-faceted face of religious discourse, and her theory attempts to unravel the imaginary constructs that have made it a potential means for subjectal renewal for so many people throughout history.

Kristeva herself was educated from an early age by French Dominican nuns in a Catholic school in her native Bulgaria. In a number of places she has stated that she came from a family of believers (Kristeva 1987a), and has referred to her father as a 'would-be Priest' who found regular solace as a member of the choir for the Orthodox cathedral in Sophia (Hughes-Hallet 1992: 26). Kristeva's background and knowledge of Christian theology, then, is both personal and academic, but she has repeatedly stated that she, herself, does not believe in God, or in the Catholic or Orthodox traditions generally (Hughes-Hallet 1992: 26; O'Grady 1998); rather, she seems to echo Freud in calling religion an 'illusion', albeit 'a glorious one' (Kristeva 1987a: 11). Kristeva's fascination with theology, rather than taking the form of a personal embrace or system of belief, stems from the wish, as a psychoanalyst, to uncover the efficacy of those imaginary constructs that enable a kind of subjective stabilisation in an individual. This means examining those religious texts and practices which are able to effect both a corporeal and psychic transference to a loving other. Religion, like poetic language, and psychoanalysis itself, offers Kristeva an entry into a complex process of sublimation that functions to abate the subjective crisis that founds each and every one of us.

So, though Kristeva neither endorses the transcendent beliefs of Christianity, as many of her critics have accused her of doing, nor views it, as do her critics, as a totalising and necessarily oppressive subjective force, I would like to submit that her theory is nevertheless inspired by the Christian theology in which she was raised and educated, and that uncovering the link between her psychoanalysis and her understanding of theology is instrumental to grasping the full range of her project.

It would, of course, take much more than this brief chapter to sketch the many possible ways of exonerating Kristeva from her critics, so I will not engage in polemic here. What I would like to proffer instead is a creative interpretation of Kristevan theory in order to suggest a means for understanding the conjunction between psychoanalysis, feminism and theology in her writings. I would like to undertake this by reading Kristeva's philosophy and narrative creations the way I have read her critics – by emphasising that which has been marginalised from the text itself – a Foucaultian gesture that detects in the margins what begs to be hidden but must come to light. Informed by this (border) logic, I will emphasise Kristeva's little-examined fictional narratives, *The Old Man and the Wolves* (1994) and *Possessions* (1998), read in relation to her theoretical work, and propose that Kristeva's writings consciously and consistently produce a doubling effect – in style and content – that evades orthodox categories (feminist-conservative, atheist-Christian) and fixed identity positions. Can Kristeva be claimed a theological daughter? A feminist sister? The answer, as always with Kristeva, is both a firm 'yes' and 'no'.

II The daughter's story: the third position of psychoanalysis

Psychoanalysis is born from the dead body of the father. Freud creates a mythical foundation for religion and patriarchy from the legend of a patricide (Freud 1985a: 202–17; 1985b). The sons of the originary family murder their violent father from fear and envy. But their consuming desire for their mother and for their father's power is not sated by the killing and the cannibalistic feast which follows (allowing them literally to ingest the father). Instead, the sons become consumed with guilt, their desires become repressed, and their remorse initiates the construction of a complex set of totemic and incest prohibitions spun out of their 'deferred obedience' to the father. This text is Freud's story – a son's story – from which so much of psychoanalytic theory has originated.

Lacanian psychoanalysis is also founded on this patricide, and another. The story of *Oedipus Rex*, as told by Sophocles, was first employed by Freud, but later augmented and reconstructed by Lacan in his theoretical work on early subjective formation. This too, is the story of a son, who mistakenly kills his father and marries his mother. Again, this murder is not a success. When the truth is discovered, the mother commits suicide by hanging, and Oedipus blinds himself and spends the rest of his years in exile. This myth has become the substratum for a set of theories (Oedipalisation, the castration complex and the 'name-of-the-father') that promise to explain a child's renunciation of desire for its mother and an acceptance of incest prohibitions, as well as other existing cultural rules and regulations.

But there is another patricide in Lacan. In order to become the golden son of psychoanalysis, Lacan had first to make of Freud a father, that is, to murder him – the 'father of psychoanalysis' (Freud himself) – and ingest him, as all good sons do, in order to replace him, albeit in his name (that is, in the 'name-of-the-father'). In a dream recounted by one of Freud's patients a man sees his father who was 'nevertheless dead, only did not know it'. From this, Freud asks himself: 'What is a Father?' And answers: 'It is the dead Father' (Lacan 1977: 292–325).[3]

I have not spent much time retelling these tales – tales of the father and the son – since they are well known, and together form the basis of much contemporary psychoanalytic criticism. What is not so well known is the third position, the missing story – perhaps there are more – which informs the psychoanalysis of Julia Kristeva. Her tale is the daughter's story and it is based on the life of St Barbara.[4]

I should begin by saying that nowhere in Kristeva's work does she explicitly recount the story of St Barbara. Instead she recalls the tale in subtle references, images and allusions, leaving a secret, though deliberate, trail for the curious reader. The first reference to St Barbara in Kristeva's work appears in a novel in which she fictionalises her own origins in Bulgaria; a novel, interestingly enough, which recounts fictively the actual death of her father. *The Old Man and the Wolves* – both a detective novel and a 'gothic roman noir' – is set in a town called 'Santa Barbara'. Kristeva has stated in an interview that the English translation of her novel renders this fictional town 'Santa *Varvara*', to prevent her English readers from mistaking the setting for a daytime soap-opera (similarly named) or a Californian coastal city.[5]

Reference to St Barbara appears in only one other place in Kristeva's work. In her most recent fictional publication, *Possessions*, also a detective novel, the mythical setting is one Santa Barbara. What is perhaps most interesting about the continuity of fictional landscape from *The Old Man and the Wolves* to *Possessions* is that Santa Barbara in the former consists of a surreal town in Eastern Europe, where the homogenising force of communism has destroyed some of the most original thinkers and artists, and turned its citizens into 'wolves' that feed on one another; the latter Santa Barbara, on the other hand, appears as a bustling city in capitalist America, where citizens fill their lives with 'fabricated smiles', 'closed faces' and endless luxury 'possessions' (as the title of the novel indicates). Quite clearly then, the oppositional setting of the two Santa Barbaras pronounces the insignificance of the material environment, while the symbolic relevance of the place-name permeates its incidental surroundings.

It is in Kristeva's theoretical work, however, that we find an account of the significance of the place-name itself. In *Strangers to Ourselves*, Kristeva provides an etymological account of the word from which the name 'Barbara' originates. The Greek *barbaros* contains the root expression 'bar-bar' or 'bara-bara' – a derogatory onomatopoeia of the foreigner's accent which produces 'inarticulate or incomprehensible mumblings' to the ear of the native speaker (Kristeva 1991: 51). '*Barbaros*', Kristeva notes, was typically used by Greeks to denote foreigners from Asia Minor, but soon became applicable to anyone who was 'non-Greek'. The word developed, as is demonstrated by its usage in the plays of Sophocles, Aeschylus and Euripides to indicate someone 'eccentric' or 'inferior'; while, similarly, current usage of 'barbaric' or 'barbarian' today conveys '*moral* inferiority', someone who exceeds the boundaries of civilised behaviour, someone savage, primitive, uncultured (Kristeva 1991: 51).

Kristeva's etymology demonstrates that the terms denoting foreignness and foreigners can be established only through a negative logic which distinguishes alterity from what cannot be embraced by the 'same'; that is, those allied characteristics which constitute the identity of any group; but at the same time, and by nature of the logic of negation, group identity, be it political, nationalistic, ethnic or religious, defines itself through the foreigner. The foreigner comes to represent that which must be shunned, marginalised, punished or even murdered, cast out from the group, in order to protect the homogeneity upon which it has been established. Yet, this expelled 'other' is, by the same token, 'the hidden face' of *any* 'identity' (Kristeva 1991: 1). Exiled from the group, the stranger exists as its lining, and exposes the tenuous identification upon which the group is established. The foreigner troubles the self-perception of the group, making it aware of its inherent gaps and breaks, insinuates its inevitable fracturing. The only certainty – identity itself – becomes shattered with the presence of the foreigner whose very expulsion from the group opens a gap, exhibits a space between.

Freud's etymology of *unheimlich*, literally, in English, 'unhomely', but more accurately and traditionally translated as 'uncanny' (Freud 1985c: 345), has as its Greek roots this element of strangeness, foreignness – the bara-bara of the outcast. It should follow that *unheimlich* would take as its meaning the opposing qualities of all that is *heimlich*, 'homely', or *heimisch*, 'native'. But as Freud indicates, the pair *heimlich/unheimlich* are not so simply defined, since there is a marked ambivalence and confusion between the two signifiers. What should function as a simple case of polar opposites, as the prefix *un* to any adjective would indicate, instead betokens that strange quality of language that permits one word to contain within itself its own undoing. Freud's further etymology reveals that while *heimlich* denotes 'what is familiar and agreeable' it simultaneously permits another, contrary usage: 'what is concealed and kept out of sight' (Freud 1985c: 345). While *unheimlich*, its antithesis, takes as its meaning the opposing qualities of the former denotation of *heimlich*, that is, it is that which is unfamiliar and troubling, it can also be used to indicate the inversion of the latter definition, 'that [which] ought to have remained secret and hidden but has come to light' (Freud 1985c: 345).[6] So the two terms, *heimlich/unheimlich*, oppose one another in the first sense, following standard grammatical construction, yet in the second meaning, shift places, take opposing denotative properties from the first, and become the antithesis, to one another once again, but on 'opposite' terms. *Heimlich/unheimlich*, each refuses a fixed position or identity, and instead they shift between their contrary significations, sometimes melding, one into the other, sometimes existing in the space between. *Unheimlich*, from the unfamiliar, becomes that which comes to light but was once concealed; while *heimlich*, once familiar, becomes that which is hidden from sight: as Freud says, 'What is *heimlich* thus comes to be *unheimlich*' (Freud 1985c: 345). This ambivalent semantics of what constitutes the 'strange' and what makes up 'the familiar' thus establishes the frame of the foreigner's story; *unheimlich* constitutes the concealed 'double' of the *heimlich*, its hidden, though implicit lining.

Kristeva's two fictional works weave their tales through the site of Santa Barbara, a fictive geographical space. Yet 'Santa Barbara' as a place-name rests on an ambivalent signification, since it does not represent a physical place or location, but, rather, an embodiment of dislocation and dis-placement, a situated subjectivity of exile and estrangement, the *unheimlich* lining of any *heimlich*; that is, simply, Santa Barbara represents a 'psychic space', the alterity at the base of identity itself. This is consonant with Kristeva's theoretical work, which places a heterogeneous foundation at the heart of subjectivity and language operation, a structuration which makes of any individual a stranger in a strange land.

In addition to the fictive Santa Barbara, the two novels – which are vastly different in style and scope – share one other element. At the centre of both detective novels is the main character, Stephanie Delacroix, a lightly veiled Julia Kristeva herself, complete with biographical details and events. And further, woven between the mythical action of the respective stories and the surreal fragments of Kristeva's autobiography are perceptible and recurrent references to the legend of St Barbara.

If there was ever any doubt that the Stephanie of *The Old Man and the Wolves* was a fictive Kristeva herself, or that the 'Old Man' represents Kristeva's actual father, the following passage sets the record straight. In the novel Kristeva recounts fictively an historic visit to Bulgaria undertaken by the French President:

As a gesture to tolerance and human rights the visiting party went to Santa Varvara Cathedral to show everyone that, wolves or no wolves [here she is referring to Communism], freedom of expression came before deals on telecommunications, high-speed trains, and so on. For me, the Gregorian chant, the incense, the ancient icons, and the gilded cupolas will always have a nostalgic charm: the charm of childhood memories, which are etched on our senses of sight, hearing and smell, and even more than words, affect our tastes – the likes and dislikes that come to us from the depths of our conscious-ness. In the midst of this reunion with a sensory past that I'd done my best to forget, I suddenly saw a hand waving from the balcony where the choir was seated. I recognised the Professor: and my smile was reticent as never before. . . . 'Do you know that man?' (The President, a humanist, always on the alert.) [Stephanie] 'Of course. . . . It's Septicius Clarus. . . . The hidden face of Santa Barbara. . . . My father. . . .'

(Kristeva 1994: 172)

Compare this fictional passage with the factual account of Kristeva's visit to Bulgaria with President Mitterrand of France in the following interview:

I had the luck, several months ago, to receive a telephone call from President Mitterrand, who asked me to accompany him on his presidential trip to Bulgaria. And it was completely overwhelming. I went. . . . Mitterrand was greeted by a crowd of students at the University. . . . And then there was another event. My father was a strong believer: he sang in the cathedral choir. Mitterrand wanted to go to religious places to show that he is for plurality of consciences and not for Communist ideology, which totalises. And so in the crypt of the Alexander Netzky church we saw this gentleman singing – it was not a mass; it was a concert of religious music – and I waved at him.

Mitterrand asked of me, 'Who is that gentleman?'
I said, 'He is my father.'

(Guberman 1996: 50–1)

It is only with the death of Kristeva's father, recounted in the factual interview and fictionalised in *The Old Man and the Wolves*, that Kristeva declares herself, through her fictional double, Stephanie Delacroix (literally, 'Of the Cross'), a daughter of the dead father. She says, echoing Freud, 'A man's not a father till he's dead', and declares Stephanie, along with all detectives (analytic or psychoanalytic), a 'sardonic and hunted disciple of the "dead" father' (Kristeva 1994: 139–40). So while Kristeva's father is, as she states 'the hidden face of Santa Barbara', it is to Santa Barbara herself that we must look to find the hidden face of Julia Kristeva.

The story of Barbara is a little-known patristic Catholic and Orthodox legend of a virgin and martyr, dated anywhere, by various sources, between the second and seventh centuries. The legend is thought to have been based on a much earlier Egyptian or Syrian myth, though its exact origins are no longer known. Most Catholic texts state that it is likely that Barbara, as a Catholic virgin and martyr, never existed, but that her story was assimilated into the Catholic canon from its original source.

Barbara is a stranger in a strange land, mourning both her motherland and her mother, whose presence is felt only through her absence from the tale. Barbara lives alone with her father, who, it is said in some accounts, wishes to find a way to protect his daughter's beauty from the vagaries of the world. So her father constructs a long, narrow tower built of stone and imprisons Barbara in his edifice for safekeeping. The father, satisfied with the enclosure that he has created for his daughter, decides that he is now able to undertake a long journey away from home without anxiety. During his absence Barbara does two things. First, she orders builders to create a third window for her in her tower, where previously there were only two. Secondly, she takes the multitude of idols that reside in her father's tower – the gods of her father – and destroys them, making sure to remove their remains from the tower.

When her father returns from his journey he is enraged by her actions. He demands that Barbara submit to his idols, but Barbara is firm in her revolt. Her father is puzzled by her addition of a third window to the tower, to which she responds: 'Two makes darkness and three makes light' [my paraphrase]. Barbara's insolence infuriates her father. Two times he attacks her 'with his sword', but Barbara refuses to bow before his gods. In a fury the father beheads his daughter, but at the very moment that she meets her death, her father himself is subsumed by flames. All that remains of the father is ashes.

This story, as I have told it, has many variations, but these features – the absence of the mother, the exile of the daughter, her imprisonment in the tower, her resistance, the death of her father and the disappearance of the father's body – occur in every telling.

Is this, as the Catholic tradition would have it, a tale of divided loyalty, of faith, and justice? Barbara is so loved by her father that he builds for her a protective tower. But despite her imprisonment, Barbara discovers the Catholic faith. She abandons the old gods of her father and removes them from the tower. In this she is rebellious. But she is also a loyal daughter since she repositions herself in his tower once again to await his return. When the father discovers the daughter's actions he murders her in anger. Barbara is taken up into the heavens.

Her death is immediately punished by a thunderbolt from God that strikes the father, and leaves his ashes to dissipate into the air. The reader is left in no doubt concerning the import of this tale: the Christian God protects and revenges his faithful followers.

But the story is not originally Catholic. It has been intricately shaped to meet the needs of those interested in proselytising the Catholic faith. There are many other ways of reading this story. I will propose just a few. As I have already suggested above, this is Julia Kristeva's story. I would like to examine this myth now as her personal tale and as a foundational myth for her theoretical work.

Perhaps this legend has the makings of a great feminist tragedy? This is how many of Julia Kristeva's critics might read this story. The daughter, having successfully freed herself from her father's tower, destroys her father's power, his gods, his tools, yet chooses to remain in the father's house. There she sits alone in an empty tower, trapped now by a captivity of her own making. Is this the story of a daughter who, having released the ties that bind her to the father, knows of no other place than the father's house? A daughter for ever estranged from her mother? A good many of Kristeva's critics would place her in this reading: the seemingly revolutionary critic who remains trapped in the male paradigms of psychoanalytic thought, resistant to leave her protective tower to find a new and unexplored path in feminist theory. That is, Kristeva's critics would view her position as that of the father's daughter.

But it is equally possible that this legend is markedly feminist. After all, the story of Barbara is above all else a celebration of a patricide. Remember that the other two patricides offered by psychoanalysis are failed murders. In Barbara's tale she outwits her father, escapes his entrapment, and destroys his power when she destroys his gods. And she does not flee the wrath of her father, but waits to confront him when he returns. She withstands his attacks and tortures, and does not relent her new-found identity, free from his influence. Her intrepidity grants her a privilege few Christian figures are rewarded with: assumption. In many versions of the tale Barbara does not die from her father's actions but is sub-sumed physically into heaven. Images of her throughout the Middle Ages and up to the present day show St Barbara holding a peacock feather, the Christian symbol of immortality. Peacock feathers are often seen in depictions of the Nativity and of the Virgin Mary (Ferguson 1954: 22; Speake 1994: 110).[7] It was once believed that the flesh of the peacock would never decay, and so its feathers are often used to symbolise this incorruptible purity, of flesh free from death. In this reading, one could believe that it is Barbara's purity itself, depicted in the tale as fire, which is responsible for the murder of her father. What is most remarkable at the end of this legend, is not so much the brutal murder of the father at the hands of his daughter, but the disappearance of his body.[8] His entire being is literally consumed by his daughter, ingested by her power, leaving only ashes behind. And where does this power come from? The story suggests that it is from Barbara's self-achieved freedom, from her new identity that is no longer fixed in the position of the father's daughter.

Supporters of Kristeva would likely view her in this reading. She has withstood the pressures and criticisms of a male-dominated French academic world, destroyed the gods of structuralism and created a radical theory that extends from her own life-experience as a woman and a mother. In her psychoanalytic work, she has swallowed up both Freudian and Lacanian theory, not to replicate their work, but to harness their power to her own aims. And where traditional psychoanalytic theory rests the foundations for subjectivity solidly on a binary logic of 'two': Father and Son in the Oedipal process, Kristeva adds a third window to her configuration: the mother, who has loves and desires outside of her bond to her child. Kristeva's agenda is not a recon-ciliation with the murdered father, like so much of psychoanalytic theory (as the two myths recounted above suggest), but a celebration of it, of the death of patriarchal structures generally – popular images of St Barbara show her trampling her father underfoot – and an incessant search for the lost mother-land. That is, Kristeva's supporters would view her position in this story as that of the mother's daughter.[9]

Barbara was one of the most renowned saints from the Middle Ages, and her image is often depicted in the art of this period. The paintings of Barbara make clear in a single image what the story can only suggest. Barbara can be recognised by the symbols that accompany her presence: a long narrow tower carried in one arm and a wide-mouthed chalice nestled in the other.[10] In some versions of the St Barbara story, she is greeted before her death with an eucharistic offering. Contemporary commentators state that Barbara – the only female saint to hold the chalice – does so because she was given the sacrament in return for her martyrdom (Ferguson 1954: 187). But it may be more appropriate to view the chalice as a symbol, not simply of her Christian religious conviction – for why then would not all female saints, necessarily martyrs, bear such a symbol? – but simultaneously, for symbols are complex constructions which can signify various and even contradictory concepts at the same time, as a representation that invokes the missing body of the mother. Barbara's symbols, the phallic tower and the uterine chalice of blood, resonate the physiognomic foundations of the daughter herself in the body of the father and the mother.

Perhaps the general structure of the Catholic reading of Barbara's story has something valuable to contribute after all. Perhaps, more than anything, hers is a story of division. Adorned with the symbols both of the mother's body and of the law (phallus) of the father, Barbara is the saintly image of Kristeva's subject-in-process. Barbara is not able to recover the missing mother, but neither is she imprisoned in her father's tower. So she wanders somewhere in the imaginary space that she has forged between the two. This is where I would like to place Julia Kristeva in this story: as the bearer of the tower *and* the chalice, as an inhabitant of 'the space between'. For, finally, is it not possible that this story, despite its polysemic resonance (or should I say, because of it?), is ultimately a stranger's story? Is this legend not the story of every migrant who lives in that nebulous space between places? The story of every subject who is, as Kristeva's theory informs us, 'a stranger to herself'? And of every psychoanalyst . . . ?

III Secret anagrams, hidden clues and doppelgängers

This chapter does not offer argument, but in its place, hazards a playful gesture: the endeavour to read a philosophy, as I have that philosophy's critics, through what has been marginalised from the body of a text. And perhaps, it is only from this strategy, located on the periphery, that I am able to submit the following: I would like to entertain the notion that Kristeva adopts St Barbara in her fictive works, as a double, as the 'other side' of Kristeva herself; and that this doubling is employed as a strategic device to frame and inform her theoretical work. I have already discussed Kristeva's early educational roots in Catholicism and her familial links to the Orthodox Church. As a young girl in a Catholic school, Kristeva may well have been required to go through the Catholic practice of choosing a saint who would provide her with a 'second name'. The chosen saint then becomes a model of virtue on which the young girl is to base her life, and a protector to whom she can turn in times of trouble. I am not suggesting, in actuality, that as a young child Kristeva selected Barbara as her saint name, or that she underwent this practice at all. I am suggesting, however, that Kristeva, aware of this practice, and also absorbed by notions of divided subjectivity, allows the image of St Barbara to permeate her later works. One has only to look at her essay on maternity, 'Stabat Mater', for a visual representation of Kristeva's fascination with 'doubling' in language and subjectivity; or look to her novels, where every character – fictitious or biographical – is always given a character that represents his or her doppelgänger.

It is also important to keep in mind that Kristeva has more than a passing interest in secret passageways and hidden entrances, in mysteries and clues. As other critics have noted, Kristeva has a fascination with pseudonyms, and many of the writers she has chosen to study over the years – Céline, Nerval, Stendhal, Lautréamont – employ pseudonyms to conceal or alter their identity, and Kristeva has even used a pseudonym herself at least once; further, she has authored a study that rejoices in the doubling of language and the concurrent doubling affects of identity (Nikolchina 1991: 238; Kristeva 1969a; 1969b; 1980b). As a student of semiotics, Kristeva has also been enchanted by anagrams and palindromes and has dedicated an entire study to Saussure's work on anagrams; 'Barbara', a mnemonic word used in logic, often used to represent the three propositions of the syllogism (bar-bar) which reveal a universal law or rule (-a), would appeal to Kristeva on these grounds alone.

However, though there are many St Barbara 'clues' evident in Kristeva's texts, I am adopting this notion of Kristeva's second name, of her 'doubling', as more of a playful strategy than the 'key to all' Kristevan 'mythologies'. I have no claim, here, for having 'cracked the code of codes', though detective fiction tempts every reader to do precisely that. And if detective fiction should be our guide, then we should already know that any code that successfully unearths a cohesive structure beneath a mass of random elements, usually does so by chance, and not at all from design. But as a method, using a fiction – the story of Santa Barbara – to unravel another fiction – psychoanalytic theory – is as good a procedure as any, so long as we are willing to risk the wager and confront the fragility within which our own life-story resides: a tenuous and divided subjectivity which is as much foreign (*unheimlich*) as it is home (*heimlich*); that is simply to say, that as the story of Santa Barbara constitutes the shadowy lining of Kristevan philosophy, so it establishes, as a stranger's story is wont to do, the 'other side' of each and every one of us.

Kristeva leaves us with one last shimmering revelation. She says, 'The *foreigner* [must] become the figure onto which the penetrating, ironic mind of the philo-sopher is delegated – *his double, his mask*' (Kristeva 1991: 134; my emphasis). In Kristeva's case, this uncanny double is none other than St Barbara, who presides as the theological sister to her philosophy; but, equally, who functions as a representation of alterity, a self-reflective, critical faculty which operates within Kristeva's own philosophical paradigms, incessantly breaking through and shatter-ing her discourse. St Barbara becomes the model on which Kristevan theory is able to remain dynamic, a renewal which resists monological discursive solidifica-tion. Modelled on her theory of poetic language, with its 'semiotic' component that disrupts, interrupts and breaks open the 'symbolic' component of univocal discourse, the stranger's trace is woven through the systematic linearity of the philosopher's scribbling; the polyphonous ruptures caused by the foreigner, whose alterity constitutes the lining of any philosophical system, anticipates its limits and fractures its fictitious unity. Like Freud's *heimlich/unheimlich* signifiers which occupy an ambivalent space between identity/non-identity, Kristevan philosophy contains within itself its own undoing; and, hence, its own renewal.

What I have hoped to offer in this chapter is a means through which readers can navigate the typology of estrangement that infuses Kristeva's work, herself '*l'étrangère*', as Barthes has often said of her; a foreignness that is presented metaphorically in narrative doubling, linguistically, through semiotic word-play, genre-bending and fluid discipline boundaries, and finally, theoretically with a subject who slips between identity positions she can never call 'home'. St Barbara is Kristeva as the quintessential stranger, a wandering theological daughter whose 'bara-bara' mutterings will continue to threaten those around her.

Notes

1   It is clear that Brennan is sympathetic to the point I am making here and not an example of its abuses.

2   She adds on p. 79 of the same text: 'Kristeva's account . . . provokes the question of what one is to make, *as a feminist*, of the description of a maternal role that consists in relaying an image of the father, associated moreover with the logos or with God.'

3   By this, Freud presumably implies the 'deferred obedience' he posits in relation to the horde of sons in *Totem and Taboo* (1985a), which create elaborate totemic and incest prohibitions. Gallop believes this dream constitutes the foundational myth for Lacanian theory generally. See Gallop 1985: 157–85.

4   This information was compiled from a number of different sources: *The Golden Legend*; *The Greek Acts*; Delaney 1980: 86; Delaney 1961: 97; Coulson 1958: 62, 47; Thurston 1981; Nevins 1980: 7, 18; Cousins 1958: 31–4; *The New Catholic Encyclopedia*, 1967: 86–7; Farmer 1978; Ferguson 1954; Speake 1994; Bond 1914; Mâle 1949.

5   Though the city also has definitive links to the saint, having been named after her in 1602, when the Spanish explorer Sebastian Vizcaino and his ship were saved from a storm after they sailed up the channel. It would have been appropriate enough to name the city after the saint who protects her devotees from lightning, but it also happened that the day the ship arrived safely was also St Barbara's feast day, 4 December.

6   Freud, echoing Schelling's definition.

7   Some commentators also attribute St Barbara's peacock feather to the city Heliopolis where she was born. This is highly problematic since her origins are largely unknown. Bond states that St Barbara holds a feather because 'the rods with which she was beaten were turned into feathers', though he is the minority in attributing her feather symbol to this aspect of her story (Bond 1914: 149). Still others state that she is not holding a feather, but a 'palm', though in the majority of depictions, it is clearly a peacock feather. For example, see the beautiful *Breviary of Martin of Aragon* (from fifteenth-century Spain), which is in the Bibliothèque Nationale, France; http://www.bnf.fr/enluminures/texte/manuscrit/aman11/i8_0080.htm

8   This is an ironic inversion of Mary's Assumption in Catholic theology, where the daughter is taken bodily into heaven by God, the Father. Here, the daughter subsumes the body of the Father, so that he leaves no corporeal trace.

9   As an interesting aside, some early versions of the story of Cinderella (of unknown origins, like many fairy-tales) refer to her as 'Barbarella'. In both stories the mother is dead, or missing, and thus the daughter is situated in

the position of 'a stranger', with no mother-land (Starbird 1993). The earliest version of Cinderella dates from the ninth century (Europe).

10   The most widely known portrait of this kind is by Guercino, who includes in his portrait of St Barbara the chalice as well as the tower, adhering to the rendition of her story as it exists in *The Golden Legend*, which states that the chalice was brought to her before her death by an angel (Mâle 1949: 191); the *New Catholic Encyclopedia* also lists Flemish and Italian artists using this symbol in addition to the tower, her more prominent symbol (1967: 86). The first known painting of St Barbara is an eighth-century fresco at S. Maria Antiqua, in Rome (Farmer 1978: 28). Interestingly, there are several depictions of St Barbara with Mary Magdalene. Since 'magdalene' literally means 'tower', the metonymic affiliation is not likely to be accidental. Many paintings attribute other symbols to Barbara as well. The Master of Flémalle's 'St Barbara' shows her with the usual tower with three windows but also with an apple, which she offers to the baby Jesus (Ferguson 1954: fig. 58); In other paintings she is found with St Margaret of Antioch (similarly beheaded for her beliefs) (Farmer 1978: 28). Jan van Eyck's St Barbara portrays the most elaborate tower construction, with an entire village operating at its base, linking St Barbara's faith to the foundation of civilisation itself (Antwerp Museum; Baldass 1951: fig. 127; cat. no. 14); while Botticelli's 'Barbara' with tower, is likely the most well-known painting of St Barbara today (Coulson 1958: 47).

Chapter 7

Martha J. Reineke

OUR VITAL NECESSITY
Julia Kristeva's Theory of Sacrifice

IN THE YEARS THAT I have been teaching feminist theory, students' reactions to course texts have ranged broadly but predictably. Generally appreciative of the readings, students also have expressed disagreement, frustration and ambivalence. But one student's singular response to a book about Freud has stayed with me. Pulling the book from her backpack one day, this student commented that she was thinking about wrapping it in brown paper lest her feminist roommates discover she was reading about someone who was 'no friend of ours'. This student's comment elicited laughter from her classmates. Weeks later, her rueful confession continued to frame our conversations together as the class struggled with the question to which the student's surreptitious approach to Freud attested: Is psychoanalytic theory a constructive and helpful resource for feminism or is it hostile to feminism's interests?

Today, what I call 'the brown paper wrapper question' has become a fixture of my course in feminist theory. It also features in the broader context of feminist theory. For some, Freud and the field of psychoanalysis that is his legacy are compelling resources (for example, Bronfen 1992; Elliot 1991; Oliver 1993, 1998); for others, they are problematic (for example, Delphy 1996; Fraser 1990; Leland 1989). Given the breadth of psychoanalytic approaches within feminist theory – for example, American ego psychologies, British object-relations theories, French psychoanalytic traditions (Wright 1992: 412, 284, 201) – those who would take up the question of psychoanalysis and feminism are best advised to skip generalised accounts and focus instead on specific examples. This chapter will examine the psychoanalytic theory of Julia Kristeva whose work is influenced by Jacques Lacan, a French psychoanalyst who recast Freud in order to make speech and language central to the psychogenesis of the human child (Ragland-Sullivan 1992: 205–6). In particular, I will demonstrate the significance of Kristeva's psychoanalytic theory of sacrifice for feminist analyses of religion.

In the first section of the chapter, I will establish the viability of Kristeva's psychoanalytic theory as a resource for feminist theory. In this discussion, a 'brown paper wrapper' becomes an apt motif. Although this phrase most commonly calls to mind the wrapped contents of a pornographic magazine, it also provokes reflection: Why and how is sexual difference associated with processes of concealment? Addressing this issue, I will establish the import of Kristeva's assertion, with Lacan, that 'women' are products of a phantasy of sexual difference. In Section II, I will examine links between phantasy and sacrifice in order to analyse violence against women. I will look closely at patterns of sexually differentiated violence in acts of sacrifice. In concluding the chapter, I will attend to religion's role in sacrificial practices in which women feature prominently. I will also discuss Kristeva's call for a non-sacrificial ethic of analysis and the implications of her call for feminism and religion.

I Why psychoanalysis?

Teresa Brennan (1991) and Patricia Elliot (1995) perspicaciously cut to the core of key feminist arguments against psychoanalysis. They argue that the diverse currents of feminism are characterised by a generosity of spirit. Feminists share a commitment to social change but under that broad rubric fall heterogeneous theories and practices. Why, then, is psychoanalysis suspect for some feminist theorists? According to Brennan and Elliot, otherwise inclusive traditions within feminism rally to exclude psychoanalytic theory when feminists assume that a theory's openness to social change is correlated *only* with socio-historical and cultural accounts of women's oppression and prospects for emancipation. Because psychoanalysis appeals to trans-historical structures of lived existence and not only to socialised patterns of behaviour, it is perceived to fall outside the purview of feminist theory and its univocal commitment to social change (Elliot 1995: 47; Brennan 1991: 117). 'Psychoanalytic feminism' becomes an oxymoron.

Christine Delphy's remarks about Kristeva exemplify such a critical perspective on psychoanalytic feminism. Delphy asserts that Kristeva 'does not address the questions raised by feminism because she does not know what they are' (1995: 220). But, as I demonstrate in this chapter, Kristeva displays a sustained interest in feminism, focusing especially on the problem of violence against women. As a consequence, Delphy's allegation is inexplicable, unless one takes into account Elliot and Brennan's observations. If asking questions about the oppression of women within the framework of psychoanalysis ipso facto constitutes 'not addressing the questions raised by feminism', Delphy's peremptory dismissal of Kristeva's work is intelligible.

In dissent from critics like Delphy, those who defend psychoanalysis as a resource for feminism reject the association between 'the historically mutable and the politically actionable' (Brennan 1991: 119). They challenge their critics' conflation of psychoanalytic feminists' call to politically engage trans-historical structures of lived existence with a condemnation of their very appeal to such structures (Brennan 1991: 115). According to Brennan and Elliot, feminist theorists should avail themselves of two interrogatory moments, not one, if they are to treat psychoanalytic theory fairly. First, feminist theorists should listen to the case that psychoanalytic feminists make for trans-historical structures. Subsequently, they should evaluate strategies for social change that psychoanalytic theorists advance based on their knowledge of these structures. When critics of psychoanalytic feminism conflate these two moments, they misrepresent psychoanalytic theory.

Brennan and Elliot's comments bring clarity to feminist theorists' concerns about unacknowledged bias in psychoanalytic feminism. When feminist theorists offer *socio-historical* accounts of women's lives, they surely are remiss if their accounts speak only of the lives of white, middle-class women in Europe and North America, rendering invisible the lives of all other women. Subject formation does hinge on articulations of power that differentially privilege some women. These power dynamics should be contested by feminists. But when feminist theorists offer accounts of subject *formation*, their accounts may rightly turn also on movements within discourse that establish the very possibilities for a difference and alterity in being that are prerequisites for subject status. The 'feminism' in psychoanalytic feminism is typified by efforts its proponents make to forge links between these distinct moments of subject formation without disavowing either. This chapter attends to the ways in which Kristeva's sacrificial theory constructs such links.[1]

Approached on terms that Brennan and Elliot suggest, Kristeva's psychoana-lytic feminism can be seen to productively overturn conventional expectations among feminist theorists about sex, gender and social change. Influenced by Lacan, Kristeva's work contrasts with pervasive trends in Anglo-American feminist theory, exemplified by Nancy Chodorow (1978, 1989), which treat the psyche as a kind of blank slate on which conventions for social relations are scripted. Feminist advocates of social change intervene when they challenge internalised norms for feminine and masculine behaviour and replace them with norms more hospitable to the goals of feminism. By contrast, Kristeva's psychoanalytic feminism is not a theory about the internalisation of gender norms. Instead, it explores, as does Lacan's theory, the 'conditions in which socially specific ideas about gender and sexuality are taken on or refused' (Elliot 1995: 45). Kristeva exchanges a cultural theory of gender for a theory attentive to trans-historical processes that produce socio-historical conditions. Not bypass-ing possibilities to promote social change and new expressions of free agency, she homes in on aspects of lived existence that are fundamental to the expression or thwarting of agency. Where proponents of cultural analysis frame constraints on agency and options for change exclusively in terms of cultural messages about gender, sometimes oppressive and sometimes emancipating, Kristeva suggests that feminist theory needs to include within its framework of analysis a focus on the most basic structures of lived existence.

Among these trans-historical structures is the 'Imaginary body'. The Imaginary body emerges out of an undifferentiated 'soup of sensations, drives, and emotions' (Minsky 1998: 64) of infant experience. Here, 'I' and 'other' are not clearly differentiated (Kristeva 1984c: 25; Lacan 1985a: 163). As it grows, the infant does attain a sense of position and perspective, experiencing its body as a body with definable boundaries. The source of its newfound boundedness is attributable to its relations with others (paradigmatically the mother) who 'mirror' for it unity and wholeness. However, the child's belief in unity afforded by this image is characterised by *méconnaissance*, or misrecognition (Lacan 1981: 74). After all, although the child believes itself in possession of the unity being promised by the image, the source of this unity still rests at the site of its image. Always, 'the I is Other' (Kearney 1986: 274). Indeed, as Kristeva notes, at the 'zero degree of the Imagination' is an insurmountable 'emptiness' (Kristeva 1987b: 24). As a consequence, at times, the child experiences great certainty in its relations; at other times, instability predominates. Insecurity is evident not only in jealousy, competition and aggression, but also in acts of idealisation and desire (Ragland-Sullivan 1992: 174; Kristeva 1987b: 32–3).

The Imaginary base of the child's sense of self-possession, which emerges in these early mirroring episodes, is never surpassed. An adult subject still achieves identity only in difference and asserts a unity of being only in the context of alienation (Lacan 1981: 205–6). As a consequence, when the word 'Imaginary' is invoked in descriptions of the sense of self-possession and internal/external coherence which humans experience in the presence of others, we should not understand 'Imaginary' to mean 'pretend'. The Imaginary is a genuine and enduring feature of existence. However, the human's sense of bounded, self-contained identity is always an investment in an *image* and dependent on mimesis.

The second basic structure in Lacanian theory, on which Kristeva draws for her own reflections, is the 'Symbolic', which marks the maturation of the subject in the world (Lacan 1968: 38–40). With Lacan, Kristeva observes that language, the currency of the Symbolic, stabilises the bounded identity which the infant first achieves in the mirror stage, securing its investments in an intersubjective world (Kristeva 1984c: 47). In earlier moments, the child had few occasions to confront the *méconnaissance* of its being because the maternal-mirror (or her substitutes) was regularly present. But the growing child experiences frequent breakdowns, interruptions and assaults on its sense of unity and stability. Mirrors fail, exposing a lack of being. Language, like wrapping paper, is made to cover this loss, disguising it. Functioning as a linguistic substitute for mirrors, language confirms and sustains the child's sense of place, offering identity packages that enable it to negotiate the world.

Examples abound; language confirms between children and their parents a familial identity. Interdependent patterns of bounded identity are also established in the pedagogy of instruction and the workplace. Nations, too, offer substantial Symbolic resources for identity (Bracher 1993; Stavrakakis 1999; Kristeva 2000, 1993, 1991). Further, such relations are dynamic and historically variable (Brennan 1993; Oliver 1998). Wherever we turn – family, school, work, nation – intersubjective patterns of relationship today differ from those of a generation or a century ago. Thus, while the Lacanian structures of subject formation (Imaginary and Symbolic) on which Kristeva builds her theory are trans-historical, the subject whose actions she critically interrogates is radically historical and social.

Two features of the Imaginary and Symbolic are noteworthy. These structures establish a framework for sexual difference distinct from concepts of 'sex' and 'gender'. Further, the achievements of the Imaginary and Symbolic are characterised by endemic fragility. Each feature has important implications for feminist theory and its commitment to social change. The former speaks to issues associated with feminism's quest for enhanced agency for women; the latter highlights risks associated with this quest. I address each feature in turn.

The relational structures of the Imaginary and Symbolic suggest a lived experience of the body that does not bifurcate along biological and social poles into 'sex' and 'gender'. Instead, the mirroring work of the Imaginary, supported by the Symbolic, creates dynamic conditions under which human subjects take up meanings in acts, joining material gestures and words. In the absence of biological mandates that predate the work of culture, 'the body is always already implicated in signification' (Oliver 1993: 156) and 'sexual difference emerges simultaneously with culture itself' (Butler 1992: 143).

With the concept of 'sexual difference', a notion of a biological pregiven that founds bodies, male and female, is relinquished in favour of a signifying practice that positions subjects differentially in relation to a 'placeholder': the phallus (Lacan 1985b: 75). Not the biological penis, the phallus is a point of division in a signifying field and sexual difference is the deployment of meaning along this division (Kristeva 1984c: 47). An arbitrary and phantasmatic construction, the phallus sets forth a shifting ground of meaning. Construed mimetically, those who are purported to 'have' the phallus are 'men'; those who 'are' the phallus are 'women' (Lacan 1985b: 75). But the phallus is not the attribute of any subject. It has currency only in the mirrored, phantasmatic play of desire. Although the phallus promises unity, jouissance – one will be all for an other – it never escapes the méconnaissance of being to deliver on this promise. The signifying work of sexual difference remains always dynamic and open.

True, Kristeva's portrait of sexual difference, informed by the work of Lacan, emphasises heterosexual expressions of desire. However, because Kristeva acknowledges that signifying practices are arbitrary, sexual difference has no essence. It is open to diverse articulations and configurations. Kristeva takes up this possibility when she recommends against the permanent institutionalisation of historically dominant erotic histories associated with the Oedipal narratives of Freud, calling instead for 'the end of amatory codes' and the exploration of 'polyvalent spaces' of desire. Her 'polylogical' thinking about desire constitutes an opportunity to conceptualise sexual difference in ways that broaden (or subvert) heterosexual privilege and the 'two-sexes' framework of gender dimorphism (Kristeva 1987b: 379–80).

Kristeva's theory of sexual difference, informed by Lacanian psychoanalysis, adds irony to the motif of a 'brown paper wrapper'. In common parlance, brown paper covers the exposed genitals of the pornographic subject, concealing them from view. But Lacan demonstrates that the phallus *is* the wrapper that covers . . . nothing. After all, because humans share a founding estrangement in being, *all* definitive claims on desire are forever deferred. The phallus is a signifying ploy that papers over a fundamental lack of being. Of course, that the phallus is a ruse does not obviate the investments humans have made in it, hoping that lack will be replaced with the fullness of being. Sexual difference is phantasmatic, but it is not 'just a fantasy'. Persistent patterns of heterosexual masculinity and femininity – hunk, *femme fatale*, womaniser, bimbo, chick, stud – attest to the enduring power of human investments in phantasmatic difference (Minsky 1998: 74). As scholars such as Teresa de Lauretis (1994) and Claudia Tate (1998) attest, so also do the fictions of lesbian desire and the 'race-ing' of desire among African Americans and between African Americans and whites confirm the power of phantasy deployed along axes inclusive of sex, race and class.

Does Kristeva's exposition of the fictions of identity within the Symbolic, informed by Lacan, lend itself to the feminist goals for social change? Feminists tend to be critical of biases and stereotypes associated with gender, race and class that mark long-standing patterns of desire in the Symbolic. Conceivably, someone could argue that these biases persist because they continue to effectively mediate the chaos of existence and offer coherent identities to those who subscribe to them. Thus, even though Kristeva suggests that these arbitrary constructions have no biological basis that grounds them as essential aspects of human life, one could draw on her work to offer a pragmatic rationale for retaining their privileged status. But feminist and other critical theorists will find more support for their criticisms of the status quo in interpretations of Lacan proffered by Rosalind Minsky and Slavoj Žižek because they emphasise the subversive potential of Lacan-influenced theories such as Kristeva's.

Minsky writes that when Lacan discloses the precarious status of the phallus, he gives the lie to the bulwark of cultural, heterosexual masculinity and its hegemony (Minsky 1998: 72). Far from valorising this phantasy, Lacan exposes its deceit, inspiring a broad spectrum of trenchant theorising on the diverse phantasies of contemporary culture. Žižek thinks that the Lacanian analytic framework has prospects for promoting social change because it offers subjects 'breathing space' (Žižek 1989: 122). When subjects assume an analytic standpoint, they become attentive to the fictional status of their objects of desire (whether framed by sex, race, nationality, or class). Their attentiveness creates a space to critically engage the lack in being which language heretofore has covered over with its stereotypic configurations of desire. Subjects are able to realise that 'the Other . . . hasn't got it' (Žižek 1989: 122). Of course, subjects who assume an analytic stance do not opt out of the Imaginary/Symbolic, circumventing lack altogether. The 'I is Other' still. However, in making constitutive lack visible, an analytic perspective allows subjects to identify their own lack with the lack in the Other (Žižek 1989: 122), creating space for an ethics of difference no longer grounded in the Identity games of the Symbolic. In the final section of this chapter, I expand on Žižek's observations and link them with Kristeva's. The framework for an ethics of analysis that Kristeva sketches has much in common with Žižek's ethics of difference.

I turn now to explore the second feature of the Imaginary and Symbolic identified earlier: the fragility of these structures. Women's experience of violence brings the frailty question to the fore. Do incidents of sexually differentiated violence arise because of the unstable status of the subject's achievements within the Symbolic, suggesting that trans-historical structures are implicated in violence against women? Or should violence be attributed to incidental socio-historical factors alone? Kristeva states that these questions have significant implications for feminism. As long as the parameters of the problem of violence are not well delineated, feminists' goals for social change may miss the mark, leaving women at continued risk. As a consequence, Kristeva thinks that violence against women is an issue of 'epochal significance' and a major social concern for women (Kristeva 1986b: 200).

II Kristeva's sacrificial theory

In her quest to understand violence, Kristeva invokes the Symbolic when she writes that sexual difference 'is translated by and translates a difference in the relationship of subject to the symbolic contract which *is* the social contract' (Kristeva 1986b: 196). Noting that what are differentiated by sexual difference are relationships to 'power, language and meaning' (Kristeva 1986b: 196), Kristeva states that far from being the equal of men in relationship, the social contract for women is 'an essentially sacrificial relationship' (Kristeva 1986b: 199). Why do women live the Symbolic sacrificially? In answering this question, Kristeva illuminates the broad context of violence against women, shedding light on the socio-historical scene on which feminism so frequently has focused its energies and elucidating the relation of violence to the trans-historical structures of the Imaginary and Symbolic.

I would like to begin my discussion of Kristeva's theory of sacrifice by considering whether 'sacrifice' has a literal referent in her work. After all, Lacan and Kristeva occasionally employ 'matricide' and 'murder' as figures of speech. For example, while discussing how language acquisition signals a child's trans-ition into the Symbolic, Lacan writes about Ernst, Freud's grandson. Describing Ernst's efforts to come to terms with his mother's absence from a room where he is playing, Lacan uses the word 'murder' in his account of what transpires. As Ernst moves a reel with which he is playing out of sight and retrieves it moments later, he says 'fort' and 'da', 'here' and 'there'. According to Lacan, with these words, Ernst makes the reel a stand-in for his mother, controlling her presence and absence. Summing up Ernst's accomplishment, Lacan states that 'the symbol manifests itself first of all as the murder of the thing' (Lacan 1968: 84). But no one interprets Lacan to mean that Ernst has killed his mother. Readers perceive that Lacan has chosen words that underscore a key observation: when Ernst makes the reel disappear, the reel mediates the lack in being which Ernst's mother's absence would otherwise predicate, given the Imaginary dictates of the mirror stage. Compensating effectively for his mother's absence by availing himself of the signifying potential of language, Ernst is able to 'master his privation by assuming it . . . [and] raising his desire to the second power' (Lacan 1977: 103; 1966: 319). Notwithstanding his dramatic turn of phrase, Lacan intends only to identify that moment when children pass from the Imaginary to the Symbolic, acquiring linguistic stand-ins for their mothers (or other intimate others) who, the reader may presume, are not at risk of physical harm from their children during this rite of passage.

Charting the same territory that Lacan covers in his discussion of Ernst, Kristeva writes that loss of the maternal is a necessary step on the subject's way to adult autonomy: 'matricide is our vital necessity, the sine-qua-non condi-tion of our individuation' (Kristeva 1989: 27). Leaving the Imaginary 'soup' of undifferentiated being, infants become children by using language to leverage autonomy and independence. Is Kristeva's use of the word 'sacrifice' a similarly innocent, if none the less striking, reference to processes of language acquisition in early childhood?

To the contrary, when Kristeva uses the word 'sacrifice', her focus most often is not on the word-play of children but on the *materialisation* of meaning in the socio-historical context of adult life. In this context, 'sacrifice' rightly conjures images of death because women experience a 'sacrificial contract against their will (*à leur corps défendant*)' (Kristeva 1986b: 200). While Kristeva shares with Lacan a focus on the hinge between the Imaginary and Symbolic orders of existence as the locus of the subject's instability, she is attentive where he is not to the life-circumstances of those who circumnavigate that hinge. Children nego-tiate this instability with far different repercussions for others than do adults. As a consequence, Ernst's sacrificial play at the threshold of the Symbolic bodes differently for his mother and the safety of her body than does the like movement of adults along that same threshold for other mothers or maternal substitutes. The articulation of this distinction is the focus of Kristeva's thinking about sacrifice.

Kristeva's sacrificial theory emerges from her observations of infancy and early childhood. Unlike Lacan, for whom the ever resourceful Ernst, playfully relishing his conquest of language, is a model for all young children, Kristeva observes early childhood through a different lens. She begins by looking closely at the 'maternal matrix' or 'maternal body' (Kristeva 1984c: 27). With this concept, Kristeva asserts that in the 'soup' of infant experience, there are no distinct mothers. Nevertheless, those that are not-yet-a-mother and not-yet-a-subject *are* differentiated because body movements articulate patterns or styles of difference. For example, a mouth turns towards or away from a breast. Only in the Symbolic will these expressions of difference create the sign 'mother'.

Even so, Kristeva recognises, as Lacan does not, that styles of difference demarcated in the maternal matrix impact the child's transition to the Symbolic. Separation from the maternal matrix of its origins 'is a violent, clumsy breaking away, with the constant risk of falling back under the sway of a power as securing as it is stifling' (Kristeva 1982: 13). Embattled and beset by mimetic conflict, the child practises boundary-making (Kristeva 1987b: 23). Not yet the accomplished subject of language, this child is 'abject'. It demarcates space and position with its mouth: chewing, spitting and swallowing sameness and difference. Its bodily fluids, expelled or retained, enable it to experience its own difference as pleasure but also as discomfort or loss. Sound and silence, echolalias and rhythms, not yet words belonging to a mother or subject-child, whirl around the abject. Alterations and checks in the movement of sound are punctuations in the life of the abject that form an 'archaic topos', a precursor to border-work that later will be formative for the subject who uses words (Kristeva 1980a: 284–5).

Material rites of division that secure for the child its most basic boundaries are bolstered by the accomplishments of language. The abject becomes a nascent subject. But never resting easily with its subject-status, the subject regularly acts to resecure the accomplishments of being. Notwithstanding its desire for the full unity of being, it is beset by manifest shortcomings. Experiencing estrangement and loss, which are markers of mortality, the subject repetitively confronts its lack of being. Summoning the resources of language and exploiting the institutions of culture, history and politics to bolster its experience of bounded identity, the subject-of-loss works in order not to die. Kristeva coins a powerful phrase to describe the subject's labor: 'death-work' (Kristeva 1983).

Although all human subjects engage in death-work, their efforts are not always sacrificial. Sacrifice emerges under conditions of acute distress, when humans second-guess *all* of their achievements in the Symbolic. This crisis is called 'thetic' in order to indicate that the subject is at risk of losing all standing in the

Symbolic. Words fade before acts that move in and through bodies, as those in the throes of crisis attempt to ritually reinvoke processes of identity-differentiation which first won them a place in the world. Kristeva names this permutation of death-work 'sacrifice' (Kristeva 1984c: 70). Precipitating factors vary: intimate and familial relationships may initiate this crisis but so also can economic, political and social conflicts (Kristeva 1984c: 76). Whatever the antecedents, when subjects are inundated by crisis, they re-enact the moments when they summoned the most archaic markers of difference in their quest to separate themselves from the maternal continent of their origins and secure their independent existence. Cutting, killing and eating, they hope to summon from the flesh over which they linger the very powers of life and death.

The parameters of sacrifice are revealed when an adult subject's re-enactment of its struggle with abject origins is compared with the actions of a tiny infant. For the infant, 'matricide' is a limited act of violence. When it summons its alimentary powers and the resources of its bowels and digestive tract to wrest from the maternal matrix the difference necessary for its independent survival, its mother may react to its struggles with concern. If she is tired, she may be upset by her baby's tears and tantrums. But she is not viscerally impacted by its rages. By contrast, under circumstances of crisis, the subject's renewed struggle with the maternal matrix more often entails an immoderate violence. The same material resources for contestation, deployed by a large and more powerful adult, evoke raw and potentially lethal violence. Is 'sacrifice' an appropriate label for this violence?

There are three reasons why 'sacrifice' is an apt term for actions undertaken by a subject in the throes of a thetic crisis. 'Sacrifice' captures the powerful gesture of killing substance (soma, matter, flesh) in order to make it signify (Kristeva 1984c: 75). Such acts enable the subject to summon *all* its signifying resources and not only signs when, travelling along the route it first navigated as a young child, it crosses once again the bridge from the maternal matrix into the Symbolic. Second, sacrifice is productive of signs, facilitating what Elisabeth Bronfen calls 'the somatisation of the idea' (1992: 196). Sacrifice marks the break between the Imaginary and the Symbolic even as it transgresses this break and sublates it. Consequently, sacrifice turns on the somatic hinge of the Imaginary and Symbolic even though a subject grasps signs in sacrifice, not soma (Kristeva 1984c: 79). Sacrifice shows Symbolic functioning, replicating it, but not as an already existing system. Instead, sacrifice reproduces the *process* of the Symbolic's production (Kristeva 1984c: 77). Third, sacrifice is an appropriate term to use when describing a subject's response to a thetic crisis because it wholly mimes the conflict sacrifice would vanquish. Reminding the reader that cultures practise sacrifice not only because sacrifice is believed to destroy forces that pose a threat to the community, but also because, in the wake of sacrifice, an entire community is purified, Kristeva notes that sacrifice destroys because victims die but sacrifice also constructs identity and place. *Pharmakos* (scapegoat) and *pharmakon* (poison and antidote) are one in sacrifice (Kristeva 1982: 84). Therefore, repeating the entire movement of the subject into the Symbolic, sacrifice re-enacts the *productive* motility that initially enabled the infant to secure its foot-hold in the world, recalling in full spectrum the early subject's formative acts of agency (Kristeva 1984c: 79).

Where is sacrifice visible? Art is a privileged discourse. It embodies in virtually complete form the three dynamics of sacrifice that Kristeva has sketched. Art breaks through the sign 'tearing the veil of representation to find the material signifying process' (Kristeva 1984c: 103). Taking on death, the artist approximates the 'scapegoat' of sacrificial ritual, differing from victims of sacrifice only because the artist does not complete the sacrificial cycle. Caught in the motility of the artistic gesture, the artist does not 'harness the thetic' and complete sacrifice as sign (Kristeva 1984c: 70). That task, Kristeva observes, is left to religions, which 'set themselves up as specialists on the discourse concerning this radical, unique, thetic event' (Kristeva 1984c: 70).

Kristeva notes also that sexual difference shapes the coded, cultural responses to thetic crisis. Identifying explosive and implosive patterns of response, she asserts that women are more likely to engage thetic crisis implosively, through gestures of depression, suicide and melancholia (Kristeva 1989: 14). Men are more likely to engage it explosively, through sacrifice (Kristeva 1989: 29). As a consequence, men's gestures figure prominently in religious traditions of sacrifice.

III Women at risk: the evidence from religion

Kristeva's account of sacrifice and her exploration of women's special vulnerability to sacrificially generated violence constitute contributions that are among the most important her work makes to feminist theory and the study of religion. Women are at special risk because those who feel imperilled by a thetic crisis regularly exploit sexual difference, making women's bodies a primary currency in a sacrificial economy. Why are women especially vulnerable?

According to Kristeva, historically and culturally specific traits of mothers are not alone reliable indicators of risk because the origins of sacrificial violence do not lie neatly in the Symbolic but at its juncture: the abject environs of the maternal matrix. Whoever bears marks of this territory is at risk. But how do we know who bears these marks? After all, within the linguistic register of the Symbolic, we do not encounter the abject in raw form. We read it in signs that point to a more archaic script, a primal mapping of meaning at the somatic hinge of human being (Kristeva 1982: 73). For the subject in the throes of a thetic crisis, the maternal matrix is revisited initially as a mimetic drama that is announced in moments of nausea and anxiety, when sweaty palms and a racing heart attest to the subject's disequilibrium in being. Falling back on the archaic possibilities of oral assimilation, now perceived in terms of reciprocal threat, the subject of crisis, now abject, bites before being bitten (Kristeva 1982: 39). Alimentary motifs together with fluids such as blood and milk form a topos, not secured entirely by the veil of representation, along which ranges the abjectified subject who would vanquish the threat that imperils it (Kristeva 1982: 54).

In historical experience, women's bodies have been identified especially with these marks of abjection. Therefore, when subjects in the midst of a thetic crisis begin to lose their grip on the Symbolic, their actions are often directed against the bodies of women. Made to give testimony that attests to the subject's maternal continent of origin, women's bodies have wrested from them renewed possibilities for being. Such violent invocations of the abject testify, Kristeva says, 'to the other facet of religious, moral, and ideological codes on which rest the sleep of individuals and the breathing spells of societies' (Kristeva 1982: 209).

Writing of these hidden facets of religious codes in *Powers of Horror*, Kristeva identifies three moments: abject violence, defilement and sacrifice. Because each moment in this typology invokes sexual difference, Kristeva's sacrificial theory is, above all, a theory of matricide. Examining religion for indications of abject violence, Kristeva locates evidence in a territory of the sacred that Freud has ignored. When he reflects on the taboos of totemism – murder and incest – Freud virtually sets aside the origins of incest dread to attend to murder, keystone of the Oedipal structure. Kristeva, aiming to give incest its due, writes that the pages of *Totem and Taboo* are 'haunted' by the mother-image which bespeaks another sacred 'oriented towards those uncertain spaces of unstable identity, towards the fragility – both threatening and fusional – of the archaic dyad' (Kristeva 1982: 58). Identifying this facet of the sacred as the 'true lining of the sacrificial' (Kristeva 1982: 64), Kristeva determines that it is structured by spatial ambivalence, a confusion of inside and outside, pleasure and pain, which rituals of interdiction mark as threat and around which they structure a protective space.

With the second aspect of this typology – defilement – Kristeva probes these interdictory processes. Rituals that inscribe boundaries and contain polluting dangers that are perceived to come from outside a society establish a ridge separating filth (abject) from that which is whole and clean. Defilement is Kristeva's Rosetta Stone, enabling her to identify in diverse narratives attestations to the maternal matrix and its threat. Parcelling bodies and creating borders, humans invoke the most archaic images: excrement and its equivalent (decay, infection, disease) stand for a danger to identity from without; menstrual and birthing blood represent a danger from within (Kristeva 1982: 71). Both form the pretext for pollution-countering ritual and myth. Rites focused on the former bound society against threats from outside; those focused on the latter protect society from dangers issuing from within. Material witnesses to the most archaic struggle of nascent subjects within the maternal matrix, these rites revisit that struggle, engage it and move subjects from the depths of chaos towards order.

Only when these rites prove ineffectual against threat is sacrifice practised. Kristeva traces a typology of catastrophe through paganism, Judaism and Christianity. Paganism wards off the impure through elaborate rituals focused on food. Still food remainders threaten. In their incompleteness they are 'residues of something but especially of someone' (Kristeva 1982: 76). Judaism inscribes impurity in an abstract moral register as potential for abomination. In repetition of the knife that cuts the umbilical cord, the knife that cuts the flesh of the foreskin 'displaces through ritual the preeminent separation, which is that from the mother' (Kristeva 1982: 100). All traces of the maternal matrix are lost to a new identity: circumcision bonds speaking beings through signs to God. Moving away from the material register, Judaism 'throttles murder': women are threats to be contained, not destroyed (Kristeva 1982: 111). Food, death and women are dangerous, not because they are occasions for impurity, but because they are occasions for idolatry. Judaism bounds itself from sacrifice when food and women are experienced not so much as polluting but as pre-texts for a Symbolic relation between Israel and God: they bespeak of order achieved in alliance of Israel's men with Yahweh.

Christianity interiorises Jewish abomination. Evil, displaced into the subject, torments not as polluting substance but as evil. Christianity swallows marks of the maternal matrix, but does not valorise or rehabilitate that matrix. Of the nourishing and threatening heterogeneity of the maternal, Christianity keeps only the idea of sinning flesh (Kristeva 1982: 117). In the Eucharist, Christianity mingles themes of devouring with those of satiating, 'taming cannibalism' (Kristeva 1982: 118). The body of Christ promises reconciliation. Absorbed in the Symbolic and no longer a being of abjection, the Christian is a lapsing subject.

Even so the account with the archaic maternal is not yet settled. Late medieval women mystics and their younger sisters, the victims of the sixteenth- and seventeenth-century witch hunts, attest to the price paid by women when a religious tradition interiorises terror as self-error. When confessors who oversee women's lives ask them to disgorge sin in words, a troubling new dynamic of abjection is introduced in Western culture (Kristeva 1982: 127–9). Because only a priestly authority can determine the truth of women's words, confession is fraught with risk. Some mystics, refusing all food but the Eucharist, are said to attain unity with Christ. But many die from starvation (Reineke 1997: 105–27). A century later, priests use torture and flames to extract from women's bodies their confessions' point of origin in the Absolute: do their words come from God *or* the Devil? Again, some women die, but the communities from which they come survive. *Pharmakon* and *pharmakos* are one (Reineke 1997: 128–60).

For Kristeva, religion has played a pivotal role among the institutions of the Symbolic that have negotiated thetic crises. Sometimes religious rites focused on abject violence and defilement have forestalled sacrifice. But religious myth and ritual also have identified women as threats to be vanquished by sacrifice. Will religion inevitably set itself up as the 'specialist' in sacrifice or can religion develop expertise in other areas? According to Kristeva, in religion can be glimpsed intimations of alternatives to sacrifice which sustain a hope that humans can come to terms with thetic crises without resorting to sacrifice.

IV An ethics of analysis – intimations of an alternative to sacrifice

Kristeva explores an ethics of analysis that, like Žižek's evocation of an ethics of difference, draws from death-work possibilities for non-sacrificial signifying practices. Where the phantasies of the Symbolic have promised to secure the subject against a lack of being, an ethic of analysis invites the subject to accept the truth of its being while offering the subject the distance it needs to acknowledge lack without fear. Likened to Žižek's 'breathing space', an ethic of analysis offers the subject room to elaborate the risks posed by death-work in order that the subject may frame these risks as promise rather than as threat. An ethic of analysis empowers the subject to articulate death-work so that there can be fewer deaths (Kristeva 1986b: 296; Oliver 1993: 147). This ethic advances as a wager: if the subject can work through and articulate that which has been barred and concealed in the course of its own formation and division, the subject need not sacrifice that which has been excluded in order to secure its own being. Instead it can enjoy an expansion of boundaries. Because this ethic challenges all property-claims made by a subject who would possess the fullness of being, it assists the subject in reconceiving the kind of space it needs to engage in death-work. Analysis prepares the subject to create meaning in the very taking up in discourse of lack as a difference to be accepted, not denied.

Religion, specialist in sacrifice, nevertheless offers intimations of an ethic of analysis which can constitute a critical intervention in sacrificial codes. The story of Ruth the Moabite elaborates just such an ethic at the heart of Judaism. At a time when Jews are forbidden to marry foreigners, Ruth settles in Judea, establishing a lineage that runs from Ruth's child, Obed, to David. God works through a stranger to effect God's relationship with humanity (Kristeva 1993: 24). Ruth's foreign difference preserves within Judaism a memory of 'breathing space': an otherness that is other in the same. In the stories of ancient Israel, the difference Ruth mirrors – exposing lack in those who would fully possess Jewish identity – is embraced as promise rather than as threat.

The Christian missionary Paul's notion of *ecclesia* and Augustine's concept of *caritas* similarly summon the possibilities of sacred difference. Forging from a heterogeneous group of merchants, sailors, exiles, sectarian Jews and women a community of those who reside in the margins – neither Greek nor Jew, slave nor free, male nor female – Paul establishes a therapeutics of exile that enables those who wander to sojourn with each other, retaining an otherness that is not made to mirror the same (Kristeva 1993: 22; 1991: 82). Augustinian *caritas* likewise celebrates a love of the other that enables Christian pilgrims to welcome foreigners in their very distinction without imposing on them any strictures of identity that confirm being for some while denying it to others (Kristeva 1991: 84). These examples suggest that when humans are able to live with difference rather than throttle it, they can create new cultural spaces that serve as safe havens, especially in times of crisis. When under circumstances of instability and change, difference appears as a threat to be vanquished, signifying practices shaped by *caritas* or *ecclesia* can invoke options for living with others that enable subjects to forestall sacrifice or put it out of play altogether.

Of course, for Christian triumphalism, that which is perceived to be alien to a Christian politics of identity is not embraced in its distinctive difference but is assimilated by force. There are penalties of ostracism or inquisition for those who remain 'other' and mirror Christians' own 'lack'. Christian practice does enter a sacrificial orbit. However, Kristeva's musings about Paul and Augustine suggest that if Christianity draws on elements in its tradition that do welcome difference as difference, it may generate anew emancipating practices similar to Pauline *ecclesia* and Augustinian *caritas*.

Kristeva's call for an ethic of analysis, suggestive of non-sacrificial approaches to identity-formation, -maintenance and -transformation, holds promise for feminism. Emerging from Kristeva's critical reflections on sacrifice and informed by her careful attention to trans-historical structures of existence that shape daily life, this call speaks directly to feminists who seek social change. Of course, feminists will want to avail themselves of many rich stores of theories and practices of liberation available to them. But this chapter has demonstrated that feminists should include Kristeva's psychoanalytic theory among their resources for promoting social change. Her thoughts about 'sexual difference' suggest a framework for construing women's lives in ways that depart from constraining stereotypes of gender, race, or class. Her analysis of sacrifice highlights the fragility of this quest, offering a cautionary alternative to analyses of violence that look only at precipitating socio-historical factors rather than at ways that the formative aspects of human experience establish pretexts for violence. Developed from this critical foundation, Kristeva's sketch of a new ethic of analysis also contributes to feminist theory. Feminist theorists with interests in religious traditions will especially want further to explore ways in which religion can promote signifying practices that offer 'breathing space' on which women can rely in their efforts to live free of violence.

Note

1   Additional examples of work informed by Kristeva that demonstrate this linkage may be found in critical analyses of racism by Reineke (1998), Noëlle McAfee (1993) and Patricia Elliot (1991). Raising suggestive questions for feminist political theory are Anna Smith's (1997) explorations of Kristeva's themes of exile and estrangement. Inspiring further feminist scholarship in this area is the burgeoning scholarship informed by Lacan that employs psychoanalytic theory to address questions of Eurocentrism and colonialism; for example, Teresa Brennan's *History after Lacan* (1993) and Stavrakakis's *Lacan and the Political* (1999).

Chapter 8

Grace M. Jantzen

'DEATH, THEN, HOW COULD I YIELD TO IT?'

Kristeva's Mortal Visions

FLASH – instant of time or of dream without time; inordinately swollen
atoms of a bond, a vision, a shiver, a yet formless, unnameable embryo.

(Kristeva 1987b: 234)

THUS BEGINS THE LEFT-HAND section of Kristeva's famous 'Stabat
Mater', a literary and psychoanalytic reflection on motherhood. It is an
epiphany, a manifestation of giving birth. Yet her essay is also a portrayal of
death, the death of Jesus, and of mourning with its complicated ties to motherhood. Much has been written about Kristeva's 'Stabat Mater' (Crownfield 1992;
Jantzen 1998a: Ch. 8); it is a rich text that repays long pondering. My present
purpose is not to expound it in detail, but rather to use it as a way of entering
into Kristeva's representation of religion through death, birth and gender.

'Stabat Mater' appears on the pages of its text sometimes as conventional
prose, but sometimes split into two columns, the left-hand column printed in
bold typeface. Whenever the text splits, the right-hand column continues the
prose presentation of the essay, which can in fact be read straight through like
any ordinary piece of prose without paying attention to the left-hand column. It
makes sense on its own, as a disquisition on motherhood and death in the representations of the Virgin Mary in Christendom. Yet the left-hand column is there,
in bold, insisting upon being noticed. And it is nothing like a standard academic
essay. It is not obviously sequential, at least not in terms of linear thought
patterns. It is staccato, full of exclamations and associations, disruptive of the
connected thought of the rest of the text. It jolts the reader out of the com-
placency of joined-up thinking and the conventional Symbolic that underlies it.

Kristeva wrote 'Stabat Mater' with direct reference to Pergolesi's musical
composition of that name, in which he represents Mary the mother of Jesus

standing with John the beloved disciple at the foot of the cross, watching Jesus die. It is this scene of motherhood and death upon which the connected prose, including the right-hand column, reflects. But the left-hand column destabilises this scene. It too presents motherhood. But here motherhood is a scene of childbirth. There is pain here too, and blood, and brokenness; there is word and flesh, indeed 'WORD FLESH. From one to the other, eternally, broken up visions, metaphors of the invisible' (Kristeva 1987b: 235). But it is represented not as theological or even psychoanalytical discourse but as pre-linguistic utterance, or − since that is not strictly possible in a written text − as just emerging into the linguistic, the flesh giving birth to word.

Kristeva's split text can be seen as the split subject itself, with the rationality and connected logic of one side containing and mastering the semiotic that always threatens to disrupt it from the other side. Yet that connected rationality is a portrayal of death and mourning, indeed of the death and mourning which is at the heart of Christendom and thus of the Western Symbolic. The split in the text can also be read as the split that constitutes the maternal body, the wound that is also a womb, from which come forth blood and birth, the disruptive possibilities of new life. It is the source of creativity, even while its other side is death. Moreover, I shall suggest that the split is also indicative of an ambiguity in Kristeva herself. On the one hand, I shall argue, she participates in and indeed promotes the deathly preoccupation of the Western masculinist Symbolic. Yet there is that in her work which disrupts it, which calls forth natality and creativity even if under the sign of a power of horror. Like religion itself, Kristeva's text both reinscribes death and opens the possibilities of life. I shall therefore press her work, partly against the grain of her own writing, to open up the gaps which beckon to natality for the love of God.

In 'Stabat Mater''s right-hand column, Kristeva presents death as the greatest and least consolable of all men's anguish. Man can deal with it only by seeing the maternal − his mother, his Mother Church, the maternal more generally − as protection: 'Man overcomes the unthinkable of death by postulating maternal love in its place − in the place and stead of death and thought' (Kristeva 1987b: 252). The maternal was the primal shelter of the newborn; Mother Church will shelter the storm-tossed soul. Hence in Western Christendom, the Church is the ark, the womb of salvation which preserves the faithful to eternal life.

The death that is most to the fore in 'Stabat Mater', the death of Jesus, has been formative of the entire constellation of the Western Symbolic which has Christendom at its centre. Death, violent death, has been lifted up as the most godly of all possibilities, simultaneously horrific and the precondition for immortality. In the Christian sacraments of Eucharist and baptism, death is ritually enacted and celebrated, in the broken body and blood of the god-man and immersion in the waters that signify death. The new life or new birth consequent upon ritual participation in the death of the god is a life born not of woman, not of flesh and blood, but of the spirit of God. It is a life of the spirit that leads to immortality, final release from the world of bodies and death. As Kristeva puts it in her meditation on Holbein's painting of the 'Dead Christ', in identification with that death 'man is nevertheless provided with a powerful symbolic device that allows him to experience death and resurrection even in his physical body' (Kristeva 1989: 134). It is such identification which has made possible within Christendom a variation on the Platonic theme that death is the gateway to immortality. This earthly life born of woman, this body which is subject to change and chance, is to be mortified (literally: put to death) so that even now the immortal life of the spirit may be begun. There are, of course, many qualifications and nuances to the broad claim that Christianity fixed death at the centre of the Western Symbolic, but they need not detain us here. My present point is the uncontroversial one that Western culture is saturated with death, of which the most crucial instance, historically and symbolically, is the death of Jesus.

Since the mortal body is the body born of woman, moreover, in the Western tradition death is symbolically linked with women, while true manliness is linked with mastery of death. Through Eve the mother of us all who introduced sin and death into the world, we find, as Kristeva puts it, that 'the unrepresentable nature of death was linked with that other unrepresentable – original abode but also last resting place for dead souls, in the beyond – which, for mystical thought, is constituted by the female body' (Kristeva 1989: 27). When in 'Stabat Mater' Mary stands at the foot of the cross watching her son die, she – 'alone of all her sex' – is linked with life rather than death precisely because of her virginity: 'The *Mater Dolorosa* knows no masculine body save that of her dead son' and can therefore stand as the negation of both womanhood and death (1987b: 250–1).

Kristeva's emphasis on death is part of her ongoing conversation with Freud and his appropriation by Lacan. Like them, she brings the significance of death right to the beginning of life. In *Powers of Horror* she asks, 'What was there in the beginning: want, deprivation, original fear, or the violence of rejection, aggressivity, the deadly death drive? Freud . . . discovered infantile, perverse, polymorphic sexuality, always already a carrier of desire and death' (Kristeva 1982: 38). Exactly how the concept of death functions, however, is, I think, sometimes obscure in psychoanalytic writings, shifting between meanings that can easily generate confusions. In a bid for greater clarity, and without meaning to imply that this is the only way it could be done, I shall draw some distinctions between what I shall call the death *drive*, death-*work* and dead *objects*.

I The death drive

In *Beyond the Pleasure Principle* (1984), Freud introduced the famous distinction between the life drives and the death drives, which he later labelled Eros and

Thanatos. As he here understood it, organisms are governed by something like a principle of entropy; they have an inherent 'urge . . . to restore an earlier state of things' (Freud 1984: 308) which stills all tension or excitation. Although the life-instincts press an individual to growth and progress, ultimately their function 'is to assure that the organism shall follow its own path to death, and to ward off any possible ways of returning to inorganic existence other than those which are immanent in the organism itself' (Freud 1984: 311). In Freud's account, death is not simply the terminator of life (thus contrasting with birth as its beginning), nor even the opposite of life, but rather is in some sense more fundamental than life. The inanimate underlies the animate, and 'the aim of all life is death' (Freud 1984: 311). Again, there is a connection with gender: the drive to return to a prior, tensionless state can be read as a longing for the womb from which one has been ejected. But the womb, once again, is a trope for the tomb: 'Dust thou art, and unto dust shalt thou return' (Genesis 3:19).

The characterisation of the life and death drives in terms of thermodynamic theories of quantum physics has not found universal favour even among psychoanalysts. However, the idea of death as fundamentally linked with separation and longing to return to the mother has been taken up much more thoroughly. Already in Freud, the young boy's separation from his mother is effected in the Oedipal stage through a fear of castration, dismemberment, which is perceived as an analogue of death: 'the fear of death [is] . . . a development of the fear of castration' (Freud 1984: 400). Because this feared event can only be averted by renunciation of the desire for the mother, it is repressed out of consciousness. The result, however, is a tendency to aggression and violence, especially violence by men against women. The aggression can be acted out in destructive, even sadistic, ways; or it can be turned inwards in masochism or melancholia (Freud 1984: 394–401).

In *Black Sun* Kristeva echoes this Freudian linkage of death, castration and women: 'the feminine as image of death' mirrors anxiety about castration and is acted out in a matricidal drive which, unless it is sublimated, 'would pulverise me into melancholia if it did not drive me to crime' (Kristeva 1989: 28). One route of sublimation is to make woman the ideal: this is the route Kristeva explores in 'Stabat Mater'. Rather than the bearer of death, Mary is seen as the one whom death cannot touch, the icon of maternal love which is stronger than death. In this way, Mary has been portrayed through the centuries of Christendom: the ideal woman, *fons amoris*, the one whose dormition is an 'avoidance of death'. 'She undergoes no calvary, she has no tomb, she doesn't die and hence has no need to rise from the dead' (Kristeva 1987b: 242).

This sublimation, however, is of course highly problematic. In the first place, it requires virginity: as already noted, death and sex are linked together, and if the former is to be avoided, so also must be the latter. But since it is precisely *maternal* love which is deathless, this requires the improbable Symbolic of the

Virgin Mother, both as a doctrine of Christendom and as an impossible ideal for actual women. Moreover, as Kristeva notes in *Black Sun*, the linkage thus far discussed takes its origin in Freud's account of the boy's Oedipal conflict: for the girl the required sublimation – if such it can be called – is altogether trickier (Kristeva 1989: 28–9). It is no accident that in 'Stabat Mater' the discourse of the Virgin Mother takes up the right-hand column of the split text, which in some respects can be read as the masculine rendition of motherhood, as contrasted with the left-hand column in which women's experience of motherhood bursts into the masculinist Symbolic and destabilises it. I shall return to this after I have discussed death-*work* and dead *objects*.

II Death-work

If Kristeva both accepts and destabilises the Freudian account of the death drive, the same can be said for her treatment of death-work. As I am here using the term, 'death-work' is the psychic work that is needed in order to deal with the destructive and aggressive energies and impulses of the death drive. It is the work I must do to prevent my death drive from killing somebody else, or, if turned inwards, killing myself: murder or suicide. Freud, moreover, represents this death-work as social as well as individual. Both *Totem and Taboo* (1985a) and *Civilization and its Discontents* (1962) are accounts of how morality, religion and society are built upon the sublimation of the death drive.

To understand more fully what is involved in death-work, it is helpful to recall Lacan's account of the mirror stage. An infant, not yet able to co-ordinate its limbs or to control its bodily functions, experiences itself, according to Lacan, not as a unified subject but as a 'body-in-bits-and-pieces' (Grosz 1990: 34). When such an infant sees itself in a mirror (actual or metaphorical) as a whole body, the result is a 'jubilant assumption of his specular image by the child' (Lacan 1977: 2). Even though its experience does not coincide with this wholeness, the child identifies with the 'Ideal I' and represses its awareness of its actual feelings and desires. Moreover, it sees itself in the mirror as separate from its mother, not a part of her, a separation that becomes deeper as the child enters what Freud had called the Oedipal stage and Lacan renames the Law/Name of the Father. It is through repression of itself and its desire for its mother that a child becomes a subject, entering into language and society: the self is thus constituted upon loss. As Ellie Ragland-Sullivan puts it, 'Loss is at the heart of language, being, representations, desire and body, and thus the death drive – jouissance effects that coalesce around loss – is central to life' (Ragland-Sullivan 1992: 58). Such loss is bound to generate rage: we are back with the aggression, outwardly or inwardly directed, which I have already discussed.

But now we have arrived at an impasse. On the one hand, the subject longs to return to the undifferentiated union with its (idealised) mother; yet on the other hand this is what it most fears, since such unity would be the end of itself in its own right. As Amy Hollywood says, 'once the subject has situated him- or herself in language, any attempt to undo this violent severing of early ties itself becomes an act of violence against the subject – a suicide, following in the path of the Freudian death drive' (Hollywood 1993: 8). The subject is therefore constituted by a split that can never be undone, the very split which Kristeva portrays as the split text of 'Stabat Mater'. And each side of the split is associated with death. The longing for undifferentiated union or stasis replicates Freud's original formulation of the death drive; but the fear of absorption generates the violence of separation and consequent mourning and/or aggression. Is there any way through this 'double bind' (Oliver 1993)?

One of Kristeva's profound contributions is her idea of the abject, a term which encompasses both the ambivalence of separation and the strength of feeling associated with it. The abject is that which demarcates the boundaries of the body. It is that which is ambiguously part of me and that against which I revolt: vomit, shit, menstrual blood and, most horrific, the corpse.

> There, I am at the border of my condition as a living being. My body extricates itself, as being alive, from that border. Such wastes drop from me so that I might live, until, from loss to loss, nothing remains in me and my entire body falls beyond the limit . . . the corpse, the most sickening of wastes, is a border that has encroached upon everything.
>
> (Kristeva 1982: 3)

This abjection is intertwined with death-work, both in its separation and in its attendant mourning.

Not only the individual but also society constitutes itself upon the abject, which it expels in order to demarcate its boundaries. Kristeva uses the work of Mary Douglas on *Purity and Danger* (1966) to show how the expulsion of what is regarded as polluting enables society, like an individual, to assume a 'clean and proper body' (Kristeva 1982: 65–72). Like an individual, a society repeats this process of separation especially when it feels its identity under threat: witness the 'ethnic cleansing' which has constituted 'others' as 'abjects', from Nazi Germany to the Balkans and Rwanda. Kristeva agrees with René Girard about the ways in which a society constructs scapegoats to carry its own abjection, and accomplishes its death-work through the 'sacrifice' – or murder – of this scapegoat (Kristeva 1982: Chs 4 and 5; Girard 1977, 1987): Martha Reineke has developed this theory to show how and why this is so often enacted upon the bodies of women (Reineke 1992, 1997). But if the death-work can be sublimated, through art or religion, if the sacrifice can be a symbolic ritual rather than continued violence and murder, only then is there hope for civilisation. Thus Kristeva follows Freud and Girard in characterising the Eucharist – the ritual consuming of the body and blood of the slaughtered man-god – as paradigmatic of the way in which the centuries of Christendom dealt with death-work. Yet even this was not enough: much violence continued to be visited upon the bodies of women, especially, as Reineke describes, on women who were mystics or 'witches' (Reineke 1997). The scapegoat, whether witch, racial 'other', or the dead god-man, bears our abjection and thus accomplishes our death-work.

Again we are back with the 'Stabat Mater' at the foot of the cross:

> Christianity has, through facilitating an imaginary identification with the death of Christ, provided a way for bringing death into the symbolic; or at least it has provided a way for enlarging the imaginary and symbolic means available for coping with death.
>
> (Lechte 1990: 188)

So long as one can keep faith, can stand with Mary mourning her dead son-god, and introject his death and his resurrection, one has a 'shield against death'. 'Man overcomes the unthinkable of death by postulating maternal love in its place – in the place and stead of death and thought' (Kristeva 1987b: 253, 252). But if we are back with the 'Stabat Mater', we are also back with its impossibilities: how are we any longer to accept a religion of a Virgin Mother or a dying god whom we ritually consume? And if we are irretrievably post-Christian, how shall we, as individuals or society, do the death-work which does not go away with the demise of Christendom?

III Dead objects and slimy abjects

The death drive and the death-work, as presented in the writings of Freud, Lacan, or Kristeva, are presented in naturalising terms; that is, they are presented as rooted in human nature. In Freud's writing, as we have seen, the death drive is treated in thermodynamic terms of the variations of energy in a biological system. This would, therefore, be applicable to all human beings, in any culture. Lacan and Kristeva are much less oriented to sheer biology and more to culture and language; yet in their writings too, the death-work, resulting as it does from separation from the mother, must be a universal human necessity, even though it could be handled differently in different cultures. The centuries of Christendom, for example, had recourse to ritual enactment of sacrifice in a way that post-Christian society does not. Nevertheless, Kristeva holds that 'matricide is our vital necessity, the *sine qua non* condition of our individuation' (1989: 27–8): the death-work is inescapable.

But is it? Even to ask that question appears psychoanalytically naïve, as though I have not grasped even the first principles. Am I suggesting that we do not have to separate from our mothers, or that we do not have to deal with the loss that entails, and the losses and separations that punctuate our lives? Am I suggesting that we can ignore the abject — that we never vomit or shit, bleed or die?

No, of course not. But what I do want to insist upon is that *not all separations are deaths; and not all deaths are murders.* We must indeed all separate from our mothers and our mother-substitutes; but the individuation that takes place need not be the death of the relationship but may be its transformation into a different phase. There is loss, but there is also gain. We do not die in this individuation; and we do not kill our mothers. To characterise individuation as death and matricide is, I suggest, already to accept and to reinscribe the fixation with death and gendered violence which saturates the Western Symbolic. Now, this insistence could appear as nothing more than a quibble about words, or, much worse, as a consolatory evasion of the necessary death-work. To show that it is neither of these, and as a basis for clarifying what I mean by 'dead objects', I return to Kristeva's representation of the abject.

Both for Kristeva and for Mary Douglas upon whom she draws in her account, the abject is paradigmatically fluid: pus, menstrual blood, vomit, the decomposing corpse. Their disgusting and horrifying nature resides partly in their borderline state between solid and liquid. Kristeva and Douglas agree, for example, that tears are not disgusting; they are clear fluid, like water, which purifies rather than pollutes (though this is not as simple as it seems, as we shall see). Douglas explicitly and Kristeva implicitly rely here on Jean-Paul Sartre's discussion of the horror of stickiness, sliminess, the viscous and its 'ambiguous character as a "substance between two states"' (Sartre 1953: 774; cf. Douglas 1966: 38). For Sartre, the viscous is disgusting because, when he touches it, it sticks to him, does not let him go. He writes:

> If I dive into the water, if I plunge into it, if I let myself sink in it, I experience no discomfort, for I do not have any fear whatsoever that I may dissolve in it; I remain a solid in its liquidity. If I sink in the slimy, I feel that I am going to be lost in it; that is, that I may dissolve in the slime precisely because the slimy is in process of solidification . . . without equilibrium, like the haunting memory of a *metamorphosis.*
>
> (Sartre 1953: 777)

Sartre associates this fear of absorption or dissolution precisely with 'the invisible suction of the past' (Sartre 1953: 778) which would refuse to let go of the emerging individual, but would stick to it, cling to it so that it could not be itself. Motherhood is slime. So also is female sexuality: Sartre continues, 'Beyond any doubt her sex is a mouth and a voracious one which devours the penis . . .' (Sartre 1953: 782). It is the old male horror of the *vagina dentata* (cf. Grosz 1994: 194).

But if the mother is the one from whom we must separate, then surely it is right to see her as dangerous? Is it not sheer denial to pretend otherwise? But to these questions, counter-questions must be posed. Why should I assume that the one from whom I must separate is dangerous to me? Would this not be the case only if I were somehow prevented from bringing about that separation? Surely we are all familiar with separations which occur, even separations involving pain and loss, which do not include either physical or psychic violence, but rather change of relationship. Consider, for instance, the end of postgraduate supervision when the candidate completes the course; or good termination of psychotherapy; or even the death of a much-loved person for whom the final months have had a very poor quality of life. We feel the loss; we grieve; but in the former cases the relationship may continue in a changed form that allows for new creativity, and even in the latter, there need have been no violence, given or received. To repeat, not all separations, not even all endings, are deaths; and not all deaths are murders. From the fact that some separations are violent, physically or psychically, because one party refuses or both parties refuse to let go, it does not follow that all losses must be seen in the same deathly terms. To assimilate them all into these violent categories makes it impossible to discriminate between healthy, well-handled separations and pathological ones.

Already the question begins to emerge whether the characterisation of the abject, and with it the death-work as Kristeva presents it, owes rather too much to an unexamined masculinist Symbolic: it is a question which will become more persistent as we go on. Kristeva distinguishes between polluting and non-polluting fluid: 'Polluting objects fall, schematically, into two types: excremental and menstrual. Neither tears nor sperm . . . although they belong to the borders of the body, have any polluting value' (Kristeva 1982: 71). But why on earth not? Tears are perhaps less difficult to understand, on analogy with water, though this still leaves many questions (for instance, about urine, which Kristeva does not discuss; and also the gendered and dangerous nature of water in the cultural Symbolic – recall Homer's barren sea; or the waters of Christian baptism which effect the death of the 'natural man'). But what is going on when semen is linked with (purifying) tears, while menstrual blood is linked with shit (cf. Grosz 1994: 206–7)?

Kristeva explains the two forms of pollution as follows:

> Excrement and its equivalents (decay, infection, disease, corpse, etc.) stand for the danger to identity that comes from without: the ego is

threatened by the non-ego, society is threatened by its outside; life by death. Menstrual blood, on the contrary, stands for the danger issuing from within the identity (social or sexual); it threatens the relationship between the sexes within a social aggregate and, through internalisation, the identity of each sex in the face of sexual difference.

(Kristeva 1982: 71)

But why is it that seminal fluid does not pose a similar threat? What emerges is that the reason menstrual blood could be threatening when semen is not is that the female – sexual and maternal – is *already* perceived as threatening and the male is not. It is thus not menstrual blood that renders the female abject; it is her abjection that renders menstrual blood horrifying. It is only in a symbolic structure in which the mother is already seen as polluting (and the male is not) that menstrual blood, but not semen, is dangerous. Therefore Kristeva's representation of the mother as the source of danger, and her insistence on the need for matricide, is in fact a reinscription and naturalisation of a gendered Symbolic which has long been part of the misogynist tradition of the West. And such a structure does indeed lend itself all too easily to matricide, not only in psycholinguistic hyperbole but in actual violence against women.

What is at stake here can be fruitfully reconsidered by asking about the *contrast* to the abject. If excrement and menstrual blood are paradigmatically abject, is there anything we could identify as paradigmatically *not* abject? We can begin with negatives. That which is not abject, on Kristeva's terms, will not be fluid. It will have definite boundaries, and will clearly be inside or outside other things. It will not be sticky or slimy or shape-shifting, but firm to the touch, capable of being grasped, handled, known, mastered. It will, in short, be paradigmatically the medium-sized inanimate object much beloved by post-enlightenment science and philosophy. In the words of Iris Marion Young:

The object is determinate and definable, with clear boundaries, separated from other objects. It is what it is, does not change its nature from one context to another. The object is passive, inert matter, having no self-mastering capacity, its movement all externally and mechanically caused. The object is what can be handled, manipulated, constructed, built up and broken down, with clear accountability of matter gained and lost.

(Young 1990: 191)

Young is writing in a different context; but it would be hard to find a clearer conceptualisation of what the abject is not. But if it is the case that in Western modernity the abject is the object's other, then perhaps it is time to reconsider the revulsion against the abject with reference to these contrasting characteristics.

Writers such as Mary Douglas and Kristeva universalise the abject, at least to the extent of saying that all cultures define themselves by contrast with what is deemed polluting; and Kristeva, like René Girard, looks to the Hebrew Bible for examples. But it is immediately clear that many of the purity laws and abominations of the biblical text are simply puzzling to us today: at least to that extent the abject does have a history. And even the assertion that all societies construct themselves against taboos should perhaps be treated with the same sort of caution with which we are learning to treat the claim that all societies have a religion: through the work of scholars like Asad (1993), King (1999) and Jensen (1997) it is becoming apparent that 'religion' is a Western construct imposed on other cultures which are then 'understood' in terms of it. Might 'taboo' operate similarly?

Be that as it may, the point here is that if the abject has a genealogy, then that genealogy is related to a genealogy of its other, the object, just as Foucault demonstrated the changing correlation of what counts as madness and rationality. From this perspective, we can see that it is no accident that the construction of the abject as slimy and fluid, paradigmatically menstrual blood, emerges at the same time as the determinable, definable, countable inert object (Shapin 1996; Poovey 1998). And it is a commonplace of feminist scholarship that the paradigmatic status accorded to medium-sized dry goods in the philosophy and science of modernity is deeply masculinist (Code 1991, 1995; Harding 1986; Bordo 1994). These are precisely the objects that can be known, manipulated, mastered, bought and sold, subjected to the gaze and commodified. And they are thought of in the same terms as men like Descartes or Locke wished to think of their own bodies: bounded, definable, hard and ultimately mechanical, mastered by the rational mind – quite different, in short, from the leaky, penetrable bodies of women.

Moreover in this Symbolic it becomes suddenly apparent why semen is not deemed polluting, since semen is the indicator of potency and it is precisely by their (literal and symbolic) potency that men assert their mastery over women and the rest of the material world. Defecation, on the other hand, becomes very private, even for men – so private that in public we act as though none of us does it. Note the contrast with sex, which male discourse often treats as a matter for boasting. And the uncontrollable seepage of menstrual blood is deemed utterly unclean and must of all things be kept secret. The violence with which the abject is associated is, as Kristeva says, surely related to the investment in a 'clean and proper body', constituted as other than these fluids, which nevertheless is constantly betrayed by their insistent demands. Even the most masterful of men has bowels, no matter how much he may pretend otherwise in his public persona. But if (as Kristeva does not say) the object were defined differently, or, better, if we could develop a different Symbolic of the object, would it be necessary to identify the abject with women? Would it call forth such strong revulsion and violence?

IV Fluidity and natality

As contrasted with solid objects, fluidity receives very bad press in Kristeva's writings, especially murky or slimy fluid. In this context it is significant to reread Luce Irigaray's work, especially her essay 'The "Mechanics" of Fluids' (in 1985b: 106–18). Irigaray, as is well known, celebrates the fluid, reconsiders it, recognises it as precisely that which is neither outside nor inside but flows between and through and around, thus overcoming the rigid binaries implicit in Kristeva's representation. Where Kristeva represents the fluid as abject, Irigaray delights in it. How could we make love if there were no lubrication? How, for that matter, could anything in the world work without fluid? Why should the fluid be abject? Who says so, and at whose expense? Irigaray writes of 'jamming the works of the theoretical machine' (Irigaray 1985b: 107), which grinds and bumps like a car without oil. Yet the theoretical works of modernity insist, she says, on 'a mechanics of solids alone', an insistence in which language, philosophy and even psychoanalysis have been heavily complicit:

> The object of desire itself, and for psychoanalysts, would be the trans-formation of fluid to solid? Which seals – this is well worth repeating – the triumph of rationality. Solid mechanics and rationality have maintained a relationship of very long standing, one against which fluids have never stopped arguing.
>
> (Irigaray 1985b: 113; emphases in original)

Irigaray calls this whole Symbolic of objects into question, in general terms, but also in terms of its representations of gender and even of God, whose spirit, she points out, is much more like fluid than like solid:

> It is surely a question of the dissociation of body and soul, of sexuality and spirituality, of the lack of passage for the spirit, for the god, between the inside and the outside, the outside and the inside, and of their distribution between the sexes in the sexual act. Everything is constructed in such a way that these realities remain separate, even opposed to one another. So that they neither mix, marry, nor form an alliance.
>
> (Irigaray 1993a: 15)

A thorough study of Irigaray's representations of fluidity has still to be done, and would, I think, be a major contribution to understanding continental philosophy of religion, particularly if it took into account the contrast with Kristeva's representation of the abject. However, I will leave that for another occasion, since what I want to do instead, in conclusion, is to return to 'Stabat Mater' and see how Kristeva's account of death and the abject is destabilised within her own writing, even whilst also being reinscribed by it.

As the left-hand column erupts into the text, it becomes evident that it is the representation of a birth, in all its inexpressible jouissance of glory and pain. It may feel like death; and in some respects it resembles death in its paroxysms and spasms which finally come to an end. Yet it is utterly different: it brings new life into the world. In this eruption, however, it refuses to fit into the categories against which death and the abject have been presented in Kristeva's work. First of all, there is the embryo that grows into a foetus in the mother's body: 'inordinately swollen atoms of a bond, a vision, a shiver, a formless, unnameable embryo' (Kristeva 1987b: 234). Is this developing life part of the woman's body or not? Inside or outside? First inside and then outside? Clarity of boundaries is not possible: long before the birth, though the foetus is indisputably inside the womb and in some ways part of the woman's very self, it is also taking on a life, an identity of its own. Not only are the boundaries unclear; they are volatile. They do not keep still. They behave like the abject in Kristeva's terms; yet in 'Stabat Mater', though there is discomfort and even severe pain, there is no sense of revulsion.

And what of the birth? It is, in one sense, certainly an expulsion; one which is simultaneously excruciating and unstoppable.

> Dark twisting, pain in the back, the arms, the thighs – pincers turned into fibres, infernos bursting veins, stones breaking bones; grinders of volumes, expanses, spaces, lines, points. All those words, now, ever visible things to register the roar of a silence that hurts all over.
>
> (Kristeva 1987b: 242)

Yet in spite of the pain of this expulsion, what sense would it make to think of the newborn infant as abject? Though it has been expelled from the woman's body with vastly more pain and insistence than excrement, the infant is not shit. It is infinitely precious. For a woman (and her baby) whose abiding feeling towards it is revulsion, something has gone badly wrong. It can happen, but when it happens help is needed; it should not be inscribed as normality.

Moreover, in birth itself there is plenty of fluid, sticky, slimy fluid, water, blood, shit, mucus. And as for the baby, towels, tissues and nappies are always needed in abundance. But when Kristeva writes of her newborn, the fluids, far from abject, take on the sounds of poetry:

> Head reclining, nape finally relaxed, skin, blood, nerves warmed up, luminous flow: stream of hair made of ebony, of nectar, smooth darkness through her fingers, gleaming honey under the wings of bees, sparkling strands burning bright . . .
>
> (Kristeva 1987b: 240)

In the terms in which Kristeva had earlier written of abjection, one would expect childbirth to be a paradigm case; yet in her own representation of it, it emphatically is not.

Moreover it seems to subvert a good deal of what she says about death. There is, to be sure, loss and grief at the separation, first in the birth itself and later as her son gradually takes on his own individual identity. It is, as Kristeva represents it, an abyss in which 'no identity holds up' for the woman as she lets her son become 'irreparably alien' (Kristeva 1987b: 255). And yet, though this is like a sword piercing her own heart, there is on the other hand still a very deep connection, beneath the level of speech. 'What connection is there between it and myself? No connection, except for that overflowing laughter where one senses the collapse of some ringing, subtle, fluid identity or other, softly buoyed by the waves' (Kristeva 1987b: 256). There is separation; but the separation is not death but the giving and receiving of new life, for both mother and child. It is nurture, not murder: to conflate the two by calling it 'matricide' will help neither mother nor child. It is necessary, indeed, for the mother to bear the pain of the changing relationship; but it is not violent. Even as her son grows and becomes 'that other who winds his way while I remain henceforth like a framework' he is still there, himself, 'his own flesh, which was mine yesterday. Death, then, how could I yield to it?' (Kristeva 1987b: 243).

Let me be clear that my intent in this is not to romanticise motherhood, let alone to collapse women into the maternal function, though arguably Kristeva herself sometimes does both. My point, rather, is that her own text renders the psychoanalytic account of death and the abject unstable and problematic. By attending to birth, by taking it as seriously as modernity has taken death, a new imaginary is suggested, a gap between the dying Christ whose image is the symbol of the West, and the emerging natal, full of new life and potential. Perhaps Kristeva is right: 'the love of God and for God resides in a gap' (Kristeva 1987b: 261).

Chapter 9

Dawne McCance

KRISTEVA'S MELANCHOLIA
Not Knowing How to Lose

CITING JULIA KRISTEVA'S remark in *Black Sun: Depression and Melancholia* (1989: 5–6), 'that there is meaning only in despair', Juliana Schiesari opens her study of *The Gendering of Melancholia* by describing the contemporary critical moment, or mode, as 'given over to a rhetoric of loss' (Schiesari 1992: 1). Like the Renaissance, ours is a great era of melancholia, Schiesari contends, for '*post*-structuralist, *post*modern, *post*-Marxist, *post*-Freudian, even "*post*feminist" theorists are both scholars of melancholia and critics positioning themselves as various kinds of melancholics' (Schiesari 1992: 2). What accounts for what Schiesari calls this 'wide-ranging work of mourning' (Schiesari 1992: 2)? Is it the case that postmodern melancholia, as Julian Roberts suggests, has a Christian-theological base, that it amounts to 'skeptical despair' over the fact that 'the connections between this world and the divine world of salvation' have been cut, and seem to be forever lost (Roberts 1995: 137)? 'Theologically, melancholy is the response to the *deus absconditus*: Christ is dead, a figure in an historical past, but no longer a presence now. Equally, the whole process of reason and signification is cut adrift', Roberts writes. Thus, 'in Dürer's celebrated etching (the "Melancholia I" of 1514), the instruments of higher mathematical learning lie useless along with all the other tools of mere human enterprise. Certainly they no longer provide us with a bridge to heaven' (Roberts 1995: 138).

Considering, for example, the first few pages of *Black Sun*, one might be tempted to read Kristeva into an account of melancholia as post-religious depressive despair. In these pages, as if to dramatise her opening sentence, that '[f]or those who are wracked by melancholia, writing about it would have meaning only if writing sprang out of that very melancholia' (Kristeva 1989: 3), Kristeva's first-person prose is languid and dispirited. 'I am trying to address an abyss of sorrow', she writes, 'a noncommunicable grief' or 'depression' (Kristeva 1989: 3); a 'despondency' or 'pain', the sense that '[a]n infinite number of misfortunes weigh us down every day', that life is 'devitalised', 'meaningless', 'unlivable, heavy with daily sorrows', and that I am 'ready at any moment for a plunge into death' (Kristeva 1989: 4). Here, to illustrate Schiesari's point, is the postmodern theorist of melancholia positioning herself as a melancholic; and here, along the lines of Roberts's thesis, is melancholia as post-religious nostalgia for a lost metaphysics:

> My depression points to my not knowing how to lose – I have perhaps been unable to find a valid compensation for the loss? It follows that any loss entails the loss of my being – and of Being itself. The depressed person is a radical and sullen atheist.
>
> (Kristeva 1989: 5)

Not knowing how to lose, Kristeva's melancholic, with all the languor and listlessness she puts into these pages, could be read as supporting a chronological definition of the *post* as, to use Schiesari's words, 'the self-critical tedium that comes *after* the euphoria of modernism' (Schiesari 1992: 3). Something akin to Christian *acedia*, Kristeva's postmodernism might then become a label for contemporary world-weariness: postmodernism as, at best, an apathy, a want of interest in issues of ethics and politics; and at worst, as *asymbolia*, complete bankruptcy, where such issues are concerned. So read, Kristeva's melancholia would complement traditional humoral pathology; and her postmodernism, diagnosed as depressive disease, a contemporary case of too much black bile, would call, individually and culturally, for cure.

In what follows, in keeping with her own definition of postmodernism, not as a chronological sequel but as the kind of signification that *spatialises* time, '*expand[s] the limits of the signifiable*' (Kristeva 1980c: 137), I read Kristeva's melancholia through her theory and practice of this 'borderline writing' (Kristeva 1980c: 139). Such writing is melancholic, I suggest, because it opens to an 'outside-of-language' (Kristeva 1989: 66), a remainder that, after Hegel, cannot be incorporated, reabsorbed or relieved. Without the relief (*relève*) of an *Aufhebung*, borderline signification revisits, rewrites, again and again, the West's religious idealisations, particularly Christianity's Virgin Mother, 'one of the most powerful imaginary constructs known in the history of civilisations' (Kristeva 1987b: 237). But no transcendence results, no theology or metaphysics.

Failure to incorporate is precisely what Freud calls melancholia, a failure of the 'devouring' that identification requires. Borrowing some of its features from 'normal mourning', melancholia is a reaction to 'object loss', to the death of a loved person, perhaps; but with melancholia, Freud says in his essay 'Mourning and Melancholia', the loss tends to be more abstract or 'ideal'. It is significant that the loss is of an ideal kind, that there has not been an actual death, that 'one cannot see clearly what it is that has been lost' (Freud 1991: 254), for it means that one cannot name the lost object of melancholia, the lost object that the ego, in normal mourning, would incorporate and so rid itself of. Unable to swallow the object (by naming it), the melancholic refuses to swallow food; he or she finds in the signifier no substitute for what is lacking and, as a consequence, cannot close over the gap that the loss opens in him- or herself, the gap that 'behaves like an open wound' in 'emptying the ego until it is totally impoverished' (Freud 1991: 262).

In *Black Sun*, approaching melancholia 'from a *Freudian point of view*', as an 'intolerance for object loss' and as a consequent breakdown in 'the mechanism of *identification*' (Kristeva 1989: 10, 11), Kristeva focuses on the way in which the signifier, for the melancholic, is a failed substitute. Reading Freud through Lacan, she attributes the breakdown in identification to a disturbance in the *process of signification* through which subject identity is produced. For the melancholic, Kristeva says, the lost object is, like a Heideggerian 'Thing', unrepresentable; it cannot be ingested because it 'does not lend itself to signification' (Kristeva 1989: 13). The lost object will not be named, but is none the less encrypted *as remains*, 'walled up within the *crypt* of the inexpressible affect' that melancholia is (Kristeva 1989: 13). The Kristevan melancholic, then, has not successfully navigated the mirror stage.

In his early work, Jacques Lacan treats the mirror stage as a developmental moment through which every would-be subject must pass. At this moment, at some time between the ages of 6 and 18 months, the toddler-child, Lacan's *l'hommelette*, identifies its self with the 'ideal unity' and 'unruffled surface' of its specular body image (Lacan 1977: 15, 19). Through this perception of the image, 'the child discovers a form (*Gestalt*), a corporeal unity' (Wilden 1968: 160), that is lacking to a toddler at this early age but that is crucial to the formation of its (fictional) present and future identity as a bounded ego, a unified and separable self. Significantly, the mirror stage misrecognition coincides with the learning of language, so that just at the moment of captation of the image, the fledgling subject posits the imaginary ego as a separate and signifiable object. As Kristeva notes in *Revolution in Poetic Language*, this positing 'constitutes a *break*', on the basis of which signification becomes established as subject/object, self/other, 'digital system', a system in which the projection of an imaginary unity entails, necessarily, a signifier/signified rupture (Kristeva 1984c: 47).

Another break is involved in the mirror stage, that between the 'semiotic *chora*' and the 'Symbolic' or signifying order that Lacan calls the locus or Law of the Father. Taken from Plato's *Timaeus*, Kristeva's term *chora* designates a state or space, a 'receptacle', which precedes the mirror stage, identity and naming. Extending back into uterine development, this pre-linguistic space is nourishing and maternal: in *Revolution in Poetic Language*, Kristeva describes the *chora* as rhythmic and as organised by instinctual drives, charges and stases, that are ordered through the mother's body. While the semiotic drives are quasi-signifying, simultaneously assimilating and fragmenting, the *chora* 'can never be definitely posited', Kristeva says; 'one can never give it axiomatic form' (Kristeva 1984c: 26). The *chora* precedes the sign, thus 'is not yet a position that represents something for someone' (that is, it is not a sign); 'nor is it a *position* that represents someone for another position' (that is, it is not yet a signifier either) (Kristeva 1984c: 26). At the mirror stage, when the child does actually posit a signifier, the *chora* is checked and constrained: 'the subject, finding his identity in the symbolic, *separates* from his fusion with the mother, *confines* his jouissance to the genital, and transfers semiotic motility onto the symbolic order' (1984c: 47).

Even as Kristeva, following Lacan, offers this account of the mirror stage as a developmental moment, instant of thetic rupture, threshold of the subject's passage from the semiotic *chora* into the symbolic, binary order of signification, she concedes that her account is in large part myth. For all that Kristeva says about the *chora* belongs to the order of representation within which, by her own definition, this pre-verbal space which 'has no thesis and no position' (1984c: 26), cannot be delimited or defined. This is the psychoanalytic theorist's double bind. Lacan recognised it increasingly throughout his career, and as he did, the mirror stage became less a narrative of child development than a way of talking about 'the logical level of the *chaîne signifiante*' (Wilden 1968: 162), the structure of the signifying process itself. From the start, Kristeva has these same two ways of talking about the mirror stage and its anterior semiotic *chora*, whereby what is at issue is not so much a moment as a *modality* of signifiance. Take the term 'semiotic' as example. From the Greek *semeion*, 'distinctive mark, trace', the semiotic, in Kristeva's second sense of the word, refers to a dimension that is anterior-exterior to the sign and syntax and that can be 'known' only through the trace or imprint of an affect, an *after-affect* (Kristeva 1984c: 25). The mirror stage, in Kristeva's second sense, refers to 'the "spatial intuition" which is found at the heart of the functioning of signification' (Kristeva 1984c: 46). As she puts it in a discussion of Bakhtin, language is not just 'an objectal surface on which pre-existing elements are combined, a structure in which the transcendental sense is mirrored and maintained by the transcendental consciousness of ever-present language-users' (Kristeva 1973: 105). With each positing of a signifier, each drive-investment in an image, the space of synchrony emerges, so that the subject and the sign become both one and an other, both position (ego, thesis) and what is heterogeneous to it. Despite the subject's drive, with each signification, to coincide with the image-ideal, there is something lacking in the signifier, lost to the subject, something that none the less leaves its mark or trace as *mood*.

Melancholia, for Kristeva, is a destabilising psychic imprint of this kind, 'imprint of separation and beginning of the symbol's sway' (Kristeva 1989: 22). In one sense, melancholia is the mark of some anterior, archaic state or space, a prehistoric *chora* if you will, long-since lost, impossible to reclaim. In another sense, melancholia is the inscription of the unrepresentable dimension of signification, an excess lost to, forgotten by, every signifier, something that, over and over again, with each signification, each repetition of the mirror stage drama, is 'inscribed within us without memory' (Kristeva 1989: 14). Melancholia inhabits a text as an uncanny, unsettling 'fringe of strangeness', the cause of which, the lost object, 'eludes representation and naming' (Kristeva 1989: 14).

How do we deal with this strangeness, this melancholic memory-trace? The work of 'normal mourning' requires identification and incorporation for cure. What makes possible a triumph over the mood of sadness, Kristeva says, is, in the first place, a *specular identification*: 'the ability of the self to identify no longer with the lost object but with a third party – father, form, schema', as happens at each 'mirror stage', when the subject assumes its place in the Symbolic and thereby refinds, recovers, the lost object in the image or ideal (Kristeva 1989: 23). What also makes triumph over sadness possible is *incorporation* of the lost object, as happens when the unnameable is given the name of the mother. In this naming of the unnameable, one deals with hatred and fear (*castration* fear, fear of losing the lost object, becomes fear of losing one's self) by putting the mother to death, abjecting the maternal body, a process Kristeva analyses at length in *Powers of Horror* (1982). Over and over again, with each signification, each loss, matricide, this culture's way of naming the unnameable, brings 'normal mourning' to a close. For the melancholic, however, who knows not how to lose, such closure cannot be had; no representation can represent what is lost to it and what inscribes in every representation a non-representational trace ('spacing of representation that is not the *sign*' [1989: 27]).

The trace is not the mother, once fully present to the individual and the culture, then swept away by patriarchal history and its heterosexual Oedipal structure. The trace is 'not the remains of something that was once present and might be rendered present once again; rather it is that which prevents any present, and any experience of presence, from being completely itself, from ever coinciding with itself' (Royle 1995: 61). Kristeva's postmodernism is not a project in linear time, not an essentialist effort to recover, as *alter ego*, an archaic, mythical mother. Indeed, 'unless one challenges precisely this myth of the archaic mother', she says in 'Women's Time', no mitigation of violence will be achieved for women-subjects in language (Kristeva 1981: 29). Kristeva's work, more synchronic than diachronic, explores the process of constituting subjects in language; shows the process to be 'sacrificial' (Kristeva 1981: 25); and expands the limits of the process – the limits of language and thus the limits of the subject – by opening to the affect of an unrepresentable. 'Never before in the history of humanity has this exploration of the limits of meaning taken place in such an unprotected manner, and by this I mean without religious, mystical, or any other justification', Kristeva observes. 'What is unrepresentability? That which, through language, is part of no particular language: rhythm, music, instinctual balm' (Kristeva 1980c: 141). That which remains, a melancholic strangeness that meaning, and mourning, cannot master.

Judging from the few biographical details she has given us, Kristeva's life is marked by this unsettling strangeness. In 1965, it was Christmas-time, she emigrated from Bulgaria, her birthplace, to a 'bleak and rainy' Paris (Kristeva 1984b: 221). In many ways, it was a moment of dis-integration. Kristeva arrived in Paris, she says, with Céline and Blanchot in her suitcase and – in a move that seems unlikely given these sources – she went immediately to midnight mass (Kristeva 1984b: 221). She was raised in such disjunction: steeped in Eastern European Catholicism and Orthodoxy on the one hand; with, on the other hand, Marx and Lenin as her 'moral textbooks', with attendance at Communist Party meetings required from age 6 or 7, and with the youthful ambition of going to Duobno in Siberia to study astronomy or physics with Soviet scholars (Kristeva 1977a). Indeed, disjunction is the signature of Kristeva's life/writing. In the oft-quoted title of his review of *Sèméiotikè*, Roland Barthes called her *l'étrangère*: a stranger, out of place in France, also someone who displaces our settled ways of seeing things (Barthes 1970: 19). Jean-Paul Enthoven has this strangeness in mind when, in an interview with Kristeva, he describes her as a counsellor to melancholic intellectuals. If an intellectual has any reason to exist, Kristeva says in this interview, it is given by the extent to which she unsettles things, 'affirms and propagates a difference [*affirme et propage de la différence*]' (Kristeva 1977a: 98).

Life and work come together under the rubric of melancholia. Under the sign of Saturn, Susan Sontag suggests with reference to Walter Benjamin, one is never just one and the same, but always one and another (Sontag 1972: 116–17). This might be why, in *A Berlin Chronicle*, when Benjamin contemplates the idea of autobiography, of setting out the sphere of life – *bios* – in writing, his first recourse is to images of wandering and of losing one's way in a city. Autobiography, as he sees it, has to do not with the conventions of coherence and self-presence that have established the Western myth of the self, not 'with time, with sequence and what makes up the continuous flow of life', but with 'space, moments and discontinuities' (Benjamin 1999: 612). Thus, as Sontag points out, Benjamin's only discreetly autobiographical work, *One-Way Street*, takes as its subject, rather than a chronology of the writer himself, his fragmentary reminiscences of place, and of dislocation in it, his endless wanderings, *flâneries*, through the labyrinth of life and work. 'A labyrinth is a place where one gets lost', Sontag reminds us (Sontag 1972: 113). Disorientation is the condition of Benjamin's melancholia.

Given what Kristeva calls '[t]he labyrinths of the *speaking subject*' (1984b: 223), getting lost is the imperative not just of autobiography, but of every attempt to posit the self. Every writing graphs the auto, repeats the mirror stage drama, on the limit-line between Law and loss. In her auto-graphical performance of this borderline identification-incorporation drama, Kristeva returns again and again to the maternal fantasy in which our culture is caught, the eternal feminine against which the sign and self emerge. Several of Kristeva's critics fault her work here. Is Kristeva's writing autobiographical? Kelly Oliver asks. 'Is Kristeva herself the "stranger" that she describes in *Étrangers à nous-mêmes?*' (Oliver 1993: 133). Is Kristeva melancholic because she cannot give up her own mother? 'She cannot replace the lost mother in her own maternal tongue; it only becomes more difficult in a foreign tongue. She is forever mourning the loss of the maternal territory, her mother/land' (Oliver 1993: 139). Consider, for example, *About Chinese Women*, a melancholy book in which Kristeva tries to convey 'the strangeness of China' (Kristeva 1984b: 233). The book was written at another disjunctive point in Kristeva's life/work, after May 1968, when it was again 'time to flee' political and textual conventions (Kristeva 1984b: 233). According to Oliver, Kristeva in this book names and claims the lost object. 'In a romantic moment', Oliver writes, 'she claims that China is less disorienting for her "who recognised my own pioneer komsomal childhood in the little red guards, and who owe my cheekbones to some Asiatic ancestor". Could Kristeva be the "Asiatic princess" of *Étrangers*, "writing her memoirs in a borrowed language"?' (Oliver 1993: 134).

The same questions have been brought to Kristeva's auto-graph text, 'Stabat Mater', in *Tales of Love* (1987b). The title of the text is taken from the mournful hymn of the Roman Catholic Church, *Stabat Mater Dolorosa*, the words of which are attributed to the medieval poet, Jacopone da Todi. A meditation on the Virgin Mary in her station at the cross, a meditation on the virginal maternal, loss and death, *Stabat Mater Dolorosa* opens with the words, 'The sorrowful mother was standing'. Kristeva mentions in her essay that the composer Pergolesi 'was dying of tuberculosis when he wrote his immortal *Stabat Mater*' (Kristeva 1987b: 252). It is as though the composer, trying to overcome his own death, mournfully returns to the lost mother, 'the primal shelter that insured the survival of the newborn' (Kristeva 1987b: 252). This primal mother, fantasy of the lost object, 'an idealisation of primary narcissism', then becomes the focus of Kristeva's 'Stabat Mater' (Kristeva 1987b: 234).

Is this essay 'autobiographical' in the sense that Kelly Oliver takes *Étrangers* to be? Does Kristeva herself, out of 'nostalgia for the Holy mother of the Catholic church' (Oliver 1993: 52), *identify* with Christianity's Virgin and thereby close off, as patriarchy does, the semiotic maternal body? In 'Stabat Mater', does Kristeva, again, name the lost object? In the essay, written shortly after the birth of her son, does Kristeva, through allusions in the essay to the birthing of the male child, assume the place of the Virgin? Here is Oliver's response:

> One of the central claims that Kristeva makes in 'Stabat Mater' is that in childbirth a mother identifies with her own mother. Kristeva as mother, then, identifies with her own mother, not just her own mother but also the Virgin Mother. 'Stabat Mater' can be read as Kristeva's own identification with the Virgin.
>
> (Oliver 1993: 52–3)

It is interesting that when Kristeva writes autobiographically, she suggests no such identification with the Virgin. Thus, in her *In the Beginning Was Love* (1987a), speaking of the 'unbelief' that goes as far back into her youth as she can remember, Kristeva recalls kneeling 'before the icon of the Virgin that sat enthroned above my bed and attempt[ing] to gain access to a faith' in Catholicism and its Mother. The trouble is that 'nothing happened' (Kristeva 1987a). Kristeva experienced none of the 'necessary melancholy' (Kristeva 1987a: 41) that accompanies separation from the mother and that, to be quelled, requires an imaginary substitute. No sadness overwhelmed her, whereupon: 'I told myself that faith could not come until I had endured difficult trials. The road to belief was blocked, perhaps, by the lack of hardship in my life' (Kristeva 1987a: 24). Nevertheless, anticipated hardships and other macabre thoughts 'soon gave way to erotic daydreams' (Kristeva 1987a: 24).

In my view, 'Stabat Mater' has little to offer as an autobiographical record of Kristeva's 'identification' with the Catholic Virgin, as 'Kristeva, the melancholy theorist longing for the lost mother' (Oliver 1993: 53). What the essay stages, rather than Kristeva's experience of giving birth, is the incessantly repeated drama, discourse of love, through which a speaking subject emerges. For Kristeva, we do not come to language, in any instance, as permanent, pre-formed subjects: 'we are subjects *in process*, ceaselessly losing our identity' (Kristeva 1987a: 9). It is the task of the analyst-as-critic to postulate this 'eclipse of subjectivity at the dawn of our life', prior to the mirror stage and prior to every signification (Kristeva 1987a: 9). Moreover, it is for the analyst-as-critic to point out that no subject emerges from the eclipse unless specular identification, identification with an Other, takes place. The Other is illusory, a fantasy, the analyst says; yet there can be no subject without it. 'I want to stress the fact that the function of the psychoanalyst is to reawaken the imagination and to permit illusions to exist' (Kristeva 1987a: 18). Psychoanalysis is not a matter of abolishing the Other, but of having the subject recognise the fantasy that it is. As Lacan puts it, 'It is a matter of the subject progressively discovering which Other he is truly addressing' (Lacan 1988: 246). With this recognition might come the kind of realignment that Kristeva talks about in her essay

'Postmodernism?' (1980c), a realignment that expands the limits of signification and the subject.

'Stabat Mater' is an experiment in 'writing-as-experience-of-limits' (Kristeva 1980c: 141). Typographically split into left- and right-hand columns, the essay oscillates on a symbolic/semiotic borderline, on what Kristeva calls, alluding perhaps to Freud's essay 'Mourning and Melancholia', the site of a wound or a scar. 'I didn't want to give an impression of coherence', she says (1984c: 24). Appropriately, then, she resorts in the essay to Christianity's Virgin Mother: an instance of a fantasy made powerful through religious consecration; an instance of a fantasy that straddles both sides of the symbolic/semiotic divide, 'this side and that side of the parenthesis of language' (1987b: 250). Revisiting Christianity's Mother, Kristeva explores the fantasy for what it is, not just by way of a discourse about, but through a performance of, its traditional role in signification: as a practice of *le sujet en procès*, the essay itself straddles the semiotic and the symbolic, crossing 'the boundaries of the self' (1987a: 6) from one side to another of the page and, synchronically, from one layer to another within the columns.

It is a mistake to read the main column as 'symbolic' and the bold-type insert as 'semiotic', for one thing because, according to Kristeva, as I have mentioned, the semiotic is unrepresentable as propositional language, as the kind of statement that the insert text makes. In both columns, both the symbolic and semiotic are in play: both dimensions are requisite to the emergence of signifier and subject. But the columns are obviously different, the main text being more of 'a knowing discourse, a discourse which pretends to some objectivity', the insert being more of a 'literary poetic text' (Kristeva 1984a: 24). From the main text, an overview and analysis of the Mary cult, we learn about the traditional role of the Virgin as Other, as an idealisation of the lost object, a fantasy enabling identification and placement in the patriarchal Symbolic. Along with the Trinity, Christianity's Virgin Mother, without a natural body and without knowing sex or death, demands incorporation, the sacrifice of a body, as the price of identification, ego-formation and placement in the Symbolic. For Kristeva, it is the genius of the Christian construct that it facilitates, perfectly, the structural requirements of signification: it makes love an experience of identification with an ideal Other, an identification that requires the repression, sacrifice or killing of the body, the 'erotic' body, that is, especially the body of woman (see Kristeva 1987b: 139–50). The poetic insert text, inclining to symbolic idealisation, yet syntactically disrupted by 'semiotic' aberrations, suggests that the repression never fully succeeds. We emerge from the 'lost territory' (Kristeva 1987b: 234) already divided, Kristeva maintains, with pre- or translinguistic semiotic processes the only access to 'species memory' we have: 'archaic traces of the links between our erogenous zones and those of the other, stored as sonorous, visual, tactile, olfactory, or rhythmic traces' (Kristeva 1987a: 8).

'Stabat Mater.' lays out, and plays out, the identification drama, the fantasy that for centuries upheld the symbolic economy of the West and its underlying grand narrative of the heterosexual family: woman/mother as passive conduit for the father's reproduction of himself, his idea, in the son. In our time the fantasy has collapsed, leading to what Kristeva calls 'the psychic sore of modernity: it appears as the incapability of contemporary codes to tame the maternal, that is, primary narcissism' (Kristeva 1987b: 235). A borderline case, situated on the site of this sore, Kristeva's 'Stabat Mater' is a melancholy text: not because in it she pines for the lost Mother, but because she shows the Christian fantasy to be obsolete. We can no longer tame the maternal through the Christian story of the Virgin, and, Kristeva suggests, we do not have another fantasy to put in its place.

This must be, in part, the message of 'Holbein's Dead Christ', where Kristeva turns to Hans Holbein the Younger's *The Body of the Dead Christ in the Tomb* (painted in 1522 on the threshold of the modern) as metaphor of the collapse of the Christian story. Inseparable from the Christian myth of the Mother is the image of the body of Christ, the son, born of the Virgin, crucified, his body resurrected/recovered as ideal. It is the Virgin's sight of the dead body of Christ that inspires the *Stabat Mater Dolorosa*. 'The *Mater Dolorosa* knows no masculine body save that of her dead son', Kristeva notes in 'Stabat Mater', and the Madonna's only pathos 'is her shedding tears over a corpse' (Kristeva 1987b: 250). Pathos it is none the less, 'Mary's outburst of pain at the foot of the cross', this outburst despite the knowledge of resurrection that she, as Mother of God, must have (Kristeva 1987b: 251). Such pathos, all affect, is missing from the Holbein painting, which portrays Christ irrevocably dead and alone: 'the expression of a hopeless grief; the empty stare, the sharp-lined profile, the dull blue-green complexion are those of a man who is truly dead, of Christ forsaken by the Father ("My God, my God, why have you deserted me?") and without the promise of Resurrection' (Kristeva 1989: 110). The painting, without 'the slightest suggestion of transcendency', does not allow for idealisation (Kristeva 1989: 110). 'Cut off from us by its base but without any prospect towards heaven, for the ceiling in the recess comes down low, Holbein's *Dead Christ* is inaccessible, distant, but without a beyond' (Kristeva 1989: 113).

If, as Kristeva says, 'Another, a new morality resides in this painting' (Kristeva 1989: 113), a modern morality in which the subject, and its constitutive signifying process, is 'isolated, pruned, condensed, reduced' (Kristeva 1989: 115), closed in on itself as is the Holbein painting, might postmodernism be an attempt to open this closure? Such, I think, is Kristeva's suggestion. In the face of the technocratic rationalism and liberal individualism that still dominate at the turn of the century and that, she says, are incapable of approaching the subject as a process in language, Kristeva sees postmodernism as a 'borderline' practice of, and experiment in, this process of the self. In particular, she says, postmodernism explores the subject's imaginary relationship to the mother, a 'body-to-body struggle' which entails 'brushing up against either enigma or void' (Kristeva 1980c: 140). This is not about a return to transcendence. Postmodern writers – Kristeva includes herself among them – work closer to the thin edge of 'the thin film of language' (Kristeva 1980c: 137), on 'the frontier between animality and symbol formations', where moods such as melancholia leave their remains (Kristeva 1989: 22).

PART THREE

On Hélène Cixous and Catherine Clément

Chapter 10

Amy Hollywood

MYSTICISM, DEATH AND DESIRE
IN THE WORK OF HÉLÈNE CIXOUS
AND CATHERINE CLÉMENT

IN AN EXCHANGE first published in 1975, Hélène Cixous, soon to be allied with the psychoanalytically oriented branch of the French women's movement, 'Psych et Po', and Marxist feminist Catherine Clément debate the political value of hysteria. Their conversation closes a volume in which Clément compares the sixteenth-century witch hunts with the nineteenth- and twentieth-century phenomenon of hysteria ('*La Coupable*'/'The Guilty Woman') and Cixous links female literary characters from Kleist and Shakespeare with Teresa of Avila and Freud's Dora, the classic psychoanalytic case study. 'I was St Teresa of Avila,' Cixous writes, 'that madwoman who knew a lot more than all the men. And who knew how to become a bird on the strength of loving.' Teresa, Cixous suggests, is an hysteric, and 'the hysterics', she claims, 'are my sisters. . . . But I am what Dora would have been if women's history had begun' (Cixous and Clément 1986: 99). The hysteric declares that she wants 'everything'. But

> the world doesn't give her people who are 'everythings'; they are always very little pieces. In what she projects as a demand for totality, for strength, for certainty, she makes demands of the others in a manner that is intolerable to them and that prevents their functioning as they function (without their restricted little economy). She destroys [*casse*] their calculation.
>
> (Cixous and Clément 1986: 155)[1]

Clément, whose essay carefully balances recognition of the witch's and hysteric's creativity and power with their ultimate containment by male-dominant society, challenges what she sees as Cixou's valorisation of the hysteric, arguing that what Dora 'broke' (*a cassé*) through her bodily symptoms 'was strictly individual and limited' and hence without larger, enduring political effect. In response, Cixous insists that she does not 'fetishise' Dora, but uses her as 'the name of a certain force, which makes the little circus not work anymore' (Cixous and Clément 1986: 157). In hysteria, repressed desire erupts. Following Georges Bataille, Cixous argues

> that what cannot be oppressed, even in the class struggle, is the libido – desire; it is in taking off from desire that you will revive the need for things to really change. Desire never dies, but it can be stifled for a long time. For example, in peoples who are denied speech and who are on their last gasp. One ceases to move the moment one no longer communicates.
>
> (Cixous and Clément 1986: 157–8)[2]

Yet Clément worries that desire can be destructive in ways inimical to the emancipatory political projects to which she and Cixous are committed. The obsessive person, she argues, through the force of his or her desire, destroys by adding to 'the rigidity of structures' and to 'ritual' rather than by loosening their hold. For Cixous, however, the obsessive and the hysteric must be kept distinct:

> When Freud says that the obsessive, on the cultural level, yields the religious and that what is hysterical yields art, it seems right to me. The religious is something that consolidates, that will re-enclose, that will seal and fasten everything that is rigid in the social realm. There is a difference between what makes things move and what stops them; it is what moves things that changes them.
>
> (Cixous and Clément 1986: 157)

The mystics, or at least 'that madwoman' Teresa of Avila, are aligned not with religion but with hysteria. Cixous's argument leads to the conclusion that mystics, in that they are *religious*, are obsessive-compulsives, whereas in that they are *hysterical*, they are artists and revolutionaries. Cixous effects a transvaluation of values, a radical reversal of the deployment of medical and psychoanalytic categories against Christian mystics – in particular, women mystics – by means of which their texts and experiences are rendered pathological.[3] In other words, where earlier readings of some Christian mystics as hysterical reduced affective and erotic forms of mysticism to disease, thereby undermining their religious value, Cixous argues that hysteria – and hence the mystical forms associated with it – marks the return of repressed desire and so unleashes a liberating force that works against the conservative and rigidifying power of religious belief and practice. She does not challenge the perceived gap between certain types of mysticism and religion, but instead reverses the valuations placed on the two. Her brief juxtaposition of mysticism and hysteria, then, works within an opposition between dominant social structures – including religion – seen as repressive and oppressive, and desire, the site, for Cixous, of a disrupting and liberatory mystical excess.[4]

This split between traditional religion and its God and the divinity released through desire, hysteria and writing runs throughout Cixous's work.[5] In *The Newly Born Woman* she asserts both that the fiction of paternity that passes itself off as truth does so with the support of the Father God and that writing, unleashed against these constraining fictions, raises 'tensions and fevers to the point of divinity' (Cixous and Clément 1986: 100, 127). In 'Coming to Writing' (1977) she claims that 'Writing is God. But it is not your God' (Cixous 1991b: 11). Writing, then, supplements and/or takes the place of hysteria and mysticism as the site in which boundless desire is unleashed. Twenty years later she still affirms the centrality of God to writing.

> I have never written without *Dieu*. Once I was reproached for it. *Dieu* they said is not a feminist. Because they believed in a pre-existing God. But God is of my making. But God, I say, is the phantom of writing, it is her pretext and her promise. God is the name of all that has not yet been said. Without the word *Dieu* to shelter the infinite multiplicity of all that could be said the world would be reduced to its shell and I to my skin. *Dieu* stands for the names that have never yet been invented. *Dieu* is the synonym. God is not the one of religions . . .
>
> (Cixous 1998: 150)

For Clément in 1975, on the other hand, hysteria and mysticism, like the writing with which Cixous links them, remain inadequate to the political goals of Marxism and feminism. 'Do you know the games like "taquin"?' she asks Cixous.

> They are games where you move a piece in a system in which you can move only a limited number of pieces to explore the possibilities of permutation without the 'taquin's' moving. One shifts an element within a perfectly rigid structure, which is all the better for it. Language only moves one square to the place of another – that's all; the real distribution of elements, the real change cannot happen on that level.
>
> (Cixous and Clément 1986: 157)

Clément insists that change occurs only through active intervention in all the material systems of oppression – linguistic, psychic, social, economic and political. Yet her search for 'the possibility of happiness', as both a 'psychic and political goal', will ultimately lead her back to mysticism and religion.[6] She comes to share Cixous's sense of a deep division between the two, although her account of mysticism (as of hysteria) is arguably more bodily, affective, experiential and tied to ritual practices than is Cixous's.[7] The result, I will argue, is the subversion of the very distinction between religion and mysticism that Clément works so hard to maintain, a subversion that leads to her continued uneasiness with the deployment of religion and of mysticism within the political realm.

Clément's turn to mysticism might be read as a retreat from politics in the name of other desires and demands. Most importantly, for Clément in the 1980s and 1990s, mysticism is a way of encountering and working through death that enables a return to life. Similarly, despite her emphasis on mysticism as the site of excessive and disruptive desire in *The Newly Born Woman*, Cixous often describes her mystical mode of writing as a way to apprehend and resolve loss, particularly that brought about by the death of the other. The two conceptions of mysticism are not antithetical, however, for desire and death – the desire for something beyond death and the refusal of death's limits, as well as the inevitable return of death as that which denies human desire – are inextricably bound together in Cixous's writing.[8] What remains unclear in both Cixous and Clément is the relationship between death, desire – and hence mysticism – and politics. Both oscillate between understanding death in terms of political repression and/or oppression and conceiving of death as irreducible to politics. In the latter instance, writing and mysticism pursue goals that cannot be encapsulated by the political. Yet even with the recognition that death will remain despite political change, the experiences of death, loss and mourning are profoundly effected by human situatedness within complex political worlds. Politics cannot contain death, desire and the work of mourning (which is perhaps inevitably religious, as Cixous and Clément both suggest), yet these experiences remain deeply embedded in the political world. Cixous and Clément pose without fully articulating or resolving the question of how to hold together the religious and the political, mourning and resistance, or, as Cixous might phrase it, the acceptance of death and its refusal.

I Cixous: writing, death and divinity

Cixous's writing is vast, diverse, protean. Although the standard bibliographies distinguish between fictions, critical essays and theatrical works, Cixous's texts continually undermine these distinctions.[9] In particular, it is impossible to separate poetry and prose or literary texts ('those to be read') and critical essays ('readings').[10] As a host of recent commentators have shown, moreover, there are marked shifts in tone, themes and metaphors across the thirty years of Cixous's career (and there will no doubt be more changes in the future).[11] Yet

if there is one set of issues that unites her work, it is this interpenetration of reading and writing, the dependence of both on forgetting and death, and the ability
of both to transcend these forces of oblivion.[12] 'Writing is God', for Cixous, and
one of the problems with which she continually wrestles is the relationship
between that future divine and present historical and political realities.

Reading, writing and death converge around the death of the father (Cixous's
own father died when she was 11) and the love of books. Cixous insists on the
close relationship between the two. *Or, les lettres de mon père* (1997) opens with
a moving evocation of reading as the one place in which forgetting is essential and
does not lead to irrevocable loss.

> But to forget is part of reading. We read to revive the happiness of
> finding again a wise person and a friend. . . . [W]e read without
> concern that we lose in reading the joy that rises up from page to
> page, because we learned a long time ago that one doesn't lose a
> book so beloved in devouring it. Because as soon as we read we
> forget it, we read and we forget we read to forget and two times to
> forget, to forget everything except for the book in as much as we are
> enchanted passengers within it, and then to forget the book that
> draws its limbs into itself, goes and lays down again in the tomb, that
> it is like a beloved dead person ready to return at the call of his name
> to bring us help when we miss him, him, only, that one there, about
> which we have forgotten everything but the name, and the power.
>
> (Cixous 1997: 11–12)

Writing's continuity, the legible trace left in the book that enables us to return
to it, renders it both faithful and immortal.[13]

Cixous ties the fidelity of the book directly to the fidelity of her dead father.

> It is for this that I love books.
> Because they come and go, die and come back to life here even in
> my room, in my office, day and night. Because they are faithful like
> my father who is a ghost on whom I believe I can count. A row of the
> dead who already breathe again. My delicate, immoderate near ones.
>
> (Cixous 1997: 12)

For Cixous, writing – at least in its feminine forms, allied with desire, excess
and the body – wrestles with death. It attempts to overcome loss (particularly
that of the father),[14] to commemorate his passing and the marks it leaves on
the daughter's body and psyche, and to encounter the possibility of one's own
death.[15] Acceptance of death and its inscription is necessary to participation in
the immortality and endless desires and pleasures of writing.

The fidelity of the book mirrors reading and writing as acts of fidelity to the other. For Cixous, as for Jacques Derrida – to whose work her own is closely linked – writing is enabled by the movement of *différance*, the differing and deferring repetition of signs through which material signifiers take on immaterial significations.[16] As repeatable and material, the signifier carries within it both presence and absence – the presence of the signifier to the reader and the absence, real or implicit, of the one from whom the signifier originates (and that absence makes it impossible ever fully to tie the signifier back to its source). Derrida's work tends to focus on loss, the absence that is inscribed within all language, and the destabilising effects of that absence on meaning. Cixous, while attentive to those features of writing, particularly as they might endanger or be deployed towards liberatory ends, increasingly highlights the ways in which writing enables the dead to speak to us, creating a bridge between present, past and future.[17]

For fidelity, Cixous claims in 'The Last Painting or the Portrait of God', is ultimately a fidelity to the 'instant', 'to what exists. To everything that exists' (Cixous 1991b[1983]: 104–5). Language both enables us to render 'what exists' present in its absence and, because of the absence constitutive to language, renders the instant impossible. Dissatisfaction, even failure, however, are necessary acts of 'faith', according to Cixous. Once again, she evokes God in order to articulate the nature of her project.

> When I have finished writing, when I am a hundred and ten, all I will have done will have been to attempt a portrait of God. Of the God. Of what escapes us and makes us wonder. Of what we do not know but feel. Of what makes us live. I mean our own divinity, awkward, twisted, throbbing, our own mystery – we who are lords of this earth and do not know it, we who are touches of vermilion and yellow cadmium in the haystack and do not see it, we who are the eyes of this world and so often do not even look at it, we who could be the painters, the poets, the artists of life if only we wanted to; we who could be the lovers of the universe, if we really wanted to use our hands with mansuetude, we who so often use our booted feet to trample the world's belly.
>
> (Cixous 1991b: 129–30)

Attempts to render the instant, through writing or painting (the object of discussion in much of 'The Last Painting'), are themselves moments of attention that render the past present and open it to the future.

Although writing can thus be read as an act of commemoration and mourning, it is also crucial to remember Cixous's insistence, in *The Newly Born Woman*, that what moves must be distinguished from that which stops movement.[18] Writing is not a crypt in which the other is embalmed and rendered incapable of change, but rather a practice through which the other lives and moves. The old gods, what in *La* (1976) Cixous refers to as the gods of men – or man as God – engender belief only when women fear death as the absence of life and confuse 'infinity' with 'death'.

> For the characteristics of our gods, those in whom for centuries we can no longer believe, is to prove that they exist precisely in these moments of trouble in which belief, in general, is about to die and in which we will be compelled to choose between madness and belief in ourself. 'I am going to encounter myself', our soul petrified with fear cries out, 'Quick, a god!'.
>
> (Cixous 1994a: 64)

For Cixous, the God of Western monotheism emerges at those moments of self-doubt in which boundaries between self and world, self and other, or self and death are about to be breached. Here language operates in its most rigid forms, promising in the existence of a clearly articulated other an escape from the supposed abyss of death. The exigencies of grammar, Cixous suggests, demand the clear articulation of the subject, leading to the reification of being, subjectivity and sexuality. With this petrification comes a refusal of movement and death, for any change marks the destabilisation of the subject.[19] Writing, however, in the grammar-defying forms practised by Cixous, allows women to give themselves what they 'would want God-if-he-existed to give' them. It allows language to operate not as the tomb in which lost possibilities are encrypted, but rather as a site of movement, change and connection across boundaries.

> It's all there: where separation doesn't separate; where absence is animated, taken from silence and stillness. In the assault of love on nothingness. My voice repels death; my death; your death; my voice is my other. I write and you are not dead. The other is safe if I write. . . . [Writing] is what never ends.
>
> (Cixous 1991b: 4)[20]

Although Cixous concedes that she does not believe revolution can be brought about through language, she also insists on the political power of writing. Her demand for fidelity to the instant, to 'what exists', and to life against the annihilating pretensions of death – what in *To Live the Orange* (1979) she understands as her 'love of the orange' – is 'political' as well as 'religious' (Cixous 1979: 26–7, 12–13). Yet she recognises the audacities and dangers of that claim, particularly in the face of history's injustices and atrocities (represented in the text, initially, by the forced veiling of women in Iran under the Ayatollah).

> For the women who know how to believe, nothing is left but
> suffering, suffering. To have known how to think, to look, to smile in
> return, is a curse, to have known how to read, to enjoy, to name, to
> have known is a misfortunate, to be human is the final catastrophe,
> now that murder is stronger than love.
>
> (Cixous 1979: 88–9)

The crucial questions, to which Cixous believes she finds an answer in the work
of Clarice Lispector, are 'how to be contemporaneous with a living rose and with
concentration camps' and how to make one's attention and joy in the former
politically meaningful in the fight against the latter (Cixous 1979: 100).

Cixous's writing evinces a continual struggle to express the political, ethical
and religious value of attention to the instant without trivialising historical
injustice and catastrophe. Moreover, the instant and 'what exists' are themselves
often moments of loss, suffering and abjection. Cixous's writing constantly moves
between pleasure and pain, beauty and horror, 'Paradise' and 'Hell', with the
role of writing and memory constantly shifting. It is both 'our human misfortune',
Cixous claims in *Manna: For the Mandelstams For the Mandalas* (1994b), 'that our
immortalities are so brief', and also 'our human chance'.

> It repairs everything, good fortune, bad fortune. And just as we lose
> one day the taste of the bread of joy and the memory of joy, so also
> will we be able to lose one day the tenacious taste of sorrow. The
> earth forgets. This is its strange privilege. It is Hell that is a prey to
> memory.
>
> (Cixous 1994b: 155–6)

And here we come to the final, unresolved tension in Cixous's work – between
the desire for immortality, that she claims to realise in writing, and recognition
of the necessity of forgetting. For Cixous, writing encapsulates the two. Yet as
long as she believes that writing keeps the other alive, can she in fact recognise
the often irredeemable nature of human suffering and loss? To which Cixous
might respond with another question: If we remain focused on that loss, can we
avoid becoming fixated on it in debilitating and life-destroying ways? And, I will
add, is this a particular problem for women?

II Clément: mourning and the 'risk of the sacred'

Clément's recent interest in mysticism and religion revolves around the same
issues, although, not surprisingly, in ways that differ fundamentally from
Cixous's. In *Syncope: The Philosophy of Rapture* (1994), *La Folle et le saint* (with

Sudhir Kakar, 1993), *Theo's Odyssey* (1999) and *The Feminine and the Sacred* (with Julia Kristeva, 2001), Clément ranges across the world's religious traditions, exploring and attempting to understand those moments of trance, rapture, ecstasy and possession that seem somehow necessary to the process of successful mourning. Clément argues in *Syncope* and *The Feminine and the Sacred* that in the modern industrialised West, depression is the only similar experience (Clément compares it to rites of initiation).

> Yes, depression is really and truly indispensable. Yes, it is a useful retreat. Yes, the posture of prostration is a withdrawal that does not do any harm: head down, eyes invisible to the other, body curled up. Yes, it precedes a rebirth and that is why I compare it to an initiation. The 'work of mourning' is one of its versions and it belongs to life, not just to death. If the depression lasts too long, in fact, it turns into melancholia, the void of the sacred becomes lost in a chasm, and rebirth does not come about. Now I am back in the danger zones. But can the danger be avoided? There is real danger only in excess, said the Greeks. That is the very definition of the tragic.
>
> (Clément and Kristeva 2001: 147)

The risk lies both in the possibility that depression and mourning might not be overcome and in the volatility of the processes through which they are successfully resolved.[21]

Clément argues that the sacred emerges in moments of crisis, experienced most often by the poor, the oppressed, the disenfranchised – and predominantly by women. These experiences of the sacred, through trance, possession and ecstasy, resolve loss and mourning, making possible rebirth and a return to life.[22] The danger in the sacred is no longer, as in *The Newly Born Woman*, that the sacred offers only private compensatory pleasures and solutions incapable of effecting larger political, social and economic change. On the contrary, Clément's primary concern in the 1990s seems to be that the sacred will infiltrate the public realm. The sacred, she suggests, is emotional, volatile and irrational, and hence leads to the spectre of fascism, totalitarianism and the rigid legal systems that Clément associates with certain forms of fundamentalism. Adolf Hitler and Eva Peron are evoked in order to reinforce her claim that it is an 'imperious necessity' for the sacred to remain in the private sphere (Clément and Kristeva 2001: 144).[23] The purportedly private nature of experiences of the sacred no longer counts against them, but rather safeguards the political from incursions of emotion, irrationality and (opportunistic?) authoritarianism.

Similarly, Clément makes a distinction between mysticism, understood as direct experiences of the sacred, and religion: 'I call "religion" any organisation of the sacred that relies on a clergy, rites, constraints and sanctions' (Clément and Kristeva 2001: 145). In a sense, she understands religion as the institutionalisation and hence the making public of the sacred, with all of the dangers that entails for the political and social realm. Yet at the same time, Clément's own work shows that the emergence of the sacred in experiences of trance, ecstasy and possession occurs in and through ritual itself. One might go further and argue that one of the reasons depression and the 'work of mourning' so often end in melancholy in industrialised parts of the world is precisely because of the paucity of rituals through which that mourning can be resolved. This is precisely the story Clément tells in *Theo's Odyssey*.

Theo is a 14-year-old French boy, raised by atheist parents and so given no religious education (although he gets a bit from school, from a Senegalese Islamic girlfriend, and from his Greek Orthodox grandmother). His parents want him to 'see for himself' when he gets older, but when Theo develops a mysterious illness, he finds himself ineluctably drawn to Greek and Egyptian mythology and the Tibetan *Book of the Dead*. The doctors are stymied by Theo's illness. Although his parents do not tell him, Theo begins to understand that he is dying. Presumably, his reading is an attempt to prepare himself for that (non)future, to think what death might mean.

Theo's wealthy, slightly 'mad' Aunt Martha has a different plan. She proposes taking Theo away from his books and on a grand tour of the world's religions – looking, not for an understanding of death, but for a cure. In Egypt, Theo wants to see the pyramids and the burial goods of the great pharaohs. Aunt Martha takes him to a local healing ritual. She spends all of her time in Benares worrying that he will see the corpses burning along the Ganges. In other words, Aunt Martha takes Theo on a religious odyssey in order to escape death – yet its spectre continually returns. Not, as it turns out, the spectre of Theo's own death, but that of a stillborn twin sister about whom he has never been told. Through his participation in ritual trances invoked by Islamic healers, Sufi musicians, a statue of the Buddha and Japanese Noh theatre (among others), Theo learns of this lost twin sister, mourns her and is cured of his mysterious ailment.

The accounts of religious traditions that intersperse Theo's travels tell relatively little about beliefs concerning death and the afterlife (Aunt Martha tends to steer the conversations away from these topics). Yet religious rituals – at least in their more 'popular', least institutionally controlled forms – are about the 'work of mourning'. The novel shows Aunt Martha and Theo coming to the realisation that religion's attention to death belongs 'to life, not only to death'. Reading is insufficient, in part because it is unable to invoke the trance-like experiences so crucial to Theo's recovery. (Writing like Cixous's, with its incantatory movement and immersion in the materiality of the signifier, may in fact engender experiences related to that of the trances evoked by music, dance and other ritual forms. Clément is not interested in this possibility, nor does she acknowledge it. This parallels her lack of interest in Christian mysticism, which, like Cixous, uses writing and reading as modes of spiritual practice.)[24] But reading also is inadequate for Clément because Theo's books focus on beliefs about the afterlife, thereby moving towards death rather than towards life. Theo's participation in religious rituals and the trance-like states that they induce are crucial to his successful mourning, which includes both welcoming and letting go of his dead sister.

The novel depicts Theo's youth and relative inexperience with religion as making him open and receptive to these states (in a way that Aunt Martha, for example, resists). The issue of the referent of belief is elided in two ways. First, in these communal rituals, Theo does not experience God, Allah, nirvana, or an *orisha*, but a private moment of familial mourning. Secondly, the novel form suspends sceptical questions that might emerge about how Theo could be mourning for a sister of whose existence he is ignorant (although there is much room for interpretation by psychoanalytically inclined readers of the novel to explore its depiction of private familial dynamics in relationship to the purported crisis of the family in Western industrial nations, especially given that the novel ends with Theo's mother pregnant, ready to provide him with a new sister – apparently the two he already has are inadequate). The supernatural element of religion is thus softened through its privatisation and fictionalisation, even as the novel seems to proclaim the need for public and bodily enacted mourning rituals.

As Clément shows in *The Feminine and the Sacred*, rituals of mourning are not completely absent from her own life, although they lack the ecstatic and supernatural elements of Theo's experience:[25]

> I'm going to tell you what my own sacred is. The memory of the family lineage, 'the head of my children' (on which one takes an oath), the alliances of love and friendship, respect for the dead, the Jewish lamp in front of the photograph of my mother during the year I have mourned her, the rites of the ancestors. Am I Confucian? No, I am truly Jewish. The rabbi who buried my mother last June told me that, for Jews, the only belief in an afterlife has to do with the survival of Israel from generation to generation: the afterlife is memory itself. That is my sacred: it is by definition faithful.
>
> (Clément and Kristeva 2001: 69)

Like Cixous, Clément returns again and again to fidelity – to the dead as to the living. The ecstasy that fascinates Clément, like Cixous's writing and reading practices, both enables and undermines that fidelity, for it is premised on an interplay of presence and absence, remembrance and forgetting, mourning and jouissance.

Writing and ritual engender paradoxical ecstatic encounters with 'what exists' and its oblivion through repetition – a repetition that always also differs, both temporally and spatially, from that which it repeats (hence the absence – or the mark of death – in all signification). Ecstasy depends on this ritual repetition and so cannot be easily removed from the realm of 'religion', understood by Clément as an encryption of the sacred. Nor can religion be so easily removed from the political realm, for it is precisely the public nature of religious ritual that is missing in Theo's life and gives rise to Clément's own nostalgic, melancholic fascination with the 'ecstatic' religions of India, Senegal and Brazil. Moreover, as she herself recognises, much of what is mourned by the practitioners of these religions is itself political – losses engendered by hunger, poverty and oppression.[26] Clément fears the incursion of religion – even, if not especially, in its ecstatic forms – into the political realm. Yet her work suggests that we need to find a place within the public realm for mourning these and other losses,[27] while at the same time working through and rectifying them, in so far as it is possible, in concrete political, economic and social terms.[28] Rites of mourning (among which might easily be included, I think, Cixous's writing and reading practices) cannot and should not replace politics, but faith in politics and commitment to life's pleasures and desires should not blind us to the necessity of mourning – a task that will remain no matter how successful emancipatory political projects may turn out to be. As Cixous and Clément both insist, this is a particularly crucial task for women, at this point in human history still so often burdened with the work of mourning and so often the victims of the greatest material and spiritual losses.

Notes

1   Allusion to the desire for everything or the all, a 'restricted little economy', and the destruction of calculation evoke the work of Georges Bataille, as does the title of Clément's essay. The desire to be everything or all is also important in the work of Simone de Beauvoir and Jacques Lacan. See Hollywood (2001).

2   Clément claims she can understand Cixous's comments only 'poetically', otherwise being unable to make sense of the idea of 'a people that doesn't communicate'. But Cixous here makes use, I think, of Bataille's more restricted conception of communication.

3   It was the neurologist Jean-Martin Charcot (1825–93), so important in the modern medical study of hysteria for his insistence that hysteria is a disease of the nerves rather than a sign of moral degeneration, malingering and laziness, who first introduced the reading of mysticism as hysteria in *La Foi qui guérit*, written shortly before his death (included in Charcot 1984[1886]).

There he argues that Francis of Assisi and Teresa of Avila were 'undeniable hysterics' with the ability, none the less, to cure hysteria in others. Charcot remains puzzled by these curative skills. (In another text, *Les Démoniaques dans l'art* – co-written with Paul Richer in 1886 – he retroactively diagnoses demonic possession as hysteria.) The association of mysticism – particularly the visionary and somatic forms of mysticism most often associated with women – and hysteria was used throughout the early twentieth century, and beyond, to disparage and denigrate women's experience and writing. See Charcot and Richer (1984); and Mazzoni (1996: 21–2). Nancy Partner and Barbara Newman recently argued for the viability of the category in explaining medieval mysticism. See Partner (1991, 1996); Newman (1998); Weissman (1982); and Hollywood (2001).

4   As I shall suggest in what follows, this split between religion and mysticism will not stand. There is a doubleness in mysticism itself – a split between the desire to be all and the recognition that one cannot be everything – that parallels the distinction Cixous tries here to establish between the mystical and the religious. This doubleness is related to the deep ambivalence of mourning, which both Cixous and Clément repeatedly associate with mysticism.

5   Her work persistently rereads, often from an explicitly feminist perspective, central texts from the Hebrew Bible, so she returns to her own Jewish tradition through its books. Her first sustained fiction, *Inside* (1986b), is a rereading of the Song of Songs in terms of the death of the father, and of human erotic relationships. For readings of 'Eve and the apple', see Cixous (1975: 180–1); and Cixous (1991b: 136–96), where she also discusses another story from Genesis that fascinates her – that of Abraham and his absolute fidelity.

6   For this formulation of Clément's project in the 1970s and early 1980s, see Jones (1987: 1). The first signs of this new interest in mysticism appear, not surprisingly, in Clément's book about Lacan. There she notes that Lacan 'classes himself among the mystics' and that he is among those 'for whom mysticism and religion have nothing to do with each other' (Clément 1983: 66). She became deeply interested in mysticism and religion, however, only after her engagement with Indian culture, first as Secretary General of the Year of India in France (1985–6), and then as ambassador to New Delhi, India, and delegate to the Festival of France in India (1987–91). She later served as ambassador to Dakar, Senegal and Banjul, Gambia (1996–9), leading to her interest in religion and possession in Africa. Cixous also became interested in India during the 1980s, perhaps under the influence of Clément. On India, see especially Clément (1993); Clément (1996); and Cixous (1987). On religion, see Clément and Kakar (1993); Clément (1994); Clément and Kristeva (2001); and Clément (1999).

7   Cixous's work for the theatre presents an important exception to this trend, for Cixous stresses the ritualistic and cathartic elements in theatre as well as its opening of her writing to the other and hence to history. See, for example, Cixous (1989: 10).

8   Reading through Cixous's fictions and essays inevitably brings to mind Caroline Walker Bynum's characterisation of the thirteenth-century beguine Mechthild of Magdeburg's *Flowing Light of the Godhead* as, in a pattern reminiscent of the Song of Songs, constantly oscillating 'between alienation and ecstasy' (Bynum 1982: 230). On the similar movement in Cixous's fictions, see Shiach (1991: 69–105).

9   In what follows I will move between a number of Cixous's texts, drawing out passages that illuminate her complex conceptions of religion, the sacred and writing. This mode of reading inevitably does violence to Cixous's complex textual practice, however, and is meant only as a preliminary attempt to draw out issues that will require more nuanced exploration through detailed readings of individual texts.

10   The lines between fiction and autobiography are also very difficult to distinguish. Elaine Marks calls Cixous's early work 'the autobiography of an unconscious'. She also suggests that the writings should be read as 'preparatory exercises' for a difficult 'spiritual itinerary', highlighting the ties between the mystical and Cixous's writing (Marks 1979: 309–10).

11   These shifts are closely tied to Cixous's political commitments and changing conceptions of how writing and politics come together. For commentary that gives attention to these issues, see especially Conley (1991[1984]); Shiach (1991); Conley (1992); Calle-Gruber (1993); and MacGillivray (1994). For Cixous's biography and its relationship to her writing, see Cixous (1989); Suleiman (1991); and Cixous and Calle-Gruber (1997).

12   Particularly in the 1970s and early 1980s, Cixous associates the forces of death and oblivion with phallogocentrism, suggesting that the emergence of new forms of femininity and feminine writing will overcome death and/or engage with loss in profoundly new ways. These two alternatives are different in important ways and the undecidability and constant move-ment of Cixous's texts between the two gives rise to my questions about the relationship between death, desire and politics. These questions also are central to Cixous's work for the theatre, which unfortunately I cannot discuss here. Cixous describes how writing for the theatre opened her to the other and enabled her for the first time to create characters. Yet the problems of memory, mourning and fidelity remain crucial to that theatrical work, arguably in a more directly political and communally oriented vein. See Cixous (1994a). The relationship between Cixous's understandings of the theatre and of religious ritual requires further study.

13   Or perhaps potentially immortal, for the book can be destroyed. Cixous tends, however, to emphasise writing's continuity and its triumph over death.

14   Although, as I have said, much of Cixous's writing from the 1970s and 1980s struggles against the Father of psychoanalytic theory and of phallogocentrism, her love of the lost father leads to ambivalence around the paternal figure and an attempt to think paternity in new ways. Arguably, this is tied to her claims to what she calls, at one point, the bisexuality of writing and all human psyches and her insistence on the fluidity of sex, sexuality and bodies. These assertions give rise to phrases like the following: *'une belle jeune mère masculine'* ('a beautiful young masculine mother'), images in which one cannot help but see an idealised image of the prematurely dead father (Cixous 1976: 87, cited by Shiach 1991: 90).

15   The trauma of the father's death marks and fractures Cixous's works in ways that change from her first book-length fiction, *Inside* (1986b), through *Or* (1997), and in ways that are not always fully analysed by the narrating voice. In addition, the father and his loss is associated with other objects of desire and their real or potential loss. The other side of fidelity is abandonment, and the affective remnants of her perceived abandonment by the father run through Cixous's work, although often without explicit acknowledgement.

16   Cixous and Derrida, both Jewish, were also both born and grew up in Algeria and although they did not know each other there, this biographical fact has brought them together in crucial ways. For an introduction to Derrida's conception of writing, see *'Différance'* and 'Signature Event Context' (Derrida 1982: 1–28, 307–30). For the relationship between Cixous and Derrida, see Cixous (1998: 117–33); Cixous and Derrida (1998); Conley (1991[1984]); and Marrouchi (1997).

17   This is tied to Cixous's rejection of a Lacanian understanding of the human being as always already split or castrated and her attempt to rethink fluid subjectivities outside of this phallic economy. From this perspective, writing is marked by the feminine – that which is other than and disrupts masculine, phallic conceptions of subjectivity and meaning. For the parallel project in the work of Luce Irigaray, see Hollywood (2001).

18   'The ideal, or the dream, would be to arrive at a language that heals as much as it separates. Could one imagine a language sufficiently transparent, sufficiently supple, intense, faithful so that there would be reparation and not only separation' (Cixous, in conversation with Conley, in Conley 1991[1984]: 146). This passage is cited on a number of occasions by the American writer Carole Maso, whose work brilliantly wrestles with the same issues. See, for example, Maso (1993); and Maso (2000).

19   Again, this is closely tied to Cixous's attempt, in the 1970s and early
     1980s, to offer an account of a feminine libidinal economy not constrained
     by phallocentrism and its 'all or nothing' – you have the phallus or you
     don't – modes of thinking. But she is in danger, at times, of disavowing
     death and the bodily mourning that it necessitates. For the problem in
     Irigaray, which is much more thoroughgoing than in Cixous, see Holly-
     wood (2001).

20   Is writing, as Kristeva suggests, ultimately a fetish in which death is both
     avowed and disavowed? And if so, is this a problem or a potential solution
     to the problem of mourning and loss? See Kristeva (1982: 37).

21   These issues are perhaps most clearly articulated by Julia Kristeva, who
     argues that whereas religion used to do the work of organising the
     emotions and allowing a place for mourning and love, that role now falls
     to psychoanalysis and literature (Kristeva 1987b). Cixous similarly posits
     literature and the theatre, both forms of writing in the particular sense
     of that term used by Cixous, as the site of mourning and its resolution.
     Clément, on the other hand, although she *uses* literature towards these
     ends, always points beyond literature to various forms of religious and
     mystical practice. In part, I think, this is because she takes writing less
     seriously than do either Kristeva or Cixous. Yet although *Theo's Odyssey*
     (Clément 1999) seems premised on a rejection of the claim that reading
     can have the affective force of ritual, the novel itself remains and is often
     more interesting in its operation than its explicit formulations of the
     relationship between reading and ritual.

22   Yet the question remains of *how* trance, possession and ecstasy accomplish
     this work of mourning. One danger in Clément's appeal to 'the sacred' is
     that it supplies an other who accomplishes this work, thereby bypassing
     this crucial question.

23   Kristeva's response is to deny that Hitler and Peron partake in the sacred.

24   Clément's disinterest in Christian mysticism emerges in her exchange with
     Kristeva, who is fascinated by the Christian mystical tradition, particularly
     the figure of Catherine of Siena. Clément does discuss the relationship
     between hysteria and mysticism (as well as hysteria and trance), arguing
     that Pierre Janet's patient Madeleine, for example, is read as an hysteric
     rather than a mystic only because her form of religiosity 'is not socially
     recognised as saintliness in our world'. Madeleine was simply born in
     the wrong era – she 'strays from an excess of memory' (Clément and
     Kristeva 2001: 122–3). In response, Kristeva rightly insists that 'a real
     effort must be made to accompany her symptoms with a certain use of
     speech' (Clément and Kristeva 2001: 135). In other words, as I have
     argued elsewhere, at issue is the interpretation of his or her symptoms and
     whether one participates in that process or merely accedes to externally

imposed interpretations (Hollywood 2001). For Clément's fuller reading of Madeleine and comparison with the nineteenth-century Hindu saint and mystic Ramakrishna, see Clément and Kakar (1993).

25   It is not clear how tightly the ecstatic and the supernatural are linked for Clément, in part because it is not clear what she understands the sacred to be. Is it simply an explosion of affect? For more on Clément's attempt to think through these issues philosophically, see Clément (1994).

26   Might this nostalgia also be for lost political opportunities and energy?

27   And although Clément does not make this argument, such public ways of dealing with loss are available, or at least more readily available, to the powerful and privileged. For a similar argument with regard to the valorisation of male melancholy and its dependence on a denigration of female mourning, see Schiesari (1992).

28   As Amy Allen pointed out to me, there is a danger here of eliding the political with publicness and losing its primary signification as the realm in which power relations are enacted. Although second-wave feminism is famously predicated on the claim that the personal is the political (that is, that the old distinction between public and private is no longer adequate to our political understanding and that power operates in regulated ways in both public and private), Clément in particular seems to suggest that publicness has a legitimating power that women and other subordinated groups need and want, both to do the work of living and the related work of mourning.

Chapter 11

Sal Renshaw

THE THEALOGY OF
HÉLÈNE CIXOUS

> True love for the other, religious without any specific denomination, brings
> about modes of exchange that are outside of any reversal.
>
> (Verena Andermatt Conley [1991:100],
> on the work of Hélène Cixous)

THROUGHOUT HISTORY THEORISTS and philosophers of love
have been preoccupied with the relationship between the subjects and
objects of love. From Plato's reflections on the divinity of a spiritual love of
knowledge to the Christian insistence upon loving our enemies, we find a re-
curring concern with understanding the mediating aspects of love. How should
we think of the kinds of exchanges that love brings about? Whether our thinking
about love concerns relations between human beings, or relations between
humans and the divine, the very notion of love as developed in Western thought
presupposes that something is loved, while someone else, as subject, does the
loving. Even if we acknowledge the possibility that love is reciprocal and the one
who is loved also loves, the notion of love has circulated around a subject/object
dichotomy that presumes that specific patterns of relating govern the exchange
between sameness and difference, self and other. As such, if and when we
presume to speak meaningfully of lover and beloved, our thinking about love is
necessarily implicated in our thinking about subjectivity.

For French feminist theorist Hélène Cixous, the sexual politics of how love
has traditionally been understood to negotiate a subject/object relation has been
a constant preoccupation of her work, which is informed by, and contributes to,
contemporary philosophical reflections on difference and subjectivity. Throughout her writing she explores the ways in which different conceptions of love have
been implicated in the production of unjust and unequal relations of exchange,

and she laments that, historically, our thinking has been mired in the dialectical structures of a patriarchal logos. Wherever dialectical relations govern the patterns of exchange, difference is subordinated to an economy of sameness in a 'battle for mastery that rages between classes, peoples, etc.' (Cixous 1986c: 78). The history of patriarchal ideals of love centres on the subject, and the otherness of the other is routinely denied in and by the privileging of subjectivity. For Cixous, the history of Western culture is 'his story' and 'the same masters dominate history from the beginning, inscribing on it the marks of their appropriating economy' (Cixous 1986c: 79). The subject of love in Western discourse is predictably masculine, and the economy of relations within which 'he' operates has been defined by reversal, by the negation of the (feminine) other. As Cixous says, 'The paradox of otherness is that, of course, at no moment in History is it tolerated or possible as such. The other is there only to be reappropriated, recaptured, and destroyed as other' (Cixous 1986c: 71). Love of the other within this masculine economy is tantamount to little more than a narcissistic love of the self. It is a kind of love that reflects back on the subject, one that loves only that which returns as profit to the lover. As the dialectic implies, the net effect of the subordination of difference leads to the 'Empire of the Selfsame', and other-regarding love is effectively a contradiction in terms (Cixous 1986c: 78).

Yet, Cixous asks, 'Is the system flawless? Impossible to bypass?' (Cixous 1986c: 78). What might happen to social relations, and indeed to love, if we were to imagine a different economy of exchange, an economy that is not structured by mastery and negation? In 'Sorties' she notes that this masculine 'system', this economy that turns love into a gift-that-takes, is in fact 'already letting something else through' (Cixous 1986c: 78). The very fact that she desires a love in which the 'other is not debased, overshadowed, wiped out' – in other words, mastered – and that she can find this kind of love represented in literature, indicates that the system already leaks (Cixous 1986c: 78). This is all the evidence she needs to begin a journey in pursuit of the conditions of a feminine relation to difference, for she believes this relation forms the foundations of a kind of love in which the other is 'truly' loved: 'I read – now driven by the need to confirm whether or not there is, on the other side of the world, this relationship between beings that alone merits the name of love' (Cixous 1986c: 78).[1]

What then, is the nature of this feminine love that permits the meeting of two equal but different subjects, who instead of feeling threatened by difference, '[delight] to increase through the unknown that is there to discover, to respect, to favour, to cherish' (Cixous 1986c: 78)? Throughout Cixous's œuvre, the answer seems to be consistently: it is divine. A love that escapes the colonising and appropriative grasp of masculine desire, a feminine love that is open to alterity, is also an expression of immanent divinity. Hence, we can extrapolate from the quote with which we began: 'True love for the other, religious without any specific denomination' escapes the problem of reversal that has defined a masculine relation to love, only to the extent that it is informed by a feminine relation to difference. In a feminine relation to the other, to otherness in general, Cixous finds the conditions of a divine love that is open to human possibility.

By tracing some of the conditions of this feminine configuration of love through a selection of moments from one of Cixous's lesser-known books, *The Book of Promethea* (1991a), I want to suggest that a picture emerges that looks uncannily like the Christian notion of agapic love. At its best, agapic love is theo-logically understood as other-regarding, spontaneous and abundant love, but it has always been a profoundly masculine vision.[2] Moreover, orthodox exegetes have historically deemed its achievement a near impossibility, for they identify an essential 'human' (masculine?) self-interest as a sustained and irrepressible obstacle to complete other-regard. Only God is sufficiently selfless to express a divine, unconditional love for the other in the patriarchal tradition of Christian-ity. Yet as we will see, Cixous's configuration of feminine subjectivity seemingly permits of a love that opens this possibility of divinity to human relations, for the feminine subject destabilises the very subject/object binary that traditional agapic love assumes, and that has been used to justify self-sacrifice as a necessary component of other-regard. While Cixous does not invoke the term 'agapic love', and moreover condemns the effects of institutionalised religion (particu-larly for women), 'her compulsive attention to the divine', as Lee Upton puts it, thoroughly informs her reflections on the possibilities of feminine love (Upton 1993: 83). To this extent then, Cixous's work, like that of both Luce Irigaray and Julia Kristeva, can be seen as contributing to contemporary reflections on the relations between religion, divinity and the feminine.

I am not, however, suggesting that the configuration of divine love that is offered by Cixous is in any way an explicit engagement with Christianity per se. Despite Cixous's pluralistic use of sacred references, it is the case that her allusions are far more frequently grounded in the Hebrew Bible rather than in the New Testament. While it is possible to read this as an implicit expression of her own Jewish background, I see no reason not to take seriously her repeated critique of institutional religion. Hence, I see her emphasis on Hebrew narratives in the same way as I see the references she also makes to the figure of Christ: as a continuation of her interest in the effects of patriarchal tales of origins.

Cixous's engagement with origin stories, be they religious or mythic, is best understood with a view to her concern with thinking through the implications of sexual difference, and it is considerably more epistemological than it is ontological. Moreover, through the influence of Jewish thinkers like Emmanuel Levinas and Jacques Derrida, in combination with her own biography, the influence of Judaism undoubtedly informs her thinking about otherness. But her work on love is typically drawn from a vast wellspring of literary allusions, thus making claims about religious affiliation considerably more difficult. It may simply be serendipity that associates Cixous's love with agape. In bringing them together here, I hope to do no more than show that Cixous's work on a feminine subject may offer a suggestive way of re-thinking the problem of self-sacrifice that has plagued the discourses of other-regarding love. Before turning to a consideration of love and divinity in *The Book of Promethea*, however, it is important to have a sense of Cixous's understanding of feminine subjectivity. It is via her theory of the feminine that she offers us the possibility of an other-regarding love that, unlike its theological corollary, agape, is not simultaneously self-sacrificial.

I The subject of love

What does Cixous mean by a feminine relation to love that is open to alterity? In what sense does a feminine relation to the other differ from a masculine one?[3] Cixous's engagement with the concept of the gift in 'Sorties' offers us one possible answer. The gift, like love, implies questions of relationship, just as, historically, it has implied a subject/object dichotomy. There are those who give and those who receive, and Cixous, like Derrida,[4] has been tantalised by the question of whether a gift can be unconditionally given. The issue is ultimately whether the relationship between giver and receiver can ever escape an economy of exchange that inevitably signals debt, an economy that itself is indebted to a subject/object dichotomy. Grounded in a feminist critique of the universal masculine subject that has implicitly dominated the discourses on gift relations, Cixous proposes instead that we think of gift relations in terms of gender. She suggests that we might think of two economies of giving, one masculine and one feminine. From a consideration of these differing relations we can begin to get a sense of what she means by a feminine relation to desire, and hence, a feminine subject of divine love. For the question of the gift that is unconditionally given can be thought of as another face of the question of other-regarding, unconditional love.

Cixous's analysis of the gift begins with Freud's enigmatic and indeed misogynist question, 'What is it that women want?' Refusing his specific question she reconfigures its centre of emphasis and poses to both men and women the question: 'When one gives, what does one give oneself?' (Cixous 1986c: 87). Within the confines of a phallocentric masculinity that is constructed around the fear of still having something to lose – castration anxiety – the question of what 'he' *gives* is clearly defined by what 'he' gets back: profit. What does 'he', the 'traditional' man, want in return? Cixous asks. The answer can only be *more* of the same: '[W]hat he wants, whether on the level of cultural or of personal exchanges, whether it is a question of capital or of affectivity (or of love, of *jouissance*) – is that he gain more masculinity: plus-value of virility, authority, power, money, or pleasure, all of which re-enforce his phallocentric narcissism' (Cixous 1986c: 87). Thus, the masculine gift is inevitably a gift to himself.

While Cixous is willing to concede that a 'free' gift may be illusory, she is reluctant to accept that the masculine relation to 'spending', defined as it is by the laws of return, is the only possible economy of exchange. What remains to be asked, she says, is the how and why of giving that are reflected in 'the values that the gesture of giving affirms, causes to circulate' (Cixous 1986c: 87). What kinds of profit does one draw from the gift, and to what uses are these profits put (Cixous 1986c: 87)? Such questions do not yield the same result for woman as they do for man.

In posing to woman, then, the question of what she gives herself through the gesture of giving, Cixous affirms that there can be no return to self equivalent to that for man. Inasmuch as woman is man's other in phallocentric discourse, woman has a very different relation to her self, to otherness, and to profiting. But, like her male 'counterpart', woman cannot simply escape the phallocentric economic implications of the gift. She too gives *for*. Like man, woman gives herself 'pleasure, happiness, increased value, enhanced self-image' (Cixous 1986c: 87). But, unlike man, woman does not attempt to 'recover her expenses' (Cixous 1986c: 87). In being constituted in opposition to the static unity of man's abstracted self, woman's self is an embodied plurality, always shifting and multiple. 'In place of the bourgeois subject, [Cixous] constructs a multiple being in perpetual metamorphosis' (Conley 1991: 31). In the face of this multiplicity of selves, to which self would woman return? To which self would the woman who 'gives' attribute the recovery of her expenses?

If, as Cixous indicates, woman's self 'doesn't revolve around a sun that is more star than the stars', then woman's self cannot be lived under the static sign of phallic unity (Cixous 1986c: 87). The gesture of giving, and indeed of love, thus becomes an occasion for feminine *becoming*, which is directed towards 'keeping the other alive', rather than masculine *being*, with its implicit affiliation with the death of the other (Cixous 1986c: 79). She alone dares and wants to know from within where she, the one excluded, has never ceased to hear what-comes-before-language reverberating. She lets the other tongue of a thousand tongues speak – the tongue, sound without barrier or death. She refuses life nothing. Her tongue does not hold back but holds forth, does not keep in but keeps on enabling. Where the wonder of being several and turmoil is expressed, she does not protect herself against these unknown feminines; she surprises her-self at seeing, being, pleasuring in her gift of changeability (Cixous 1986c: 88).

Unlike man, the trajectory of woman's subjectivity is oriented towards the future. Without a desire to profit from experience by returning experience to her self, woman literally finds *her/self*, variable and changing, in an endless movement *towards* the other. Thus, as Cixous emphasises, inasmuch as we can speak at all of a self that might be proper to woman, 'it lies in [her] capacity to depropriate herself without self-interest . . .' (Cixous 1986c: 87). But, this willing depropriation is not to be mistaken for either passivity or selflessness.

What is 'depropriated' is not a self that pre-exists the moment of its encounter with another but rather a possessive relation to self that would necessarily order the encounter around a subject/object dichotomy.

> But I am speaking here of femininity as keeping alive the other that is confided to her, that visits her, that she can love as other. The loving to be other, another, without its necessarily going the rout [*sic*] of abasing what is same, herself. As for passivity, in excess, it is partly bound up with death. But there is a nonclosure that is not submission but confidence and comprehension; that is not an opportunity for destruction but for wonderful expansion.
>
> (Cixous 1986c: 86)

For Cixous, it is a mistake to read woman's refusal to be in possession of her self as self-sacrificial. On the contrary, woman's non-possessive relation to subjectivity is the very occasion of her encounter with the other as other, the occasion of wonderful, mutual expansion.

In escaping the reflective grasp of one/self that underpins the 'principles of unity' that have shaped masculine discourses on subjectivity, Cixous's feminine subject reconstitutes the subject/object structure of the gift, and indeed the structure of love, as it has typically been configured in dialectical terms. Hence, she reopens the question of the genuine gift just as she reopens the question of other-regarding love. The multiplicity and fluidity of feminine subjectivity that orients it towards becoming rather than being, forecloses on the inevitability of the return of the gift to one/self for it has already decentred the origin of the gift, the unified subject. Thus, feminine subjectivity opens an intersubjective space of invitation to the other, rather than enacting a gesture of self-assertion, however benevolent. Cixous is aware that 'if there are traces of origin, of the I give, there is no gift – there is an I-give' (Conley 1991: 159). A gift that is pure gift must be like grace; 'it must fall from the sky' in the manner of a blessing (Conley 1991: 159). Throughout the following reading of *The Book of Promethea* (henceforth *Promethea*) we will see that the very possibility of a truly other-regarding love is predicated upon this multiple, plural and feminine relation to one/self. In it, Cixous finds a place for a love that is other-regarding without being self-sacrificial. In it, she finds the humanly, femininely, divine.

II The presence of Promethean love

Located at the interstices of many genres, *Promethea* is simultaneously journal, notebook and diary; autobiography and biography; fiction and non-fiction. It is an unconventional text that attempts the seemingly impossible: to convey in writing a new and passionate love between two women, the narrator and Promethea, in the very immediacy of love's presencing: 'It is a book completely in the present. It began to be written the moment the present began' (Cixous 1991a: 15). And, as is appropriate to Cixous's theoretical concerns with *écriture féminine*, form maps content as she displaces syntactical conventions in favour of a writing that flows from one encounter to the next with few markers of separation. The speculation of *Promethea* revolves around the narrator's struggle to understand the differences between 'love as assertion', captured in the phrase 'I love you', and 'love as invitation', which Cixous identifies as a unique capacity of the 'other woman' of this book, Promethea. In 'love as invitation', Cixous finds a feminine structure of relations that breaks with the conventional subject/object dichotomy and that signals the arrival of Paradise.

As is also typical of Cixous's commitment to working with the 'realities' of human being, *Promethea* refuses to transcend the everyday in its reflection on divinity. For instance, Promethea's simple, almost banal, gesture of arriving with a tray of sandwiches at the precise moment that Cixous has lost herself in the 'hell' of trying to write the present, ushers in the divine as it restores Cixous's shaking confidence in her ability to 'render in writing the infinity that [Promethea] bathes in' (Cixous 1991a: 100). By returning to the everyday, Cixous offers us a conception of divinity and love that is bound to the temporal complexities of human existence. She was indeed in hell before the appearance of the sandwiches, before Promethea's gesture of love enables her to experience the arrival of Paradise in the present.

Paradise in Cixous's work must be understood as a moment within time, rather than a state beyond existence, for she recognises that as human beings, we are beyond Eden.[5] Paradise begins the instant that the self-consciousness of subjectivity is lived differently – specifically, when the subject relinquishes a possessive, masculine relation to itself as the subject of knowledge. But perhaps, and most innovatively, *Promethea* entertains the idea that Paradise is to be found in the present *with* the other, a present that is only possible in the abrogation of self-interested subjectivity.

Throughout this text, Promethea symbolises feminine multiplicity; the subsequent possibilities this affords her with respect to 'living' the immediacy of the present, in the absence of self-interest, are offered as the key to divinity. Hence, Cixous says, 'what makes Promethea so rare is her way of living every day on nature's scale, inside the seething of Creation. Every morning, she throws herself out the window into infinity' (Cixous 1991a: 156). Promethea is all immediacy, all presence, and Cixous is clear that inasmuch as she is able to live the present, she approaches God. Indeed the final words of this book foreclose upon any ambiguity about how we should think of Promethea's relation to presence, love and divinity. In a playful exchange over titling the book, the women propose a number of suggestions ranging from the silly – 'Promethea at the Police Station', 'Promethea on Vacation' – to the suggestive – 'Promethea Reads the Bible'. In the end, Promethea suggests it should be called 'Promethea Falls in Love', and to this suggestion Cixous offers the last words: 'Falls? – Is' (Cixous 1991a: 209). Promethea *is* love; she is synonymous with love, and in the synthesis of Promethea's subjectivity and love we find the echo of agape.

Cixous seems to be suggesting here, and indeed throughout this text, that Promethea's relation to presence is the source of a divine other-regarding love. 'Promethea is the astounding Present given me by God. I am astounded. I accept' (Cixous 1991a: 91). And again, 'Under Promethea's leadership, we have a taste of God' (Cixous 1991a: 185). Through the figure of Promethea, Cixous underscores and develops her thinking on the relationship between presence, divinity and woman's capacity to depropriate herself without self-interest, for Promethea's ability to live 'on nature's scale' derives from her detached, feminine relation to her self. In a play on both the Lacanian pre-symbolic and biblical Eden, Cixous suggests that Promethea is a 'survivor from divine times, unconscious of [herself] in the way the earth is unconscious of itself' (Cixous 1991a: 154). This very unconscious humility with respect to self-possession, rather than to self-consciousness per se, is the source of an abundant, feminine love that does not look to return to itself, but rather permits a genuine meeting with the other. Promethea's 'boundless giving of herself' is anything but the sacrificial gift of self that underpins the orthodox configuration of divine love in Christianity (Cixous 1991a: 152–7). Promethea has nothing to lose. Giving of her self is no more and no less than giving space to the present via a relationship to her self that, in its detachment from singularity, is understood to be multiple and feminine.

As the love between the women in *Promethea* constantly changes, the narrator finds her task of writing the immediate increasingly insurmountable, and she suggests that to continue doing so actually requires the assistance of God. Throughout this book there are innumerable prayers and appeals, made by the author, that underscore the religious dimensions of the text: 'Oh my God, I must want to want to do what I will not succeed in doing; God make me at least strong enough to reach the foot of the mountain and break there, to wash up in pieces at the edge of the sea' (Cixous 1991a: 101). Given the association of Promethea with God/divinity, it is interesting to note that on some occasions the narrator appeals to Promethea for assistance in this difficult task of writing, and on others, she invokes the signifier 'Dieu'. In a moment that reverberates with agapic allusions, and that also demonstrates Cixous's thinking about feminine self-dispossession, she suggests that she is in fact little more than a channel, a scribe for Promethea, who writes through her. The structure mimics agape, which is always attributed to God, even in an exchange between humans. It is never 'we' who are the source of agapic love; rather, inasmuch as it is agapic, it is God's love working through us. '[E]verything that follows has moved through my hand and onto the paper when there was real contact with Promethea. I have often put my left hand between her breasts and with the rapid motions of my docile right hand it was written. I am only that cardiograph' (Cixous 1991a: 53).

Elsewhere Cixous has noted that ultimately 'no one can write without the aid of God', though she speaks not of the patriarchal Gods of Judaism or Christianity (O'Grady 1996: 8). God, she says, is a synonym for that which 'goes beyond us, of our own projection towards the future, towards infinity' (O'Grady 1996: 8). The construction of God here is unmistakably evocative of her construction of feminine subjectivity. In *Promethea*, the Cixousian God is to be found in escaping the fixed identity of a subjectivity constituted in singularity. God, for Cixous, is that which breaks the subject's immersion in the past and gives birth to the future – now.

If the opening pages of *Promethea* are any indication, Cixous is clearly daunted by the paradoxical task of writing the present of loving the other. She dreads so much the violence that singularity imposes both upon herself and, potentially, upon the other, that she hesitates to begin at all, for fear that the very structure of the written logos will inevitably privilege *her* subjectivity. To begin with the first-person narrative voice would be to betray the spirit of the love the author wants to write/convey, a love that is able to encounter and express the otherness of Promethea. To avoid this imposition of her self upon the text, yet to remain none the less in the closest possible proximity to Promethea, Cixous introduces two narrative voices: H and I. Because of the extraordinary nature of this love, Cixous says, that love has already reconfigured her self-identity. She is no longer who she was. She is no longer the same as the author of her previous books, and her former authorial identity could not accomplish this task of writing the present of love. Love and writing are inseparable in Cixous's work: 'Because I write for, I write from, I start writing from: Love. I write out of love. Writing, loving: inseparable. Writing is a gesture of love. *The Gesture*' (Cixous 1991b: 42). To write the present of loving the other, Promethea's mysterious immediacy, 'before memory gets there, before it has begun its embalming and forgetting and storytelling', requires something different on the part of the author; it requires the plurality of a feminine relation to self (1991a: 91).

Cixous's use of two narrative voices simultaneously stages and displaces the dilemma for self/other relations that flow from a unified subject. Yet potentially, those two voices herald the introduction of yet another binary structure. Thus, Cixous extends her commitment to plurality and her opposition to self-possession still further by underscoring Promethea's role in the process of writing:

> I warn her: 'I am writing on you, Promethea, run away, escape. I am afraid to write you, I am going to hurt you!' But rather than run away, she comes at a gallop. Through the window she comes,

breathing hard, and alive as can be, she flings herself into the book, and there are bursts of laughter and splashes of water everywhere, on my notebook, on the table, on my hands, on our bodies.

(Cixous 1991a: 15)

Through Promethea's embodied immediacy in the authorship of the text, Cixous highlights the fact that it is not *hers*, but Promethea's book, at the same time as she underscores the feminine aspect of this moment by emphasising its corporeality. This is the book *of* Promethea, the first of Cixous's works not to be 'her' own. Questions of possession and ownership of the text are subverted in this innovation to literary convention, as Cixous withholds from the author possession and ownership of her self. She is at least two, hence plural, before the arrival of Promethea whose 'soul-scale', she says, so vastly exceeds singularity that she signifies 'a people' (Cixous 1991a: 16). As Susan Sellers notes, Cixous has always considered the need for a 'third term to break the current symbiosis of self/other relations' (Sellers 1996: 58). And in *Promethea*, Cixous is clearly proposing that the disruption to relations lived as discrete binary structures heralds the arrival of a collective, intersubjective subject of the present, which is the arrival of Paradise – the divine.

Through this divided authorial self Cixous broaches one of the most important ethical questions of *Promethea*: Who is the subject of a writing/loving that is of, or with, the beloved, as opposed to on, or from, the beloved? Who is the subject of a writing/loving that escapes the impulse to colonise the other's otherness – since love, as we have known it, cannot be presumed to escape the dialectical legacy of patriarchy? Who, then, is the subject of an enabling love that borders onto the divine? Neither I nor H alone is sufficient for the task; it requires both/ and. Such love invokes the multiplicity of a feminine subject who is schooled in the practices of 'dispossession of one/self', a subject who willingly surrenders a grasping attachment to her own knowledge of knowledge, her knowledge of the other. The goal of Cixous's writing in *Promethea* is to move near enough to feel, to brush surfaces with Promethea, but never to get so close as to inscribe her, never so close as to assume her otherness to her self. Self-dispossession – not the sacrifice of either self or other – is to be understood here as the ethical pre-condition of a divine love of the other that is thoroughly other-regarding.

III The Paradise of presence with the other

Not all that is recognisable as love in *Promethea* is also divine love. Nor is all the love that is expressed, other-regarding. In particular, the author/s, H and I, labour with the question of other-regarding love, as the task of writing the immediacy of love with Promethea forces them to consider a love that escapes binary structures. Unlike Promethea, whose ability to live the 'Present Absolute' has been so thoroughly emphasised, H and I continue to get stuck in identity categories like 'woman'. Such categories appeal to a unity that fixes time, and thus functions to inhibit the ability H and I might otherwise have to experience the present with Promethea. Yet it is clear that the notion of Paradise that this text invokes is one that is ultimately found *with* the other. As Sarah Cornell notes, 'Paradise is living the present, but it is also living the immediate non-deferred happiness of paradise with the other. *The Book of Promethea* is about the discovery of the Promised Land, about the unhoped for encounter with the humanly divine other: Promethea' (Cornell 1988: 131). So, if divinity is Paradise, and Paradise is a meeting with the other that is beyond an opposition between self and other, then Paradise is the moment where self and other are constituted in the very meeting of their differences. But in Cixous's theology of love, we are always temporal beings, made for an 'eternity cut to our size': thus this divine encounter is necessarily a moment (Cixous 1991a: 87).

Cixous notes that love is one thing she thought she knew something about (Cixous 1991a: 104). Indeed, she describes herself as a 'passionate devotee' (Cixous 1991a: 104). But her encounter with Promethea and the difference that Promethea represents – Promethea's 'yes' to life that frees her to *be* in the present – forces Cixous to acknowledge the binary constraints of her previous devotions. She has, she realises, always contented herself with loving (Cixous 1991a: 104). But Promethea insists that if this is truly to be a book of love, Cixous must write that she too is loved. In so doing, Promethea forces Cixous to reflect on the structure of reciprocity, itself a concept that is concerned with the economies of the self/other relation.

Within many discourses of love, reciprocity or mutuality is typically con-figured as occurring when two parties engage in loving each other: 'I love you' evokes an 'I love you, too'. But Promethea's insistence raises for Cixous the more difficult question of receiving love. Giving, she says, 'requires no courage, but to receive love so much strength, so much patience, and so much generosity must be extended' (Cixous 1991a: 105). Why would this be the case? Why would receiving love invoke such hyperbolic description? It seems clear that Cixous is again referring to ways of living subjectivity, namely, to the relational possibilities that a feminine love generates. To receive love requires the willingness to risk moving out of one/self, towards the other. It requires the surrender of one/self, and in Cixous's understanding of feminine subjectivity, as we have seen, such an act amounts to surrendering an attachment to unity, not surrendering self. Loving, on the other hand, makes no such necessary demand upon the self. One can love without being loved. One can love that which cannot return love; Kierkegaard's perfect love in remembrance of the dead is perhaps the most unsettling example (Kierkegaard 1962). But the love relation that is divine for Cixous is one that is predicated on the acceptance of love as well as the gift of love. Only then, she says, 'can love descend upon us the way it wants, in one of its bewitching forms' (Cixous 1991a: 105). Only then will love itself emerge in the intersubjective space of meeting. It seems clear that if one is locked into a notion of subjectivity as singular and unified, the notion of self-dispossession that lies at the heart of Cixous's other-regarding love will raise the spectre of sacrifice and hence of annihilation. But a feminine relation to self recognises dispossession of *one* self, not as sacrifice, but as the continual birth of a new self and/with the other, in the present.

In speaking elsewhere of love, Cixous suggests that '[o]nly when you are lost can love find itself in you without losing its way' (Cixous 1991b: 39). She refers here to specific ways of living subjectivity. Only when one is lost to one/self, can love find itself without losing its way, for only when we are dispossessed of a grasping relation to ourselves, and hence dispossessed of the need always to return to unity, can we possibly encounter the otherness of the other without feeling threatened. Having at the outset taken up the challenge of writing of love in the present, *Promethea*, the 'love' story, has all along been a book of love as 'relinquishment, dispossession and possession' (Cixous 1991a: 136).

By the conclusion of *Promethea*, it seems clear that there are important differences between H, I and Promethea. Promethea's capacity to live a feminine relation to herself, her willingness to immerse herself in the moment, provides a foundation for divinity, but this is not in itself an *experience* of divinity. Not until there is a meeting with the other, not until H and I are able to relinquish their attachment to unity, does love transcend the structure of formal reciprocity. Only when both subjects are simultaneously 'lost to themselves' does love in *Promethea* go beyond the love of binary relations. Only then does the feminine 'fray a passage to the divine' that allows the gift of love to emerge in the intersubjective space of meeting between two different but equal subjects (Cixous 1992: 71).

IV Concluding remarks

The sheer diversity and volume of Cixous's writing have inevitably led to a search for thematic and conceptual continuities. Typically these have been found in her ongoing reflections on the implications of sexual difference for our understanding of subjectivity; her interest in the place of love in social relations; and her critique of patriarchy's affiliation with death and loss, rather than with life and birth. Few commentators have remarked on the extent to which the religious has been her constant 'poetico-philosophical' companion. Yet, from her earliest collection of short stories, *Le Prénom de Dieu* (1967), God or divinity, in one form or another, has found its way into her writing. Indeed, it would be hard to find a Cixousian text that does not in some way refer to the religious, be it via her interest in biblical narratives, her passion for invoking religious concepts like spirit and soul, grace and innocence, or even, as Verena Conley observes, in the 'messianic tone' that she adopts in much of her writing (Conley 1991: 108). However, – unlike, for example, Luce Irigaray – Cixous has not gone the route of suggesting that what women need is a divine conceived in their own likeness.[6] Her commitment to understanding the feminine as a different way of living being, as a different relation to subjectivity, thus displaces the divine from its object form, and permits it to be understood as an aspect of human relations. Cixous's engagement with questions of religion and sexual difference remains one of the most suggestive areas of her work that clearly calls for extended consideration.

Notes

1   Cixous's use of the term *écriture féminine*, writing that is of the feminine, derives from her observation that a few remarkable authors have been able to express, rather than suppress, difference and otherness in their texts. The bulk of her examples are male authors, again underscoring her assertion that masculinity and femininity are not determined by morphology.

2   A thorough engagement with the concept of agape is beyond the scope of this project. Suffice it to say, for many theologians it is one of the defining features of Christianity as a religion of love. However, the 1930s work of two Protestant theologians, Anders Nygren and Reinhold Niebuhr, understood agape as essentially hostile to the self. As a corrective to what they took to be humanity's essential narcissism, Nygren and Niebuhr focused on the Second Commandment concerning neighbour love as a justification for their assertion of a radical form of self-sacrifice as normative in relations of other-regard. Yet, as many feminist theologians have noted, the Christian insistence on selflessness has been especially problematic for women who have routinely been excluded from the benefits of a positively constituted subjectivity. Thus, without consider-able reinterpretation, agape has not been taken up as an ideal of love in much of the work in feminist theology. (On orthodox agape see Nygren [1982(1938)] and Niebuhr [1932]. See also Gene Outka [1972] and Colin Grant [1996], for contemporary engagements. On feminist critiques, see, for example, Valerie Saiving Goldstein [1979], Margaret Farley [1975], Rosemary Radford Ruether [1983], Carter Heyward [1982] and Anne Bathurst Gilson [1995].)

3   Cixous's use of the terms 'masculine' and 'feminine', 'woman' and 'man', has been subjected to considerable critique by Anglo-American feminist scholars who have been concerned with the possibility of an underlying

commitment to essentialism. Cixous has responded to this assertion on numerous occasions by rejecting any pre-discursive implication in her work, and she does so very explicitly in 'Sorties' (Cixous 1986c: 81).

4   See Jacques Derrida (1992) and (1995).

5   Cixous's essay 'Grace and Innocence' (1992) deals extensively with the question of Paradise. In it she proposes the conditions of a 'second innocence' that she understands to be humanly possible, as opposed to the first and impossible innocence of Eden. There are many parallels between her concerns in 'Grace and Innocence' and her concerns in *Promethea* as she offers a different way of living knowledge, as the condition of a second innocence. We have to know 'how not to know', she says, how not to possess what we already have.

6   See Irigaray (1993c) and (1991).

Chapter 12

Charlotte A. Berkowitz

PARADISE RECONSIDERED
Hélène Cixous and the Bible's Other Voice

And . . . God made a deep sleep fall on the *adam* and . . . God constructed . . . a woman.

(Genesis 2: 22–3)

What we hope for at the School of Dreams is the strength . . . to look straight at the face of God, *which is none other than my own face*, but seen naked, the face of my soul. The face of 'God' is the unveiling, the staggering vision of the construction we are. . . . An unveiling that happens by surprise, by accident, and with a brutality that shatters: under the blow of the truth, the eggshell breaks. Right in the middle of life's path: the apocalypse; we lose a life.

(Cixous 1993: 63)

FOR HÉLÈNE CIXOUS, as for the practitioners of conventional Western religion, God embodies the sacred. But in Cixous's lexicon, God is not the Father. For, in the psychoanalytic terms that ground Cixousian theory, the function of the father is to facilitate the child's acquisition of linguistic identity via separation from the mother. This separation represses the child's prelinguistic bodily recorded experience of interconnection with the mother and, through her, with all life. Cixous finds holiness in precisely this experience, a felt knowledge of what it means to be 'human', not only a subject of the separating Law of the Father, but also a creature of the soil (humus), one with all the life of the earth (Cixous 1993: 41, 38–9, 156). Poetic language can recall this repressed knowledge, for, like dreams, poetic language exceeds the laws of grammar, gender, time and place (inside-outside) that reciprocally uphold Paternal Law (1991b: 148). Because of the capacity of poetic writing to overcome the divisions of the Law, Cixous has been moved to call such writing 'Other-Love' and 'God' (1986c: 99; 1991b: 11, 23).

Cixous was born just prior to the outbreak of the Second World War to a Jewish family living in French-occupied Algeria. As a female she was an outsider to the Law that governed her own tradition; as a female and a foreigner, a 'Jewoman', she experienced a double invisibility in the eyes of the Christian French, who ruled Algeria at the time (1986c: 70, 101; 1991b: 11–12). But in work on poetic texts and in the research seminars on poetic texts that Cixous conducted throughout the 1980s and 1990s at the University of Paris VIII, she traded the double disenfranchisement of her formative years for citizenship in an alternative 'country'. In a 1986 interview, she explains that the borders of this country are fluid, 'a country on the side of freedom, where we talk from one language to another, from one civilisation to another, from one memory to another' (Sellers 1988: 142). In such a 'country' Cixous finds the potential for an alternative 'religion'. For, if religion is etymologically a means of 'binding', then the collective search for meaning within poetically written texts is 'a religion of thinking' that exceeds the Law. Such thinking binds one to another while 'keep[ing] alive . . . the beauty . . . and mystery . . . of the thing most subject to obliteration', 'the thing' that is otherwise 'lost in the uproar of our daily life' (Sellers 1988: 142).

Cixous finds evidence of the human reality that is this lost 'thing' not only in certain modernist and contemporary texts, but also in the texts of antiquity, Mesopotamian stories, Greek plays and the Bible. Although she disdains those parts of the Bible that represent Paternal Law, Cixous is drawn to biblical stories, especially to stories from the Torah, the first five books of the Bible (Cixous 1986c: 73; 1993: 117). In the condensed language of these stories, as in the fluidity with which they treat time, place and character, Cixous finds a narrative mode subversively near to dream, that is, to the unconscious which preserves the memory of time before the Law (1993: 67). An instance of such discovery occurs in her brief but brilliantly revolutionary reading of Genesis 3, the scene in which the Bible's first woman transgresses the Law to eat of the forbidden fruit of 'the tree of knowledge of good and evil'. In what follows immediately, I will summarise and discuss this analysis, which opens new paths to human self-knowledge through the biblical story. Then I will explore some of those paths from a vantage provided by Cixous's work. This exploration will enable the Torah to be seen as a place in writing where, in an era which acknowledges the exhaustion of the Law, the paternally oriented religious cultures that the Torah has been influential in shaping according to the Law can recuperate the knowledge repressed with the (m)other and so begin anew.

For Cixous, for whom reading is (like) writing – a therapeutic and liberating exchange with the other (1986c: 86; 1993: 21, 38–9) – the alterity of the biblical text 'astonishingly' emerges in the Edenic scene of female transgression to provide a moment of profound revelation. Here the Bible can be seen both to expose the meaninglessness of 'the word of the Law' and also to illuminate the way to recover the knowledge that the Law forbids. Cixous explains the first of these insights in terms of common logic: the meaninglessness of the Law is revealed in the incomprehensibility of the prohibition of the fruit. God forbids the 'apple' on pain of death (1991b: 151).[1] But '[f]or Eve, [the threat] "you will die" means nothing, since she is in the paradisiacal state where there is no death'. The only power of the Law here, Cixous observes, as she has observed elsewhere of God Himself, is 'in its invisibility, its force of denial, its "not"' (1986c: 101–2; 1991b: 151). However, opposed to this absence is the concrete reality of the object of the woman's desire for knowledge. It is not the Law but the 'apple' that *is*, and the 'apple' is 'good' (1991b: 151).

If the application of everyday logic to the biblical story overturns the binary opposition (paternal presence/maternal absence) that mutually maintains the Law, the logic of dream discovers in acting on the impulses of woman's desire the way to effect that overturning. This (other) logic recognises, condensed in the woman's eating and sharing the fruit, a metaphor for 'the genesis of "femininity" [which] goes by way of the mouth', by way of a 'taste' for the self-knowledge internalised with the maternal breast (1991b: 151–2). For the 'apple' has an inside, and in stating that Eve eats of the 'apple', Cixous observes, 'our oldest book of dreams relates to us in its cryptic mode that Eve is not afraid of the inside, neither of her own nor of the other's' (1991b: 152). Indeed, Eve can be said to demonstrate the courage of an artist, a willingness 'to lose oneself' in experiencing 'a certain oral' and specifically 'feminine' pleasure (1991b: 120–1, 151–2).

Such pleasure (feminine jouissance) will guide the reading that follows below. Before beginning this reading it will be helpful to recall several facts about the Torah, and about the way that it is written, which offer departure points for such an approach. The first of these facts is that while the Hebrew[2] word *torah* tends to be translated 'Law' and, like the God who is its author, to be associated with an Oedipal economy of separation, *torah*, in etymological fact, does not mean Law, but 'teaching'. A feminine noun, *torah* is derived from the root *yarah*, to 'cast', to 'shoot', hence, to 'point out', to 'guide', to 'teach' (Klein 1987: 264). (I do not mean unduly to exploit the femininity of the word *torah*. On the contrary, this reading will demonstrate that the Torah teaches the way to overcome the gender divisions that plague [us in] language.) The second fact that needs to be recalled is that religious tradition allies the Torah with the female via an association with the book of Proverbs's female figure of Wisdom. Many scholars recognise in Wisdom the vestige of an ancient Canaanite goddess, Asherah, 'In Wisdom Mother of the gods' and their wet-nurse (Patai 1967: 37; Bickerman 1962: 64).[3]

The liturgy of the Torah service limns the Torah in words that the book of Proverbs applies to Wisdom: 'She is a tree of life. Her ways are ways of pleasantness and all her paths are peace' (*shalom*, wholeness) (Proverbs 3:18, 17). But – and this is the third fact that needs to be emphasised – this ascription of wholeness notwithstanding, the narrative of the Torah is, as Cixous has observed, 'cryptic', 'dream'-like. It is riddled with interruption, word- and sound-play, repetition, ambiguity and ellipsis. Ambiguity and ellipsis are heightened by the mode of writing prescribed by Jewish religious law for Torah scrolls. Namely, in order to be legitimate (*kosher*), a Torah scroll must be devoid of both vowels and punctuation. These graphic absences, like the gaps in the narrative, historically have been understood as insurance that the Torah will remain open to interpretation throughout time, silent places that provide room for an ongoing, world-renewing 'dialogue with God' (Boyarin 1990: 15; Faur 1986: 116–17). However, just as the femininity of the Torah has long been defined in the terms of the Law,[4] this dialogue until very recently has taken place almost exclusively between men, in a Father–son line of communication.

As Cixous's analysis of the meal in the garden suggests, the (mono)logic of that line is inadequate to read the Torah's narrative, whose fractured and tortuous surface, once treated by the framers of the documentary hypothesis as a 'patchwork' of sources, more recently has been recognised by literary scholars as a supple and sophisticated art form, a self-reflexive 'labyrinth' (Alter 1981: 21, 27, 157, 158). For Cixous, it is precisely such a labyrinthine structure that makes a written work a 'text', a 'weaving' in which the reader is implicated with/as the writer. For a labyrinth grants 'access to the passage, to the *trans*, to the crossing of borders, to the de-limitation of genuses-genders-genres and species, to construction and deconstruction, to metamorphosis' (Cixous 1998: 105). Hence, as Wendy Faris observes in a work on modernist labyrinthine texts, even when, as in the Daedalus myth, labyrinths are of the 'sky-father's' making, they tend ultimately to recall the realm of the 'earth mother' – 'the fertile, all-conceiving realm of undifferentiated wholeness, of female desire' (Faris 1988: 6–7). As we shall now see, the nature of the Torah's narrative is such that, when the reader is so inclined, it can facilitate passage(s) to this repressed realm. Here the identity of God and humanity can be endlessly reconceived in the course of an exchange with the (m)other.

Mindful of the difference of the Hebrew text from its many translations, I will begin my passage by exploring the scene in Eden where God 'builds' or 'constructs' the woman whose actions Cixous has analysed in terms of female desire, as discussed above. This exploration, like the remainder of this chapter, will suggest that the woman is not only a character in the story but also a figure for the text (authored by God). Consonant with Cixous's ongoing meditation on the capacity of poetic language to transform human identity by calling into question the self constructed according to the Law (1986c: 86; 1993: 63), what follows next will demonstrate that this woman/text calls for such a deconstructive and (self-)transformative analysis. The woman is 'constructed' upon a body part called a *tzela*, a 'rib' or, in an equally valid translation, a 'side', which is taken from a creature whom God has sent for the occasion into a 'deep sleep' (Genesis 2:21–2).[5] This creature, like the human creatures of Genesis 1, is called an *adam*, a name that signifies both the individual 'human being' and the collective 'humanity'.[6] Just as etymology allies the English 'human' with humus, soil, Hebrew etymology affiliates *adam* with *adamah*, the earthen ground or soil whose 'dust' the narrative says is both the *adam*'s origin and the (non-)matter to which the *adam* is destined to return (Genesis 2:9, 3:19). But, when the *adam* receives and names the newly constructed woman, the *adam* linguistically breaks the human connection with the earth to identify 'himself' in a term new to the narrative: 'This now shall be called *ishah*, woman, for from *ish*, *man*, she was taken' (Genesis 2:23).

In this naming speech, with its narcissistic assumption 'that woman is created out of [man's] body', Ilana Pardes, a feminist biblical scholar, has remarked upon a 'dream-like reversal of the [natural] order of things' (Pardes 1992: 47–8). Pardes's observation that the *adam* expresses 'himself' as one in a dream, like Cixous's reading the Torah as a 'book of dreams', gains credibility from the narrative, which nowhere states that the *adam* awakens from the 'deep sleep'. This narrative silence, I would suggest, permits the reader to choose to under-stand the story as a dream. To make such a choice is to agree to be transported from the hierarchically ordered realm of the Law into the 'borderless' realm of the unconscious and, in Cixous's terms, to perform the 'work of love' that translates an other system of (self-)representation to language, to logic (Cixous 1986c: 98; Sellers 1988: 146).[7]

In Cixous's analysis the logic of dream reveals in Eve's eating the fruit a meta-phor for acting on female desire. Now this logic reveals in the *adam*'s reversal of bodily reality a 'distortion' of the self that refuses that desire, a 'dissimulation' by which the ego of the dreamer defends against what it fears to know (Freud 1965: 174–5). Given that the *adam*'s nominal break with the earth occurs in the same breath with 'his' reversal of bodily reality, the latter would seem to conceal a fear not only of the creative power of woman's body but also of (the human origin in) the earth. In Cixous's terms, both these fears signal fear of 'death', for it is death more than life that the subject of the Law sees in woman's ('castrated') body and in the (life-receiving as well as -giving) earth (Cixous 1986c: 69, 80, 109–10). But this Oedipal fear of death and its concomitant self-distortion can be overcome by continuing to approach the text from the position of artistic cour-age and openness to the other that Cixous identifies with the feminine and with 'life' (Sellers 1988: 7; Cixous 1986c: 79, 86; 1991b: 36–41; 1993: 113). In what follows below, the woman/text constructed by God facilitates the artistic pro-cess that Cixous defines in terms of 'crossing over borders', 'dying' to the self constructed as 'separate' under the Law and 'reintegrating the earth' (1993: 130–1, 150–1). Undergoing this process pays 'the life debt' (to the mother) and so restores the creative 'side' of the human being that is 'woman': the side that knows the eternal human interconnection with all life (1986c: 103; 1993: 151–6).[8]

Like dreams, where identities decompose and transmute into new forms, the earth is a 'school' where we learn that our roots are in an order of things that contradicts the Law (Cixous 1993: 118–19, 151–6). Given the circumstances of her 'construction', the woman in Eden may well be affiliated with such a counter-order, for she is the fulfilment of a promise made prior to the deep sleep of the *adam*. This promise is made by God when, observing that 'it is not good for the *adam* to be alone', God determines to make for the *adam* an *ezer k'negdo* (Genesis 2:18). Translated in the King James Version of the Bible as 'an help meet' for the *adam*, that is, a 'befitting' helper, the phrase *ezer k'negdo* requires careful (re)consideration. While the noun *ezer* means 'help' or 'helper', the modifying *neged* (in *k'negdo*) suggests 'fitness' in terms of both 'correspondence' and 'opposition', 'contradiction', 'resistance'.[9] Therefore, we may anticipate in the 'resistant helper' one who will alleviate the *adam*'s solitary condition not by echoing the separating message of the Law, but by speaking in 'a different voice'.

The woman's voice would seem to be condemned when God speaks to the *adam* of the consequences of eating/consuming the fruit. God says, 'Because you listened to the voice of your woman [*ishah*] . . . the ground [*adamah*] is cursed. . . . In suffering you will eat of it all the days of your life . . . until you return to the ground from which you were taken, for you are dust, and to dust you will return' (Genesis 3:17–19). Given that the Hebrew phrase 'listen to the voice' means also 'obey', it is easy to understand God's speech here in terms of the Law, which privileges with paternal presence paternal voice and authority while condemning woman to the role of obedient, silent partner to man (Cixous 1986c: 79–80). However, continuing to read from the perspective of dream – which subverts, along with the Law, such hierarchical constructions of human identity – exonerates the woman and enables the reader to hear the curse and the death sentence recast in terms consonant with Cixous's life-renewing 'return to earth'.

It seems fair to state that readers of the Bible are accustomed to hearing anger and even misogyny in the voice in which, in the speech quoted above, God allies the voice of the woman with cursed ground and death. But the feminine reading position defined by Cixous involves an intense and specifically aural attention to the text (Sellers 1988: 7). By daring, with Eve's courage for a model, to cross the barrier imposed by God's angry voice and to 'listen' closely to the text, the reader may hear a nuance that inspires reflection upon the source of this misogynistic anger. This nuance is in the pronominal inflection 'your' with which, when speaking to the *adam*, God identifies the woman whose voice brings the curse and the death sentence (Genesis 3:17). This identification suggests not only that God does not hold culpable the generic 'woman's voice', but also that, although God has constructed her, God disidentifies with the woman whose voice brings death.

She is now the *adam*'s possession. This is so not only because she is God's gift to the *adam*, but also because of the power that God has earlier granted the *adam*: the power of naming. The preceding has shown in the moment when the *adam* breaks with the earth to name the woman as 'his' issue and to rename 'himself' 'man', the moment that the narrative calls into question 'his' knowledge of human identity, 'his' fitness to name. The scene that next comes under consideration will continue this critique. This time the question of identity is posed in the context of voice, and the reader is implicated with/as the *adam* who, knowing only the woman(/text) whom 'he' has identified and confined within the framework of Oedipal understanding, cannot adequately hear her voice nor/in the voice of God.

The scene in which this question arises occurs when, following the couple's eating the fruit, their 'eyes . . . were opened and they knew that they were naked' (Genesis 3:7). After covering themselves, they hear the *kol*, the 'sound' or 'voice' of God, and they hide from God among the trees of the garden, or, in a literal if awkward translation, 'in the middle of (a) tree of the garden' (Genesis 3:7).[10] God 'calls' to the *adam*, asking, 'Where are you?' But the *adam* does not respond in terms of this location. 'He' replies only that, having heard God's voice, 'I was afraid because I am naked, and I hid' (Genesis 3:9–10). In other words, the *adam* knows 'his' position, 'his' place in the world (of the garden), only in relation to God's voice. Like 'his' relation with the side of 'himself' that is woman and with the ground of his origin, this relation is a fearful one. Therefore, just as earlier 'he' hides behind the dissimulating mask of reversal from the 'naked truth' of that relation, now 'he' hides his 'nakedness' from a God whose voice, as the following will show, 'sounds' in consonance with the reader's position vis-à-vis the (m)other.

The tenability of this thesis may begin to be established with a reconsideration of the moment when God responds to the *adam*'s reply, 'I was afraid because I knew I am naked', by posing two questions: '*Mi higid l'kha?*' – 'Who told you?', or, in an equally valid translation, 'Who related?' or 'Who narrated to you [that] you are naked?' – 'From the tree I commanded you excepting your eating from it, have you eaten?' The *adam* insists on God's responsibility for the woman, while responding to these questions as one, 'The woman that you gave me . . . she gave me from the tree and I ate' (Genesis 3:10–12). According to the terms of the Law, the *adam*'s shifty answer constitutes an admission of guilt. Thanks to the 'evil' deed of the woman, 'he' has eaten from the forbidden tree, and having thus broken the Father's Law, 'he' must die.

But to read a story as a dream is to recall Freud's famous pronouncement that in the unconscious, there is never a 'no'. Nor, as Cixous reminds us in a passage quoted earlier above, does death exist in the deepest layer of the unconscious, from which dreams arise. Close reconsideration of this moment when God questions the *adam* about why 'he' has hidden will now discover that the 'no' and the death sentence spoken in the loud Paternal voice may cover a countering life-oriented (m)other's 'yes'. God asks, 'Who told/narrated to you that you are naked? From the tree I commanded you excepting your eating from it, have you eaten?' I think it is fair to say that conventional biblical reading considers these simply rhetorical questions, which, like the curse and the death sentence, are spoken in a Father's loudly angry voice. But the work of reading as described by Cixous encourages recognising in such a voice a means by which a text mimes the *resistance* of the earth by refusing easy assignments of meaning, while 'calling' upon the reader to descend ever deeper within (Cixous 1993: 5–6). Responding to such a call in the biblical story discovers in God's questions a stunning feat of condensation and displacement. This delicate compression and exchange of terms is coupled with an inquiry into the source(s) of 'man's' self-knowledge. And this inquiry by God can be heard in the hushed voice of the (m)other. Cixous calls this voice the 'equivoice', whose Oedipally invisible written manifestation is the 'white ink' in which poetic language recalls the experience of 'eternity' that a child ingests with its mother's milk (Cixous 1986c: 93–94).[11]

God questions the source of the *adam*'s knowledge of 'his' nakedness. The narrative states that the *adam* knows his nakedness via vision: 'Their eyes were opened and they knew that they were naked.' Yet God does not invoke vision but 'telling', 'relation', 'narration'. Hence, God can be seen delicately to raise the issue of narrative voice, the voice of the text. Blurring the borders between aural and oral ingestion, God translates hearing this voice, which imparts self-knowledge (nakedness), to the act of eating from a tree. In other words, God may be said to ask these questions in what Cixous calls the 'fundamental language', the (m)other tongue, which recalls a time before vision gains priority over the other senses, the time(lessness) of interconnection at the maternal breast (Cixous 1991b: 52). And surely when reading is understood as (self-)questioning, 'letting oneself be read by the text' (Sellers 1988: 147; Cixous 1986c: 86), God's questions here are addressed to the reader as well, the human being who may recognise that via the eyes (s)he is a participant in the textual dream, implicated in hearing and producing its voice(s).

God's questions are posed in language that recalls the bodily recorded knowledge of the Oedipally concealed (inter-)relation with the mother and all life. This is the knowledge the *adam* lacks, who consequently hides from 'himself' behind the distorting mask of reversal as later, with 'his' woman, 'he' hides from God 'in the centre of a tree of the garden' (*b'tokh etz ha-gan*), where 'he' positions himself in a fearful relation to God's voice. The *adam* is banished, or 'dispossessed' (*garash*), of Eden and the tree of life at its centre (*etz ha-khaim b'tokh ha-gan*) for listening to the voice of the woman he has come to possess within the framework of Oedipal identity. This woman tells him his 'nakedness' by feeding him from a tree that is assumed to be the forbidden 'tree of knowledge of good and bad'. But what follows will demonstrate that the text can be seen to question this assumption and in so doing to provide a ground on which to change the relation of human beings (*adam*) to themselves as well as God.

Participating in this change reveals that, like the tree that hides the *adam* and his woman at its centre, this tree too is a figure for both the text and the reading subject, whose Oedipally hidden centre is everywhere and is capable of both posing and responding to the question of identity in terms of the relation with the (m)other. Discovering the presence of this omnipresent centre through the process of the reading exchange calms the anger that has tended to be heard in the voice of God. For, as Cixous's work suggests, that anger is the projected Fury of a concealed subject, who, having sacrificed its (m)other to the Law, lacks a source of human self-knowledge, of human self-representation (1986c: 103–12).

Venerable tradition recognises as the Law the teaching (*torah*) in which this reading discovers such a source. But the same tradition allies this teaching with female Wisdom, 'a tree of life'.[12] The biblical tree of life is located at the centre of the garden of Eden (delight, delicacy, exquisiteness). The tree that is forbidden to the *adam* prior to the woman's construction is called 'the tree of knowledge of good and evil' (Genesis 2:17). But when the woman speaks of the tree that she finds desirable she calls it only 'the tree that is in the centre of the garden' (Genesis 3:3). In Genesis 2:9 the narrative states that God 'made spring from the ground every tree pleasing to the sight and good to eat and the tree of life in the centre of the garden and the tree of knowledge of good and evil'. By blurring the border between the two trees, like the woman's description of the tree whose fruit she desires, this description poses questions.

Do two trees occupy the centre of the garden? Does the tree of life stand alone at the centre, separate from the tree of knowledge of good and evil? Or, in keeping with the logic of dreams, a logic which displaces desire into each dream figure, are the Edenic trees not only separate but also at some level one, like nature's trees whose roots begin in the processing earth? And if these trees are one, do not both figure the text, which, like the human subject, not only is made of separating Paternal Law (socially constructed knowledge of good and evil) but also contains the profound knowledge of eternal interconnection (life)? What tree/text/vision of her human self is this that the woman sees, which promises to gratify her desire and from which she eats and feeds the *adam*, who does not know his connection with the ground (*adamah*)? Or, in another version of the same question, what desiring woman is this who sees the tree?

From Cixous's perspective, the meaning of a text is grounded in the desire, which is to say the desiring body, of the reader-writer (Cixous 1993: 6). Is it not possible then that, like the trees that grow from the ground, the ground itself here figures the desiring, mediating body of the reading-writing subject as well as the woman/text, who mediates the *adam*'s self-knowledge when she tells him his nakedness by feeding him from the tree? Perhaps the *adam*'s linguistic divorce from his human roots is foretold in his origin in the 'dust' of the ground. For if the ground figures the desiring body of the reader and the text, then dust figures the most superficial layer of that body, (desire for) the unmediated Law. The curse on the ground renders the latter so unyielding as to make painful work of earning bread until the *adam*'s return to dust (Genesis 3:18–19). Could this curse not be a consequence of listening to the voice of the woman/text, which tradition allies with 'the tree of life', with ears that can hear only the words of the Law, as figured by 'the tree of knowledge of good and evil'? With no access to the deeper bodily ground in which the Law is rooted its cultural subjects are doomed to die. Consumed by the very consumability of the Law that attempts like the breast to sustain, such subjects painfully work increasingly barren (a-)textual ground for 'bread' that, like the fruit of the tree, can provide self-knowledge. The voice of the woman to which Cixous's work encourages and provides ways to listen guides the reader to richer (bodily) ground, ending the curse while returning to the dust of superficial reading any notion that the human is a monological being, 'man'.

When the *adam* who calls himself 'man' is banished from Eden for listening to the voice of 'his' woman and eating from the forbidden tree, the way to the biblical tree of life is barred (Genesis 3:24). But, as the preceding suggests, the story in which this occurs is one in which the reader not only encounters the resistance of barriers, but is also enabled by these encounters to discover that barriers can be rendered permeable, that one can be one and also the other. Without access to the permeability of our borders, 'mankind', like the *adam* to counter whose solitary state God constructs the woman, is 'alone'. Indeed, in the first instance of negative judgement in the Bible, God, as we have seen, deems this aloneness 'not good'. But if it is not good for the *adam* to be alone, then when God sends the *adam* away from Eden 'lest he stretch forth his hand and take from the tree of life', God participates in this 'not goodness' by perpetuating the *adam*'s aloneness.

Or so the verses that treat the banishment would seem to suggest. For, although the narrative states that God made garments for both 'the *adam* and his woman' and clothed 'them', God's following rumination on the fate of the *adam* is couched in the singular: 'See, the *adam* has become like one of us, knowing good and bad, and perhaps now he will stretch forth his hand and take also from the tree of life and eat/consume and live for ever.' So God sends the *adam* away 'to work the ground from which he was taken'. Then God places barriers 'to keep the way to the tree of life' (Genesis 3:21–4).

Although Eve will reappear after Eden, there is, then, a sense in which the *adam* is alone when he goes forth from the garden, where, with the tree of life, the woman remains off-limits (Bal 1987: 114). In the narrative silence about the woman's accompanying the *adam* from Eden, there is room to see that whether or not the *adam* leaves Eden with the woman he has construed according to the Law, he leaves Eden alone because he lacks a (m)other, a balancing other. If the *adam* should stretch forth his hand and take from the tree of life/text, he would replicate the act of eating from the hand of the Oedipally construed woman because he would understand what he ingested only in terms of the Law. He would indeed consume the text. But, unrecognised, this 'woman' is present in the text as in the reader, and 'she' can be fruitfully re-cognised through the work that leads through the barriers that prevent access to the (m)other side of the self. By discovering the (m)other in the text that 'God' has written, we discover the goodness (connection) of God in ourselves. Thus, we discover a source of ethics, of laws governing human relations, that is grounded in the infinite love of the (m)other.

Paradise, Cixous writes, is 'not given' but 'down below', accessible via the humanising work of 'unburying' that is (reading-)writing (1993: 6). To bring this potentially endless reading to a close, we will now leave the paradise that is barred to the Oedipal *adam* to go to a place in the Bible that reveals that Eden is never lost but is potentially everywhere, hidden within. Here, unlike the *adam* who must work cursed ground, Moses, to whom God is later said to have dictated the Torah, stands on ground that God calls 'holy'. On this ground Moses asks and is told God's name (Exodus 3:5, 13–14). This experience begins when Moses sees a 'messenger' of God in 'a flame of fire' that emanates 'from the centre of [*mitokh*] the . . . bush that burned . . . unconsumed' (Exodus 3:2). 'Seeing that [Moses] turned aside to see' this sight, God calls to Moses and tells him to lead the children of Israel to 'a good and large land . . . flowing with milk and honey' (Exodus 3:8). Moses responds with two questions. The first question is, '*Who am I* to go to Pharaoh and to lead the children of Israel out of Egypt?' The second question may be summarised as follows: 'When the children of Israel ask me the name of God, what shall I say?' (Exodus 3:11, 13).

The first question tends historically to be dismissed as merely an indication of Moses' modesty, while the response to the second is apotheosised. This response is: 'Thus shall you say to the children of Israel, I will be what I will be. . . . This is my name . . . forever. . . . I will be' (Exodus 3:14–15). If this scene takes place in waking reality, then, like the prohibition in Eden perceived within the context of the Law, God's answer is meaningless, an insoluble mystery encountered on the exclusionary linear path of masculine 'sacred writing' (Cixous 1991b: 14–15). But, like Moses on seeing the burning bush, the logic that has guided this reading until now 'turns aside' from such linearity to discover a different 'sacred (ground of) writing'. Positioned on this ground, one can discover encapsulated in the 'I will be' a response to Moses' two questions understood as one, a reciprocal question of identity ('who-you-me?') such as characterises Cixous's work (1998: 14). This 'I will be' is not the easily heard boast of an unchanging (dead) Father, but the whispered 'I-who-am-you' of a (living) presence unknowingly ingested with the woman/teaching recognised only as the embodiment of the Law but which is capable of endless transformation with(in) the subject reconceived through the textual exchange.

The 'song' of the (m)other resonates throughout poetic writing to tell a story of likeness that keeps difference alive (Cixous 1986c: 93). An instance of such resonance at the burning bush serves momentarily to bring together Adam, and hence the reader, with Moses, who with God is the co-author of the text. This brief moment of synthesis occurs when, like the *adam* who fearfully hides from himself and from the God whose voice he fears, Moses responds to God's presence by hiding his face, 'afraid' to look at God (Exodus 3:6). The teaching that its readers, like Moses, write 'from the mouth of God', uncovers our faces with that which (in the Name of the Father) we fear. In Exodus 3 such an uncovering can again occur when one sees that the messenger of God appears to Moses *b'labat-esh* – in a 'flame', which can also be read as a 'heart' of fire. This flame is contained at the 'midst/centre' of not simply '*a* bush', as translations tend to render it, but '*the* thorn-bush, which burned . . . and was not consumed' (Exodus 3:2). For one who quest(ion)s for self-knowledge, the image of a heart of fire enclosed in thorny branches can suggest that the voice from the burning bush speaks (and the eye of the god sees) from the internal position of the (m)other. There the heart of the text beats the rhythm of its story, the human self-knowledge which is love and which, as the bordering thorns suggest, is painfully inaccessible (Cixous 1998: 16; 1993: 85). The potential for the work to ease this pain depends on the reader's being able to recognise a play of identity and difference in the image of the bush burning unconsumed, with the heart of flame barricaded at its centre, and the image of the tree of life in the centre of the garden of Eden, which is guarded by flame *against* being consumed. Blurring the border between the two, which are structurally alike and yet different in appearance, this echo subtly links the burning bush with the tree of life/text. The link suggests that the text, too, is *de*-centred and that it is not only difficult to access but implicated in revealing the name according to an other logic of meaning, an uncanny logic that exceeds the limits of Paternal ('phallocentric') discourse. This logic, as the preceding reading has attempted to demonstrate, is the key that reciprocally unlocks the gate to the knowledge of eternal interconnection represented by the tree of life. This is the paradise Cixous's work facilitates finding: the internal 'good and large land flowing with milk and honey' (Exodus 3:8).

Notes

1   The apple, in fact, does not exist in the biblical narrative, which names only the 'fruit' of the Edenic tree.

2   In order to transliterate Hebrew words accessibly, I have followed such scholars as Susan Handelman and Michael Fishbane in avoiding the International Phonetic Alphabet, whose symbols can confuse those unfamiliar with it.

188 CHARLOTTE A. BERKOWITZ

3   See also Rich, who cites work by Otto Rank and Theodore Reik that recognises in the Torah vestiges of 'the primal female goddess' (1979: 75). Also, Gadon provides an extensive discussion of Asherah's embodiment of the nurturing qualities of the primal goddess (1989: 167–88).

4   As Tikva Frymer-Kensky points out, Rabbinic Judaism's identification of the Torah with the feminine 'made sacred study a search for woman' (1992: 182).

5   In Exodus 25 and 26, for example, *tzela* denotes a 'side' of the ark of the covenant and of the tabernacle.

6   All Hebrew nouns are gendered masculine or feminine. The neutral noun *adam*, 'human', is masculine; therefore masculine pronouns are used to refer to *adam*. However, the textual work reveals that '*adam*' need not be thought solely in masculine terms. Therefore, when referring to the *adam* of the early Eden story, I enclose masculine pronouns in quotation marks. As the story moves on, we see that the *adam* seems to have 'his' way. In Genesis 3:6 and 3:16 the narrative calls 'him' not, as it otherwise does, *adam*, but the woman's *ish*, man/husband (a title whose status the text continually questions). Therefore, as this reading proceeds, I cease using the quotation marks.

7   Because reading recognises and attempts to preserve the difference of the other, Cixous compares work on poetic texts with 'the work of love that can take place between two human beings' (Sellers 1988: 146).

8   By 'woman' I do not mean to imply an essence common to all women. Rather, I am attempting, in Cixous's terms as I understand them, to name the repressed, permeable side of the human subject, which knows itself one, through the mother, with all life.

9   Permutations of *neged* occupy nearly three columns in Alcalay's *Complete Hebrew–English Dictionary* and make clear its predominantly oppositional sense (1990: 1576–8).

10 *B'tokh etz ha-gan*. '*B'tokh*' can be translated 'in the middle' or 'in the midst'. *Etz ha-gan* means literally 'tree of the garden', or, since the indefinite article does not exist in Hebrew but is implied in the absence of the definite article (*ha*), 'a tree of the garden'. The King James Version makes sense of the awkward phrase with 'amongst the trees of the garden'.

11 See also Julia Kristeva on 'the voiced breath that connects us to an undifferentiated mother' (Kristeva 1980b: 195).

12 Erich Neumann explains that 'the self-regenerative tree is the centre of the Great Goddesses' vegetative symbolism. As fruit-bearing tree of life it is female: It bears, transforms, nourishes . . .' (1963: 48). No doubt it is for this reason that pre-biblical iconography affiliates the nursing mother goddess Asherah with trees (Frymer-Kensky 1992: 159, 161).

PART FOUR

On Monique Wittig

Chapter 13

Erika Ostrovsky

RELIGION IN THE FICTION OF MONIQUE WITTIG

I am at the Golgatha. . . . *I* implore the great goddess m/y
mother and *I* say to her mother mother why have you
forsaken m/e. . . . *I* cry out in m/y distress mother
mother why have you forsaken m/e.

(Wittig 1975: 122–3)

Artemis laced in leather over her bare breasts. . . .
Aphrodite, the black goddess with the flat belly. . . .
[T]riple Persephone . . . sun-headed Ishtar. . . . [D]ark
Isis . . . red Hecate . . . Pomona and Flora. . . . [B]londe
Cybele . . . Ceres with the corn in her hair. . . .
[M]oon-headed Rhamnusis . . . Minerva the daughter of Zeyna.

(Wittig 1975: 69)

PASSAGES SUCH AS THESE in the fiction of Monique Wittig, although
probably the most arresting examples, are by no means isolated or atypical
instances of her treatment of religion. A consideration of the entire corpus of
her work shows that it is an important component of all her novels, from
The Opoponax to *Across the Acheron*. Yet although the studies devoted to her now
number in the hundreds and treat every conceivable aspect of her writing, to
date, none deals specifically with the role religion plays in her fiction. This is not
as surprising as it at first appears. For, since she is a feminist (or rather, lesbian)
author, it is assumed that other issues directly connected with such an orientation
are of primary concern to her. Moreover, there are no direct references to
religion in her theoretical, political, or philosophical writings to aid the literary
critic in the interpretation of its function and significance.

In order to gain an understanding of the key concepts that underlie her attitude towards the subject of religion, then, it is necessary to venture rather far afield and look for the answer in texts outside her fiction. After much searching, it is found in an essay which does not actually deal with religion but rather treats the characteristics and aims of avant-garde writing: 'The Trojan Horse' (Wittig 1992: 68–75). Originally published in French in 1984, twenty years after the appearance of Wittig's first novel, *The Opoponax* – and thus a backward glance by the author at her own writings after having reached maturity as an artist – it contains invaluable information concerning her fundamental outlook and also unequivocally defines her stance as a writer. With its help it becomes possible to clarify the factors that determine her treatment of religion, even though it contains no actual reference to this subject.

'The Trojan Horse' contains two main concepts that define 'any important literary work . . . with a new form' (Wittig 1992: 69). The first is that it 'operates as a war machine, because its design and goal is to pulverise the old forms and formal conventions . . . [to] sap and blast out the ground where it was planted' (Wittig 1992: 69). The second is to achieve universalisation or, as Wittig states it, to create a 'global form of . . . work', that is, one that goes beyond the narrow confines of any particular point of view (Wittig 1992: 75). The latter receives further clarification in another essay, 'The Point of View: Universal or Particular?', where Wittig affirms that the writer 'must work to reach the general, even while starting from . . . a specific point of view' (Wittig 1992: 67).

In applying these concepts to her treatment of religion, it appears likely then that it will involve violent attack, subversion or overthrow of existing traditions, as well as an emphasis on various ways of achieving universalisation or a 'global form'. While Wittig does not totally elucidate the meaning of the latter, it becomes clear in a consideration of her fiction that universalisation in the realm of religion involves a movement away from and beyond a limited system such as that of the predominant Judeo-Christian one of Western society. It can be seen that it manifests itself primarily in syncretism, that is, the union or fusion of conflicting religious beliefs. In this practice, Wittig is not alone. One of the most striking examples occurs in the sonnets of Gérard de Nerval, especially those entitled 'Myrtho', 'Horus', 'Antéros' and 'Artemis', written more than a century ago (Nerval 1949: 23, 33, 39, 53). However, it is, surprisingly, outside the field of literature that Wittig's concept of universalisation finds its closest parallel. It appears in the last published work of Joseph Campbell, *The Inner Reaches of Outer Space: Metaphor as Myth and Religion* (1985). There, Campbell is concerned with what he calls 'elementary ideas', an important aspect in the constitution of religions everywhere, which contrasts with 'ethnic ideas' or local systems locked into a particular belief. It is the identical attempt to transcend any narrow worldview and to attain universality which also preoccupies Wittig. It is expressed in her essays mentioned above, although only obliquely applicable to religion. One must turn to her fiction in order to see it most clearly illustrated. Moreover, as Wittig's writing progresses, so does the importance as well as the complexity of her treatment of religion, which causes it to be increasingly interesting to the critic.

In her first novel, *The Opoponax* (1966), it can be observed that the 'war machine' approach is uppermost. It takes the form of a direct attack that has the power to 'blast out the ground where it was planted' – in this instance and in its setting, the prevailing Christian doctrine. The first clue is that most of the action takes place in a Catholic school run by nuns and that they are presented in such a way as to make them appear anonymous, anodyne, practically indistinguishable. They form a unified group, an impression achieved by the ingenious device of citing their names in a long list, uninterrupted even by commas:

> Mother of Saint John the Baptist . . . Mother of Saint Bonaventura Mother of Saint Apollinaire Mother of Saint Hippolytus Mother of Saint Nicholas Mother of Saint Gregory Mother of the Infant Jesus Mother of Saint Jules Mother of Saint Francis of Assisi Mother of Saint Thomas Aquinas Mother of Saint Sylvester Mother of Saint Ignatius of Antioch.
>
> (Wittig 1966: 173)

Their undifferentiated and submissive character is even more clearly established in a scene that takes place during a Holy Mass at the moment of Communion when all the nuns monotonously intone the same formula: '*Domine, non sum dignus*' (Wittig 1966: 174). It is striking that they thus not only express their subservience to the male God of Christian tradition but, by using the masculine form of the adjective (that is, *dignus*), they accept a traditional formula which denies their female identity.

The opposing forces, those that explode existing modes of thought and action, are the children. Characterised by their wildness, their freedom, their irreverence, they form a group that stands in direct contrast to the prevailing religion and traditional behaviour. Their transgressive, sacrilegious, 'heathen' activity saps and blasts out 'the ground where it was planted', that is, Catholicism (Wittig 1966: 169–72, 182–4, 253). They are a living negation of the doctrine of sin, repentance and punishment. This is clearly shown in an incident involving the irreverent behaviour of one of the central characters, Valerie Borge, who, instead of participating in the ritual, traces the outline of coins in her missal during a solemn requiem mass (Wittig 1966: 172–3). However, it reaches its greatest intensity in the depiction of the love relationship between Valerie and Catherine Legrand, full of erotic overtones, which would certainly constitute a serious transgression of religious doctrine. The children, taken as a group, show no reverence for the rituals of the Church, the sanctity of death, or various figures of authority in the Christian world, such as priests or bishops.

There is further evidence of subversion in the book in the affirmation of paganism, evident on the very first page, by means of a character's name: 'Robert Payen' (pronounced the same way as 'païen' which, in French, means 'pagan'). While only a single pagan divinity, Artemis, appears in this text, her choice is already significant since she is the Greek goddess of the hunt and Lady of the Beasts, and is in these ways linked to some of the unorthodox activities of the protagonists of the novel who hunt, carry weapons and consider ammunition a suitable love gift (Wittig 1966: 190, 206–7). Moreover, even if Artemis shares certain traits with the nuns (virginity and refusal of contact with males) she nevertheless stands in direct opposition to them and, for that matter, to the entire doctrine of which they are the representatives by virtue of her identity as a Greek (pagan) goddess.

Wittig's second book, *Les Guérillères*, goes much further in its attack on the religious establishment but does so in ways different from those that appeared in *The Opoponax*. First of all, the concept of a work of art as a 'war machine' is extended to the entirety of the text, since *Les Guérillères* is an epic of warfare against the established order, primarily that of male domination. However, it also includes the overthrow of various elements of Judeo-Christian religion. Among the best examples is the one dealing with Eve as represented in the Hebrew Bible. In Wittig's version she is alone in Paradise, without Adam, and certainly not created from his rib, but accompanied by her favourite serpent, named Orpheus.

> [H]e keeps advising her to eat the fruit of the tree in the centre of the garden. . . . [A]s soon as she has eaten the fruit, she will become taller, she will grow, her feet will not leave the ground though her forehead will touch the stars. . . . [S]he will acquire knowledge. . . . [She] will have a clear understanding of the solar myth that all the texts have deliberately obscured.
>
> (Wittig 1985: 52)

Thus, rather than causing the Fall and the expulsion from Paradise by eating the forbidden fruit from the tree of knowledge on the advice of the evil serpent, as in the Old Testament, Wittig's Eve attains superhuman stature and joyful knowledge of the solar myth that she believes all traditional texts have sought to hide.

As a matter of fact, one of the most important examples of the subversion of numerous ancient (and modern) traditions which associate women with the moon and lunar divinities consists of Wittig's introduction in *Les Guérillères* of a variety of solar goddesses. They include, among others, Amaterasu and Cihuacoatl, as well as Koue Fei, 'mistress of the sun' (Wittig 1985: 26, 27, 65). By these means, Wittig has not only undermined existing beliefs but has also introduced the second basic notion which, in 'The Trojan Horse', she affirmed to be of paramount importance in the creation of a work of art: universalisation. To this end, a number of 'other' religions are juxtaposed with or even supersede Judeo-Christian doctrine. Buddhist and Hindu elements, as well as 'pagan' types of worship, appear here (Wittig 1985: 127, 136). Probably the most striking example occurs in a description of 'monuments whose basic design is the circle in all its modalities':

> The principal building is a hemisphere. Paths encircle it at different levels. One follows them in the direction of the sun. Thus one passes at the four cardinal points [and] arrives by an ascending path at the zenith, [where there] is an immense musical stave that instruments progressively decipher. This is what has been called the music of the spheres.
>
> (Wittig 1985: 136)

This is clearly an instance of a 'global form' or religious syncretism in the creation of a structure involving worship, since it evokes a three-dimensional mandala, a labyrinth, and a reference to Heaven in Christian scripture. A great variety of other original elements that are 'pagan' or outside of Judeo-Christian tradition are also present in this text. Examples include the practice of exposing mummified corpses, the adoration of a goddess named Eristikos, and the stupas, dagbas and chortens found in Buddhist and other Asian religious traditions (Wittig 1985: 16, 24, 136).

By all the various means apparent in *Les Guérillères*, both goals Wittig holds up as vital in 'The Trojan Horse' are arrived at simultaneously. Subversion joins religious syncretism; destruction of established concepts is allied with the creation of a broader horizon – with global concepts.

In her next book, *The Lesbian Body*, Wittig achieves the most profound upheaval as well as the greatest degree of universalisation in all domains, including that of religion. Its very title is, of course, an immediate statement of transgression. Not only does it challenge traditional notions of love and/or eroticism, but it attacks a rule present in most established religions forbidding any sexual relationship that is not aimed at reproduction. Lesbianism is thus a sinful act, yet it is glorified by means that not only shock most conventions but also defy an important, quasi-universal religious interdiction.

A further challenge consists of the entire nature of the text. *The Lesbian Body* invites comparison with the Song of Songs and thus the Hebrew Bible, fundamental in Judeo-Christian religion and part of its male-dominated tradition. This makes it the perfect target for the author, a challenging bastion to be stormed. Moreover, the Song of Songs is considered among the finest love poems in which a male subject addresses a female object of desire. The greatest defiance then consists of subverting the poet's (and the Bible's) aims by making both lovers female.

Central in Wittig's text is the place given to the Egyptian divine couple of Isis and Osiris, both of whom are rendered female here. They function as key figures in this book. This is especially true of the goddess Isis, who is described as being instrumental in the rebirth of her beloved, Osiris, after Osiris's annihilation. The echoes of the death and resurrection of Christ are clearly evident, as is the subversion of this most fundamental of Christian beliefs. In Wittig's version, it is the pagan female divinity who accomplishes the resurrection, not God the Father or Christ the Son.

The constant subversion of phrases from Christian scripture and ritual is also striking. Most pronounced is the repeated use of one of the sayings ascribed to Jesus: 'So be it'. In this text, it appears in contexts that are entirely different and would most certainly be considered sacrilegious. For example, it is addressed by the (female) lover to the (female) beloved, and a variation, 'now and for ever, so be it' is part of a highly erotic sequence (Wittig 1975: 25, 131). At other times, it is connected with Sappho, here treated as a divinity (Wittig 1975: 97). Even more arresting is the instance when this phrase is combined with a formulaic expression from one of the most important Christian sacraments, 'I baptise you'. This is particularly subversive since, instead of John the Baptist or a priest performing the ceremony of baptism, it is one of the female lovers who pronounces the sacred formula that is central to Christian orthodoxy (Wittig 1975: 29).

When Christ himself appears in this text he is totally transformed – that is, feminised – and renamed 'Christa the much crucified' (Wittig 1975: 35). The most marked instance is that which refers to the moments before Jesus' death. Here, as was seen at the beginning of this chapter, all the well-known elements are changed into their opposites (Wittig 1975: 122–3). It is evident that the famous seven last words of Christ, when spoken by a female human being and addressed to a mother goddess rather than to God the Father of the New Testament, are diametrically opposed to the established version sacred to Christians. It is one of the most clear-cut instances of subversion.

Another figure of central importance to Christian belief, the Virgin Mary – revered for her role as the mother of Jesus and the merciful goddess who intercedes for sinners – is replaced by a divinised version of Sappho, the Greek (and reputedly lesbian) poet. She is glorified, implored, addressed in prayer and praised in terms that echo those habitually used to refer to the Virgin – such as 'the all-attentive' and 'the very tender goddess' – in this further instance of religious subversion (Wittig 1975: 57, 97, 61, 115). Other striking changes, reminiscent of Christ's being renamed 'Christa', but affecting other religions, include the re-envisioning of the great Greek god Zeus as 'Zeyna the all power-ful she who grasps the lightnings in her hand', while Minerva (unlike Athena who sprang from the head of Zeus, her father) now claims Zeyna as her mother (Wittig 1975: 42, 69). Thus, not only is the central figure of Christianity feminised but the major male Greek divinity is equally transformed.

Aside from such subversion, Wittig elevates goddesses from various other religions. Examples include 'Ishtar goddess of goddesses'; '[t]he glorious sup-remely divine Astarte she who has no beginning who has no end she who is'; 'Persephone the triple goddess'; and a nameless goddess with multiple attributes and varying, even contradictory, traits: 'I am the triple one, I am the formidable benevolent infernal one . . . I am the sovereign one, I thunder with my three voices the clamorous the serene the strident' (Wittig 1975: 93, 111, 145). Most striking, however, is the universalisation Wittig achieves by creating an entire pantheon of female divinities, drawn from a great variety of religions and whose traditional characteristics are frequently also changed, as seen in the second epigraph at the beginning of this chapter (Wittig 1975: 69).

In the sequences devoted to Isis and Osiris, Wittig accomplishes such intricate interweaving and establishes so many cross-references that a number of divinit-ies (and their actions) are united and even superimposed, suggesting that they are one and the same (Wittig 1975: 79–80, 113). Thus, Isis resurrects Osiris as Christ resuscitated Lazarus; breathes life into her as did the God of the Hebrew Bible when he created the first man; dances, as did Shiva, to cause the world to come into being; and affirms that the result of Osiris's rebirth and the union of the couple will be the birth, not of a male divinity, but of human females ('little girls'). In the last of these, reproduction will occur by means that are a biological impossibility – 'XX plus XX = XX' – thereby suggesting a miraculous birth with links to the nativity stories from the life of Christ (Wittig 1975: 128). Thus the couple of female lovers, Isis and Osiris, the Virgin Mary and Christ, Yahweh and Shiva, are combined into an entirely new whole, constructed from elements of a great variety of beliefs. It is indeed a most outstanding example of religious syncretism, and proof of Wittig's unusual powers of invention.

The work which follows, *Lesbian Peoples: Materials for a Dictionary*, is quite different in nature from *The Lesbian Body*. Not only is it a most unusual dictionary, full of lacunae, with a mock bibliography and unexpected definitions, but it handles those words dealing with religious matters in a novel way. It introduces humour and playfulness into a type of work (the dictionary) and a domain (religion) that are traditionally treated with seriousness, respect, even reverence, thus displaying a subversive attitude from the very outset. For example, Wittig does not hesitate, in the 'bibliography' included in this text, to give as the author of a book named *Genesis* a woman called Beni Amer – whose last name, in French, is a play on words, with *amer* meaning 'bitter' (Wittig and Zeig 1979: 169).

Various entries in the body of the work also supply facetious or non-traditional definitions. For example, Eve and Lilith are defined as '[t]wo famous companion lovers who lived in Palestine', while a definition of 'sirens' cites New Testament figures 'Mary the Egyptian and Mary the Bohemian who emerged from the sea', noting that 'Mary was later celebrated as Venus, a goddess of love, who emerged from the waters' (Wittig and Zeig 1979: 52, 141). Subversion and syncretism, however, are not present only in references to the Hebrew Bible and the New Testament. Various other religions are subjected to similar treatment. Thus, Thetis and Carmenta, coming from two widely different cultures, are associated with the beginnings of written language – since they were 'credited with giving the world an alphabet' – as is Kali, the dread Hindu goddess (Wittig and Zeig 1979: 150, 4).

Important too, is subversion by omission. Nowhere in the text is there a mention of a divine Creator, of Adam as the first human being, of Eve as temptress and sinner, or of the Fall. When it is referred to at all, Paradise is called the 'terrestrial garden', and is thus a profane rather than a sacred abode (Wittig and Zeig 1979: 1). There is no angel with a flaming sword to cause expulsion from this original, blissful place inhabited by a tribe of 'amazons'. They lived there, we are told, in total harmony until the establishment of cities, when schism and banishment occurred and they were dispersed all across the globe (Wittig and Zeig 1979: 15–16).

Moreover, various religions are subjected to lusory treatment, consisting mostly of amusing mixtures and transformations. Thus Athena becomes an 'ancient Libyan amazon'; Demeter and her daughter, Persephone, are described as 'famous . . . companions and lovers', as are the sister goddesses, Isis and Nephtys; Ares, the Greek god of war, and Menelippa become 'companion queens'; Hera is 'the Leader of War'; and Kali 'invented an alphabet, composed of fifty signs, [each appearing] on her effigy figured by the skulls on her necklace' (Wittig and Zeig 1979: 11, 42, 85, 9, 71, 4). Syncretism also occurs when the latter is 'celebrated as Kali the Black, the Devourer who dances on cadavers. . . . [S]he is, along with Artemis, Athena, and Diana, the favorite warrior of the companion lovers' (Wittig and Zeig 1979: 89).

Sometimes, amusing effects are achieved by pure invention on the part of the author. One example is the mention of a goddess named 'Trivia the Thunderer' (Wittig and Zeig 1979: 154), whose name indirectly pokes fun at Zeus, the king of the Greek gods, and one of his major attributes. Another is 'Bacche', who is worshipped by the Bacchantes (Wittig and Zeig 1979: 15) and whose name, as a feminisation of 'Bacchus', is a playful adaptation of that Greek god's original name and a reference to his reputedly hermaphroditic nature.

As a matter of fact, the treatment of religious matters with humour (in the form of good-natured laughter, irony, bitterness, or malice) is one of the predominant features of this 'dictionary'. It is exemplified, for instance, by the description of the Holy Grail, in which the Knights of the Round Table are feminised and the number twelve is replaced by thirteen, comparable to the number of amazons in a witches' coven (Wittig and Zeig 1979: 66–7); further, Joan of Arc, the Christian heroine and virgin, is eroticised and given a female lover, Haiviette (Wittig and Zeig 1979: 88). Reproduction – which, in most religions, is considered the duty of believers and thus a sacred act – is mocked in a variety of ways, such as in the image of birth by way of the ear (Wittig and Zeig 1979: 49). On the other hand, dying – an equally important moment in every religion – is here given the profane meaning, common in Elizabethan times, of extreme pleasure or orgasm (Wittig and Zeig 1979: 43–4).

Many other instances of amusing subversions can be found in the 'bibliography'. For example, a work entitled *Demeter Revisited* is attributed to Phyllis Chesler, the American feminist (Wittig and Zeig 1979: 169), while the famous French philosopher, Pascal, is feminised and becomes 'Pascale' (Wittig and Zeig 1979: 170). Another humorous feminisation is that of the Greek god of war, Ares, who is turned into the queen of a tribe of amazons (Wittig and Zeig 1979: 9), and Hera, originally the Greek goddess of marriage and the hearth, becomes 'she who does not reconcile' (Wittig and Zeig 1979: 71).

In the book that follows, translated as *Across the Acheron*, the English title gives the impression that Wittig will deal primarily with Greek religious ideas, when in fact its original French title, *Virgile, non*, contains entirely different references. Virgil, the guide who leads Dante in his journey through Hell and Purgatory to Paradise in *The Divine Comedy*, although referred to as 'the gentle Virgil' in Wittig's text (Wittig 1987: 30) – when, indeed, he is far from gentle – is refuted as well by the word '*non*'. This instantly constitutes a negation of one of the world-famous literary works that celebrates Christian doctrine. Further subversion occurs on the very first page of Wittig's text, in the transformation of Dante's male guide into a female one, 'Manastabal', who leads a female narrator, bearing the author's own name, 'Wittig'. Moreover, the voyage described in *The Divine Comedy*, which traces Dante's descent into Hell, his travels through Purgatory and his final ascent into Paradise, and is thus based on concepts sacred to Christian tradition, becomes, in *Across the Acheron*, 'a journey which is both sacred and profane' (Wittig 1987: 7).

This notion of duality is reinforced by anachronisms and by the numerous place-names and botanical references (Golden Gate Park, Castro Street, eucalyptus trees . . .) that suggest that the setting is modern San Francisco. Moreover, although *Across the Acheron* is divided into three zones that at first resemble the 'Inferno', 'Purgatorio' and 'Paradiso' of Dante's poem, these have nothing to do with the concepts of sin, damnation, repentance and redemption or salvation that are so important in Christian doctrine. This is instantly evident in the dual nature of various places. For example, a laundromat is the first circle of Hell (Wittig 1987: 17); Purgatory is replaced by the term 'Limbo' and is usually a billiard parlour or a bar; and Paradise resembles a site that overlooks the Golden Gate Bridge (Wittig 1987: 117–18).

Furthermore, treating with irreverence, ferocity and ribald humour a subject that echoes *The Divine Comedy* (Wittig 1987: 41) amounts to profaning the vast edifice of Christian doctrine upon which that trilogy is based. This is also evident in a negation of the 'divine' order of Dante's work, a negation achieved in *Across the Acheron* by disorder – a purposeful mixture of sequences that deny the progression from Hell to Paradise – as can easily be seen in the Table of Contents of the work. There are many ways in which subversion occurs in this text, most of which are amusing (although the laughter is at times gallows humour, especially in the sequences set in Hell or Limbo). One of the methods for achieving this is to mix various genres or, as 'Manastabal' says to 'Wittig', through a 'confusion of styles [that] is sometimes quite barbaric' (Wittig 1987: 55). An example of such fusion (or confusion) can be seen when 'Wittig' acts as if she were in a cowboy movie during one of the visits to Hell.

Humorous mixtures are also achieved through a mingling of the sacred and the profane. This can be seen when 'Wittig', like Jacob in the Hebrew Bible, wrestles with the angel – using 'boxing . . . judo grips . . . karate blows, shutos' (Wittig 1987: 114–15) – or when the text depicts angels with laser guns (Wittig 1987: 36), who ride motorcycles (Wittig 1987: 117) and resemble jazz musicians who play the piano, the saxophone and percussion instruments (Wittig 1987: 118), as well as preparing gourmet (vegetarian) meals while singing a song from *Alice in Wonderland* (Wittig 1987: 117).

Paradise itself, which is in most traditions a purely spiritual concept, the abode of disembodied beings, divine and saintly figures, is here a palpable place in which a person can participate in a variety of sense experiences and where every joy of the body can be fully realised. In some sense, this is once again an example of syncretism, although not explicitly stated, since such an image of the afterlife is also that of the Egyptians, the Hindus (with the presence of the voluptuous Apsaras), or Walhalla (where the Walkyrie welcome dead heroes). Wittig's depiction had already been hinted at in earlier episodes than those dealing with the arrival in Paradise, when it became clear that angels do have a sex (and it is female), that they live in a land of sunshine and that, in the celestial city, joyous music is heard.

All this is most evident in the final pages of *Across the Acheron* (Wittig 1987: 116–19). The setting is the magnificently coloured countryside overlooking the Pacific Ocean near the Golden Gate Bridge, which has the double advantage of being a real landmark and alluding to the Gates of Heaven. Strikingly lacking in Wittig's version are the Christian divinities, the saints and blessed spirits, as well as the Mystic Rose so central in Dante's ultimate vision of Paradise. Even the dread angel who, according to Christian doctrine, announces the Day of Judgement with the sound of his trumpet is replaced here by a naked cherub who resembles a human infant and announces the start of a joyous feast. In a kind of negative syncretism, also lacking is the radiant image of the thousand-petalled lotus and the dissolution of both the beheld image and the beholding mind which characterises the arrival at the highest *chakra* in Buddhism.

The accent everywhere is on sense experiences and Wittig (the author) uses her excellent descriptive talents to evoke every one of these. She appeals to the visual through the images of the angels who, as in a painting, are presented in the full array of their skin tones (mostly black and golden, suggesting their various races – another example of the subversion of a traditional view, as well as a desire for universalisation). The varying colours of the landscape, vividly pictured, also contribute to the pleasure of the eyes that can be experienced here. As for the auditory, there is the long list of birds from every part of the globe whose songs join the chorus of the angels. The gustatory and olfactory are stimulated by the mention of various aromatic herbs and spices used in the preparation of the feast cooked by the angels.

Finally, instead of Dante's divine guide, Beatrice, the central figure in Paradise is the beloved of 'Wittig', who refers to her on numerous occasions as 'she who is my Providence' (Wittig 1987: 76, 109 and 117) but never actually pronounces her name (suggesting parallels with the prohibition that exists in many religions concerning the name of God, yet here referring to a human being). The joyful arrival in what appears to be a very sensual, earthly paradise and the happy meeting of the lovers both echo 'the poem that Dante called a "comedy" because it ends well' (Wittig 1987: 41) and differ greatly from the beatific vision that concludes *The Divine Comedy*. And, although the beloved in some ways resembles Beatrice, in that she is accompanied by a whole cohort of seraphim, archangels and angels of every kind (Wittig 1987: 76, 117), she is totally unlike the latter in that she is a palpable, flesh-and-blood creature.

Other echoes and divergences occur regarding such elements of Christian religion as references to Saint Christopher which, here, deal with 'Wittig' and her guide, 'Manastabal' (Wittig 1987: 10, 109); the pronouncement, 'Dust you were born and to dust you will return', attributed to a monstrous eagle (Wittig 1987: 11); and the epithet 'the word made flesh' used in a context totally different from the traditional one (Wittig 1987: 20). Most striking, however, are the seven last words of Christ quoted (this time in their original version) by the women in the laundromat, who are described as 'damned souls' who accept the doctrine of male supremacy in both religious and worldly matters (Wittig 1987: 14), thus giving a double meaning to their damnation.

Further duality or mixture of opposites is nowhere clearer than in the author's use of language. What she calls 'word work' (Wittig 1992: 72) is, of course, central to every writer. It is therefore not surprising that it will reflect the most important dichotomy of the 'journey that is both sacred and profane' (Wittig 1987: 7) which is to be undertaken here. Wittig's 'word work' takes the form, in *Across the Acheron*, of slang – a very up-to-date and low version – which is arresting in the context of the allusion to a lofty, poetic, religious text such as Dante's, written in language fitting to its subject. Yet slang, in Wittig's work, is by no means omnipresent. It coexists with noble style and poetic utterances. The two registers alternate and intertwine. Sometimes lofty pronouncements are challenged and even mocked by 'Manastabal'. This is especially true in circumstances of suffering (in the various hells depicted in this text). 'Figures of style' are out of place there. Poetry is only fitting in the sequences that depict tragic events or those evoking paradise. Yet, even in those instances, poetic language frequently deals with both sacred and profane matters. For example, while jubilation characterises the end of the 'long pilgrimage through hell' and the arrival of the beloved amidst a crowd of archangels and seraphim, the latter is described as disembarking from an aeroplane (Wittig 1987: 117) and the sumptuous, poetic descriptions of the processions and activities in Paradise are juxtaposed with the mention of a song from *Alice in Wonderland*, 'Soup, beautiful soup' (Wittig 1987: 117) – quite a different and certainly profane register.

In looking back at the entire corpus of Wittig's fiction, it becomes evident that, in the realm of religion, as in every domain of her writing, her central aims have been fully realised: to abandon, attack, subvert and destroy established traditions and dominant modes; and to attain a point of view that goes beyond the singular and manifests itself in the creation of global concepts. As in all other aspects of her work, she has achieved this by a great variety of means which range from simple reversal to complex transformations, and from the use of various types of humour, to the most intricate and innovative creations. Her treatment, at times subtle and indirect, at others blunt and even brutal, is, in every instance, proof of her great originality and boldness as a writer. These are perhaps nowhere more evident than in the daring manner in which religion is depicted in her fiction. Moreover, while Wittig nowhere speaks of the important place religion occupies in her work, from her earliest to her most recent texts, this silence exemplifies the value she assigns in numerous instances to an absence of enunciation (Wittig 1966: 18), to what is not said or named (Wittig 1975: 46, 87) – proof of her intense preoccupation with religion and the deep meaning she attaches to it.

Bibliography

Afzal-Khan, Fawzia and Sesadri-Crooks, Kalpana (eds) (2000) *The Pre-occupations of Postcolonial Studies*, Durham, NC: Duke University Press.

Alcalay, R. (1990) *The Complete Hebrew–English Dictionary*, Israel: Massada.

Alter, Robert (1981) *The Art of Biblical Narrative*, New York, NY: Basic Books.

Amadiume, Ifi (1987) *Male Daughters, Female Husbands*, London: Zed Books.

Anderson, Pamela Sue (1998) *A Feminist Philosophy of Religion*, Oxford: Blackwell.

Armour, Ellen T. (1993) 'Questioning "Woman" in Feminist/Womanist Theology: Irigaray, Ruether, and Daly', in C. W. M. Kim et al. (eds), *Transfigurations: Theology and the French Feminists*, Minneapolis, Minn.: Fortress Press.

—— (1997) 'Questions of Proximity: Women's Place in Derrida and Irigaray', *Hypatia* 12, 1: 68–74.

—— (1999) *Deconstruction, Feminist Theology, and the Problem of Difference: Subverting the Race/Gender Divide*, Chicago, Ill.: University of Chicago Press.

—— (2001a) 'Beyond Belief? Sexual Difference and Religion after Onto-theology', in J. Caputo (ed.), *The Religious*, London: Blackwell.

—— (2001b) '"Through Flame or Ashes": Traces of Difference in *Geist*'s Return', in N. Holland and P. Huntington (eds), *Feminist Interpretations of Martin Heidegger*, University Park, Pa.: Pennsylvania State University Press.

Asad, Talal (1993) *Genealogies of Religion: Discipline and Reasons of Power in Christianity and Islam*, Baltimore, Md. and London: Johns Hopkins University Press.

Bachofen, Johann J. (1967) *Myth, Religion and Mother Right: Selected Writings of J. J. Bachofen*, trans. R. Manheim, Princeton, NJ: Princeton University Press.

Bagchi, J. (ed.) (1995) *Indian Women: Myth and Reality*, Hyderabad: Sangam Books.

Bal, Mieke (1987) *Lethal Love: Feminist Literary Readings of Biblical Love Stories*, Bloomington, Ind.: Indiana University Press.

Baldass, Ludwig (1951) *Jan Van Eyck*, London: Phaidon Press.

Barthes, Roland (1970) 'L'Étrangère', *La Quinzaine Littéraire* (1–15 May): 19–20.

Belenky, Mary F. (ed.) (1986) *Women's Ways of Knowing: The Development of Self, Voice and Mind*, New York, NY: Basic Books.

Benjamin, Walter (1999) *Selected Writings*, Volume 2, *1927–1934*, ed. M. W. Jennings et al., trans. R. Livingstone et al., Cambridge, Mass.: Belknap Press.

Bhattacharya, N. N. (1999) *History of the Tantric Religion: An Historical, Ritualistic, and Philosophical Study*, New Delhi: Manohar.

Bickerman, Elias (1962) *From Ezra to the Last of the Maccabees: Foundations of Post-Biblical Judaism*, New York, NY: Schocken.

Bloodsworth, Mary K. (1999) 'Embodiment and Ambiguity: Luce Irigaray, Sexual Difference, and "Race"', *International Studies in Philosophy* 31, 2: 69–90.

Bond, Francis (1914) *Dedications and Patron Saints of English Churches: Ecclesiastical Symbolism, Saints and Their Emblems*, London: Oxford University Press.

Bordo, Susan R. (1994) 'The Cartesian Masculinization of Thought and the Seventeenth-Century Flight from the Feminine', in B.-A. Bar On (ed.), *Modern Engendering: Critical Feminist Readings in Modern Western Philosophy*, Albany, NY: State University of New York Press.

Bourdillon, Michael (1987) *The Shona Peoples*, Harare: Mambo Press.

Boyarin, Daniel (1990) *Intertextuality and the Reading of Midrash*, Bloomington, Ind.: Indiana University Press.

Bracher, Mark (1993) *Lacan, Discourse, and Social Change*, Ithaca, NY: Cornell University Press.

Braidotti, Rosi (1994) 'Of Bugs and Women: Irigaray and Deleuze on "Becoming-Woman"', in C. Burke et al. (eds), *Engaging with Irigaray: Feminist Philosophy and Modern European Thought*, New York, NY: Columbia University Press.

Brennan, Teresa (1991) 'An Impasse in Psychoanalysis and Feminism', in S. Gunew (ed.), *A Reader in Feminist Knowledge*, London and New York, NY: Routledge.

—— (1993) *History after Lacan*, London and New York, NY: Routledge.

Bronfen, Elisabeth (1992) *Over Her Dead Body: Death, Femininity, and the Aesthetic*, London and New York, NY: Routledge.

Bühler, G. (trans.) (1969) *The Laws of Manu*, New York, NY: Dover.

Bulbeck, Chilla (1998) *Re-Orienting Western Feminisms*, Cambridge: Cambridge University Press.

Butler, Judith (1992) 'Gender', in E. Wright (ed.), *Feminism and Psychoanalysis: A Critical Dictionary*, Oxford: Blackwell.

Bynum, Caroline W. (1982) *Jesus as Mother: Studies in the Spirituality of the High Middle Ages*, Berkeley, Calif.: University of California Press.

Calle-Gruber, Mireille (ed.) (1993) *On the Feminine*, trans. Catherine McGann, Atlantic Highlands, NJ: Humanities Press.

Campbell, Joseph (1985) *The Inner Reaches of Outer Space: Metaphor as Myth and Religion*, New York, NY: A. van der Marck Editions.

Campbell, June (1996) *Traveller in Space: In Search of Female Identity in Tibetan Buddhism.* New York, NY: George Braziller.

Cannon, Katie G. (1988) *Black Womanist Ethics*, Atlanta, Ga.: Scholars Press.

Cavarero, Adriana (1995) *In Spite of Plato: A Feminist Rewriting of Ancient Philosophy*, Cambridge: Polity.

Chakravarti, Uma (1989) 'Whatever Happened to the Vedic *Dasi*? Orientalism, Nationalism and a Script from the Past', in K. Sangari and S. Vaid (eds), *Recasting Women: Essays in Indian Colonial History*, New Delhi: Kali for Women.

Chanter, Tina (1995) *Ethics of Eros: Irigaray's Re-writing of the Philosophers*, London: Routledge.

Charcot, Jean-Martin and Richer, Paul (1984 [1886]) '*Les Démoniaques dans l'art' suivi de 'La Foi qui guérit'*, Paris: Macula.

Chase, Cynthia (1987) '"Transference" as Trope and Persuasion', in Shlomith Rimmon-Kenan (ed.), *Discourse in Psychoanalysis and Literature*, London: Methuen.

—— (1989) 'Desire and Identification in Lacan and Kristeva', in *Feminism: Psychoanalysis*, Ithaca, NY: Cornell University Press.

Cheah, Pheng and Grosz, Elizabeth (1998) 'Of Being-Two: Introduction', *Diacritics* 28, 1: 3–18.

Chodorow, Nancy (1978) *The Reproduction of Mothering: Psychoanalysis and the Sociology of Gender*, Berkeley, Calif.: University of California Press.

—— (1989) *Feminism and Psychoanalytic Theory*, New Haven, Conn.: Yale University Press.

Christ, Carol P. (1991) 'Mircea Eliade and the Feminist Paradigm Shift', *Journal of Feminist Studies in Religion* 7: 75–94.

Cixous, Hélène (1967) *Le Prénom de Dieu*, Paris: B. Grasset.

—— (1975) *Souffles*, Paris: Des femmes.

—— (1976) *La*, Paris: Des femmes.

—— (1979) *Vivre l'orange/To Live the Orange*, Paris: Des femmes.

—— (1980) 'The Laugh of the Medusa', in E. Marks and I. de Courtivron (eds), *New French Feminisms*, trans. K. and P. Cohen, Brighton: Harvester.

—— (1981) 'Castration or Decapitation?', trans. A. Kuhn, *Signs* 7, 1: 36–55.

—— (1986a) *La Bataille d'Arcachon*, Laval, Québec: Trois.

—— (1986b) *Inside*, trans. Carol Barko, New York, NY: Schocken.

—— (1986c) 'Sorties', trans. B. Wing, in H. Cixous and C. Clément, *The Newly Born Woman*, Manchester: Manchester University Press.

—— (1987) *L'Indiade ou l'Inde de leurs rêves; et quelques écrits sur le théâtre*, Paris: Théâtre du Soleil.

—— (1988) 'Extreme Fidelity', in S. Sellers (ed.), *Writing Differences: Readings from the Seminar of Hélène Cixous*, trans. A. Liddle and S. Sellers, Milton Keynes: Open University Press.

—— (1989) 'From the Scene of the Unconscious to the Scene of History', in Ralph Cohen (ed.), *The Future of Literary Theory*, trans. Deborah W. Carpenter, New York, NY: Routledge.

—— (1990) *Reading with Clarice Lispector*, trans. V. Conley, Minneapolis, Minn.: University of Minnesota Press.

—— (1991a) *The Book of Promethea*, trans. B. Wing, Lincoln, Nebr.: University of Nebraska Press.

—— (1991b) *'Coming to Writing' and Other Essays*, trans. S. Cornell et al., Cambridge, Mass.: Harvard University Press.

—— (1992) 'Grace and Innocence', in her *Readings: The Poetics of Blanchot, Joyce, Kafka, Kleist, Lispector, and Tsvetayeva*, trans. V. Conley, New York, NY: Harvester Wheatsheaf.

—— (1993) *Three Steps on the Ladder of Writing*, trans. B. Wing, New York, NY: Columbia University Press.

—— (1994a) *The Hélène Cixous Reader*, ed. Susan Sellers, New York, NY: Routledge.

—— (1994b) *Manna: For the Mandelstams For the Mandelas*, trans. Catherine A. F. MacGillivray, Minneapolis, Minn.: University of Minnesota Press.

—— (1997) *Or, les lettres de mon père*, Paris: Des femmes.

—— (1998) *Stigmata: Escaping Texts*, New York, NY: Routledge.

Cixous, Hélène and Calle-Gruber, Mireille (1997) *Rootprints: Memory and Life Writing*, New York, NY: Routledge.

Cixous, Hélène and Clément, Catherine (1986) *The Newly Born Woman*, trans. Betsy Wing, Minneapolis, Minn.: University of Minnesota Press.

Cixous, Hélène and Derrida, Jacques (1998) *Voiles*, Paris: Galilée.

Clarke, J. J. (1997) *Oriental Enlightenment: The Encounter between Asian and Western Thought*, London: Routledge.

Clément, Catherine (1983) *The Lives and Legends of Jacques Lacan*, trans. Arthur Goldhammer, New York, NY: Columbia University Press.

—— (1993) *Pour l'amour de l'Inde*, Paris: Flammarion.

—— (1994) *Syncope: The Philosophy of Rapture*, trans. Sally O'Driscoll and Deirdre M. Mahoney, Minneapolis, Minn.: University of Minnesota Press.

—— (1996) *Gandhi: The Power of Pacifism*, trans. Ruth Sharman, New York, NY: Discoveries.

—— (1999) *Theo's Odyssey*, trans. Steve Cox and Rose Schwartz, London: HarperCollins.

—— (2000) *Jésus au bûcher*, Paris: Éditions du Seuil.

Clément, Catherine and Kakar, Sudhir (1993) *La Folle et le saint*, Paris: Éditions du Seuil.

Clément, Catherine and Kristeva, Julia (2001) *The Feminine and the Sacred*, trans. Jane Marie Todd, New York, NY: Columbia University Press.

Code, Lorraine (1991) *What Can She Know? Feminist Theory and the Construction of Knowledge*, Ithaca, NY and London: Cornell University Press.

—— (1995) *Rhetorical Spaces: Essays in Gendered Locations*, New York and London: Routledge.

Cohen, A. (1983) *The Soncino Chumash*, London: Soncino.

Colebrook, Claire (1997) 'Feminist Philosophy and the History of Feminism: Irigaray and the History of Western Metaphysics', *Hypatia* 12, 1: 79–98.

Collins, Patricia Hill (1991) *Black Feminist Thought*, London: Routledge.

Conley, Verena A. (1991) *Hélène Cixous: Writing the Feminine*, Lincoln, Nebr.: University of Nebraska Press; expanded from 1984 edition.

—— (1992) *Hélène Cixous*, Toronto: University of Toronto Press.

Cornell, Sarah (1988) 'Hélène Cixous's *Le Livre de Promethea*: Paradise Refound', in S. Sellers (ed.), *Writing Differences: Readings from the Seminar of Hélène Cixous*, Milton Keynes: Open University Press.

Coulson, John (ed.) (1958) *The Saints: A Concise Biographical Dictionary*, New York, NY: Hawthorn.

Cousins, Mary (1958) *Tell Me about the Saints*, London: Hutchinson.

Crownfield, David (ed.) (1992) *Body/Text in Julia Kristeva: Religion, Women, and Psychoanalysis*, Albany, NY: State University of New York Press.

de Lauretis, Teresa (1987) 'The Female Body and Heterosexual Presumption', *Semiotica* 67, 3–4: 259–79.

—— (1994) *The Practice of Love: Lesbian Sexuality and Perverse Desire*, Bloomington and Indianapolis, Ind.: Indiana University Press.

Delaney, John J. (1961) *Dictionary of Catholic Biography*, New York, NY: Doubleday.

—— (1980) *Dictionary of Saints*, New York, NY: Doubleday.

Deleuze, Gilles (1990) *The Logic of Sense*, trans. Mark Lester and Charles Stivale, New York, NY: Columbia University Press.

—— and Guattari, Felix (1987) *A Thousand Plateaus: Capitalism and Schizo-phrenia*, trans. Brian Massumi, Minneapolis, Minn.: University of Minnesota Press.

Delphy, Christine (1995) 'The Invention of French Feminism: An Essential Move', *Yale French Studies* 87: 190–221.

—— (1996) 'French Feminism: An Imperialist Invention', in D. Bell and R. Klein (eds), *Radically Speaking: Feminism Reclaimed*, North Melbourne: Spinifex Press.

Denton, Lynn Teskey (1992) 'Varieties of Hindu Female Asceticism', in J. Leslie (ed.), *Roles and Rituals for Hindu Women*, Delhi: Motilal Banarsidass.

Derrida, Jacques (1981) *Positions*, trans. A. Bass, Chicago, Ill.: University of Chicago Press.

—— (1982) *Margins of Philosophy*, trans. A. Bass, Chicago, Ill.: University of Chicago Press.

—— (1992) *Given Time: I, Counterfeit Money*, trans. P. Kamuf, Chicago, Ill.: University of Chicago Press.

—— (1995) *The Gift of Death*, trans. D. Willis, Chicago, Ill.: University of Chicago Press.

—— (2002) *Acts of Religion*, ed. G. Anidjar, New York, NY: Routledge.

—— and Vattimo, Gianni (eds) (1998) *Religion (Cultural Memory in the Present)*, trans. D. Webb, Stanford, Calif.: Stanford University Press.

Deutscher, Penelope (1994) '"The Only Diabolical Thing about Women . . .": Luce Irigaray on Divinity', *Hypatia* 9, 4: 88–111.

—— (1997) *Yielding Gender: Feminism, Deconstruction, and the History of Philosophy*, London: Routledge.

—— (1998) 'Mourning the Other, Cultural Cannibalism, and the Politics of Friendship (Jacques Derrida and Luce Irigaray)', *Differences* 10, 3: 159–84.

Doane, Janice and Hodges, Devon (1992) *From Klein to Kristeva*, Ann Arbor, Mich.: University of Michigan Press.

Douglas, Mary (1966) *Purity and Danger: An Analysis of the Concept of Pollution and Taboo*, London: Routledge & Kegan Paul.

Dziva, Douglas (1996) *A Critical Examination of Patterns of Research in the Academic Study of Shona Traditional Religion*, Pietermaritzburg: University of Natal.

Eliade, Mircea (1958) *Yoga: Immortality and Freedom*, trans. W. R. Trask, 2nd edn, *Bollingen Series LVI*, Princeton, NJ: Princeton University Press.

—— (1969) *Patanjali and Yoga*, trans. C. L. Markmann, New York, NY: Funk & Wagnalls.

Elias, Norbert (1994) *The Civilizing Process: The History of Manners and State Formation and Civilization*, trans. E. Jephcott, Oxford: Blackwell.

Eller, Cynthia (2000) *The Myth of Matriarchal Prehistory*, Boston, Mass.: Beacon Press.

Elliot, Patricia (1991) *From Mastery to Analysis: Theories of Gender in Psychoanalytic Feminism*, Ithaca, NY: Cornell University Press.

—— (1995) 'Politics, Identity, and Social Change: Contested Grounds in Psychoanalytic Feminism', *Hypatia* 10, 2: 41–55.

Fanon, Frantz (1986) *Black Skin, White Masks*, trans. C. L. Markmann, London: Pluto Press.

Faris, Wendy B. (1988) *Labyrinths of Language: Symbolic Landscape and Narrative Design in Modern Fiction*, Baltimore, Md.: Johns Hopkins University Press.

Farley, Margaret (1975) 'New Patterns of Relationship: Beginnings of a Moral Revolution', in W. Burkhardt (ed.), *Woman: New Dimensions*, New York, NY: Paulist Press.

Farmer, David Hugh (1978) *The Oxford Dictionary of Saints*, Oxford: Clarendon Press.

Faur, J. (1986) *Golden Doves with Silver Dots: Semiotics and Textuality in Rabbinic Tradition*, Bloomington, Ind.: Indiana University Press.

Ferguson, George (1954) *Signs and Symbols in Christian Art*, London: Zwemmer.

Feuerbach, Ludwig (1957) *The Essence of Christianity*, New York, NY: Harper.

Feuerstein, Georg (1989) *Yoga: The Technology of Ecstasy*, Los Angeles, Calif.: Jeremy P. Tarcher.

—— (1998) *Tantra: The Path of Ecstasy*, Boston, Mass.: Shambhala.

Fishbane, Michael A. (1989) *The Garments of Torah: Essays in Biblical Hermeneutics*, Bloomington, Ind.: Indiana University Press.

Fraser, Nancy (1990) 'The Uses and Abuses of French Discourse Theories for Feminist Politics', *boundary* 17, 2: 82–101.

Freud, Sigmund (1962) *Civilization and its Discontents*, trans. J. Strachey, New York, NY: W. W. Norton.

—— (1965) *The Interpretation of Dreams*, trans. J. Strachey, New York, NY: Basic Books.

—— (1984) *Beyond the Pleasure Principle* and *The Ego and the Id*, Vol. 11 of the Penguin Freud Library, trans. J. Strachey, Harmondsworth: Penguin.

—— (1985a) *Totem and Taboo*, trans. James Strachey, Harmondsworth: Penguin.

—— (1985b) *Moses and Monotheism*, trans. James Strachey, Harmondsworth: Penguin.

—— (1985c) 'The Uncanny', in *Art and Literature*, trans. James Strachey, Harmondsworth: Penguin.

—— (1991) 'Mourning and Melancholia', in his *On Metapsychology*, Vol. 11 of the Penguin Freud Library, trans. J. Strachey, Harmondsworth: Penguin.

Frye, Marilyn (1983) *The Politics of Reality*, Trumansburg, NY: Crossing Press.

—— (1992) *Willful Virgin*, Freedom, Calif.: Crossing Press.

Frymer-Kensky, Tikva (1992) *In the Wake of the Goddesses: Women, Culture, and the Biblical Transformation of Pagan Myth*, New York, NY: Free Press.

Gadon, Elinor (1989) *The Once and Future Goddess*, New York, NY: Harper.

Gallop, Jane (1983) '*Quand nos lèvres s'écrivent*: Irigaray's Body Politic', *Romanic Review* 74, 1: 77–83.

—— (1985) *Reading Lacan*, Ithaca, NY: Cornell University Press.

—— (1988) *Thinking Through the Body*, New York, NY: Columbia University Press.

Gatens, Moira (1996) *Imaginary Bodies: Ethics, Power, and Corporeality*, London: Routledge.

Gilson, Anne Bathurst (1995) *Eros Breaking Free: Interpreting Sexual Theo-Ethics*, Cleveland, Ohio: Pilgrim Press.

Girard, René (1977) *Violence and the Sacred*, trans. P. Gregory, Baltimore, Md.: Johns Hopkins University Press.

—— (1986) *The Scapegoat*, trans. Y. Freccero, Baltimore, Md.: Johns Hopkins University Press.

—— (1987) *Things Hidden Since the Foundation of the World*, Stanford, Calif.: Stanford University Press.

Goldstein, Valerie S. (1979) 'The Human Situation: A Feminine View', in C. P. Christ and J. Plaskow (eds), *Womanspirit Rising: A Feminist Reader in Religion*, San Francisco, Calif.: Harper & Row.

Grant, Colin (1996) 'For the Love of God', *The Journal of Religious Ethics* 24, 1: 3–21.

Grosz, Elizabeth (1989) *Sexual Subversions: Three French Feminists*, St Leonards, NSW: Allen & Unwin.

—— (1990) *Jacques Lacan: A Feminist Introduction*, London and New York: Routledge.

—— (1993) 'Irigaray and the Divine', in C. W. Kim et al. (eds), *Transfigurations: Theology and the French Feminists*, Philadelphia: Fortress Press.

—— (1994) *Volatile Bodies: Toward a Corporeal Feminism*, Bloomington, Ind.: Indiana University Press.

Guberman, Ross Mitchell (ed.) (1996) *Julia Kristeva Interviews*, New York, NY: Columbia University Press.

Gulati, Leela (1995) 'Myth and Reality: In the Context of Poor Working Women in Kerala', in J. Bagchi (ed.), *Indian Women: Myth and Reality*, Hyderabad, India: Sangam Books.

Günter, Andrea (2001) 'Reflections on Material Transcendence, the Relationship between Women, the Word and the Maternal Order of Life, Emanating from Luce Irigaray, Luisa Muraro, the Philosophers of DIOTOMA and the Women of the Women's Bookstore, Milan', in K. Biezeveld and

A.-C. Mulder (eds), *Toward a Different Transcendence*, Berne: Peter Lang AG – European Academic Publishers.

Gupta, Sanjukta (1992) 'Women in the Śaiva/Śakta Ethos', in J. Leslie (ed.), *Roles and Rituals for Hindu Women*, Delhi: Motilal Banarsidass.

Handelman, Susan A. (1982) *The Slayers of Moses: The Emergence of Rabbinic Interpretation in Modern Literary Theory*, Albany, NY: State University of New York Press.

Harding, Sandra (1986) *The Science Question in Feminism*, Ithaca, NY and London: Cornell University Press.

Heidegger, Martin (1962) *Being and Time*, trans. J. Macquarrie and E. Robinson, New York, NY: Harper & Row.

—— (1971) 'What are Poets for?', in his *Poetry, Language, Thought*, trans. A. Hofstadter, New York, NY: Harper & Row.

—— (1977) *Martin Heidegger: Basic Writings*, ed. D. Krell, New York, NY: Harper & Row.

Heyward, Carter (1982) *The Redemption of God: A Theology of Mutual Relation*, New York, NY: University Press of America.

Hirsh, Elizabeth and Olsen, Gary (1995) '"Je – Luce Irigaray": A Meeting with Luce Irigaray', *Hypatia* 10, 2: 93–114.

Hollywood, Amy M. (1993) 'Violence and Subjectivity: *Wuthering Heights*, Julia Kristeva, and Feminist Theology', in C. W. Kim et al. (eds), *Transfigurations: Theology and the French Feminists*, Minneapolis, Minn.: Fortress Press.

—— (1994) 'Beauvoir, Irigaray, and the Mystical', *Hypatia* 9, 4: 158–85.

—— (1998) 'Deconstructing Belief: Irigaray and the Philosophy of Religion', *Journal of Religion* 78, 2: 230–45.

—— (1999) '"Divine Woman/Divine Women": The Return of the Sacred in Bataille, Lacan, and Irigaray', in F. Ambrosio (ed.), *The Question of Christian Philosophy Today*, New York, NY: Fordham University Press.

—— (2001) *Sensible Ecstasy: Mysticism, Sexual Difference, and the Demands of History*, Chicago, Ill.: University of Chicago Press.

hooks, bell (1982) *Ain't I a Woman?* London: Pluto Press.

Hopkins, Jeffrey (1999) *The Tantric Distinction: A Buddhist's Reflections on Compassion and Emptiness*, Boston, Mass.: Wisdom Publications.

Hove, Chenjerai (1990) *Bones*, Oxford: Heinemann International.

Hughes-Hallet, Lucy (1992) 'Egghead out of Her Shell', *The Independent on Sunday* (9 February): review, p. 26.

Inden, Ronald (1986) 'Orientalist Constructions of India', *Modern Asian Studies* 20, 3: 401–46.

Irigaray, Luce (1983) *L'Oubli de l'air: chez Martin Heidegger*, Paris: Éditions Minuit.

—— (1984) *Éthique de la différence sexuelle*, Paris: Éditions Minuit.

—— (1985a) *Speculum of the Other Woman*, trans. G. C. Gill, Ithaca, NY: Cornell University Press.

—— (1985b) *This Sex Which Is Not One*, trans. C. Porter, Ithaca, NY: Cornell University Press.

—— (1988) 'Un plaidoyer pour la différence', *Il est une foi* (mai–juin): 14–15.

—— (1989a) 'En mémoire de lui?', *Il est une foi* (mai): 14–20.

—— (1989b) 'Sorcerer Love: A Reading of Plato's *Symposium*, Diotima's Speech', trans. E. H. Kuykendall, *Hypatia* 3, 3: 32–44.

—— (1991) *Marine Lover of Friedrich Nietzsche*, trans. G. C. Gill, New York, NY: Columbia University Press.

—— (1993a) *An Ethics of Sexual Difference*, trans. C. Burke and G. C. Gill, Ithaca, NY: Cornell University Press.

—— (1993b) *Je, tu, nous: Toward a Culture of Difference*, trans. A. Martin, New York, NY: Routledge.

—— (1993c) *Sexes and Genealogies*, trans. G. C. Gill, New York, NY: Columbia University Press.

—— (1994a) 'Equal to Whom', in N. Schor and E. Weed (eds), *The Essential Difference*, Bloomington, Ind.: Indiana University Press.

—— (1994b) *Thinking the Difference: For a Peaceful Revolution*, trans. K. Montin, New York, NY: Routledge.

—— (1996a) *I Love to You: Sketch of a Possible Felicity in History*, trans. A. Martin, New York, NY: Routledge.

—— (ed.) (1996b) *Le Souffle des femmes*, Paris: ACGF.

—— (1999a) *The Age of the Breath*, trans. K. van de Rakt et al., Russelsheim, Germany: Christel Gottert Verlag.

—— (1999b) *Entre Orient et Occident*, Paris: Grasset.

—— (1999c) *The Forgetting of Air in Martin Heidegger*, trans. M. B. Mader, London: Athlone Press.

—— (2000a) 'Tâches spirituelles pour notre temps', *Religiologiques* 21: 17–34.

—— (2000b) *To Be Two*, trans. M. M. Rhodes and M. F. Cocito-Monoc, London: Athlone Press.

—— (2001) *To Be Two*, trans. M. M. Rhodes and M. F. Cocito-Monoc, New York, NY: Routledge.

—— (2002) *Between East and West: From Singularity to Community*, trans. S. Pluhácek, New York, NY: Columbia University Press.

Jantzen, Grace (1997) 'Feminism and Pantheism', *The Monist* 80, 2: 266–85.

—— (1998a) *Becoming Divine: Towards a Feminist Philosophy of Religion*, Manchester: Manchester University Press.

—— (1998b) 'Disrupting the Sacred: Religion and Gender in the City', in Kathleen O'Grady et al. (eds), *Bodies, Lives, Voices: Gender in Theology*, Sheffield: Sheffield Academic Press.

—— (2001) 'Before the Rooster Crows: John Locke, Margaret Fell, and the Betrayal of Knowledge in Modernity', in *Literature and Theology* 15, 1: 1–24.

Jensen, Lionel M. (1997) *Manufacturing Confucianism: Chinese Traditions and Universal Civilization*, Durham, NC and London: Duke University Press.

Jones, Ann Rosalind (1987) 'Editor's Introduction', in Catherine Clément, *The Weary Sons of Freud*, trans. Nicole Ball, London: Verso.

Jones, Serene (1993) 'This God Which Is Not One: Irigaray and Barth on the Divine', in C. W. M. Kim et al. (eds), *Transfigurations: Theology and the French Feminists*, Minneapolis, Minn.: Fortress Press.

—— (1995) 'Divining Women: Irigaray and Feminist Theologies', *Yale French Studies* 87: 42–67.

Jonte-Pace, Diane (1992) 'Situating Kristeva Differently: Psychoanalytic Readings of Women and Religion', in D. Crownfield (ed.), *Body/Text in Julia Kristeva: Religion, Women, and Psychoanalysis*, Albany, NY: State University of New York Press.

Joy, Morny (1990) 'Equality or Divinity: A False Dichotomy?', *Journal of Feminist Studies in Religion* 6, 1: 9–24.

—— (1996) 'No Longer Docile Daughters or Handmaidens of the Lord: Women in Religion Contest Their Divine and Human Condition(ing)s', *Women's Studies International Forum* 19, 6: 601–19.

—— (1998) 'What's God Got to Do with It?: Irigaray and the Divine', in K. O'Grady et al. (eds), *Bodies, Lives, Voices: Essays on Gender and Theology*, Sheffield: Sheffield Academic Press.

—— (2000) 'Beyond a God's Eyeview: Alternative Perspectives in the Study of Religion', in A. W. Geertz and R. T. McCutcheon (eds), *Perspectives on Method and Theory in the Study of Religion*, Adjunct Proceedings of the 17th Congress of the International Association for the History of Religions, Leiden: Brill.

Kearney, Richard (1986) *Modern Movements in Philosophy*, Manchester: Manchester University Press.

Keller, Mary L. (2001) *The Hammer and the Flute: Women, Power and Spirit Possession*, Baltimore, Md.: Johns Hopkins University Press.

Kierkegaard, Søren (1962) *Works of Love: Some Christian Reflections in the Form of Discourse*, trans. H. and E. Hong, New York, NY: Harper Torchbooks.

King, Richard (1999) *Orientalism and Religion: Postcolonial Theory, India and 'The Mystic East'*, London and New York, NY: Routledge.

Klein, Ernest (1987) *A Comprehensive Etymological Dictionary for Readers of English*, New York, NY: Macmillan.

Kristeva, Julia (1969a) 'Pour une sémiologie des paragrammes', in *Sèméiotikè*, Paris: Éditions du Seuil.

—— (1969b) as Julia Joyaux, *Le Langage, cet inconnu*, Paris: Éditions du Seuil.

—— (1973) 'The Ruin of a Poetics', in S. Bann and J. Boldt (eds), *Russian Formalism*, Edinburgh: Scottish Academic Press.

—— (1977) 'Julia Kristeva: à quoi servent les intellectuels?', an interview with J.-P. Enthoven, *Le Nouvel Observateur* (20 June): 97–134.

—— (1980a) 'Place Names', in *Desire in Language: A Semiotic Approach to Literature and Art*, ed. Leon S. Roudiez, trans. T. Gora and A. Jardine, New York, NY: Columbia University Press, pp. 271–91.

—— (1980b) *Desire in Language: A Semiotic Approach to Literature and Art*, ed. Leon S. Roudiez, trans. T. Gora and A. Jardine, New York, NY: Columbia University Press.

—— (1980c) 'Postmodernism?', in H. R. Garvin (ed.), *Romanticism, Modernism, Postmodernism*, Lewisberg, Pa.: Bucknell University Press.

—— (1981) 'Women's Time', trans. A. Jardine and H. Blake, *Signs* 7, 1: 13–35.

—— (1982) *Powers of Horror: An Essay on Abjection*, trans. L. S. Roudiez, New York, NY: Columbia University Press.

—— (1983) 'Within the Microcosm of the "Talking Cure"', in J. H. Smith and W. Kerrigan (eds), *Psychiatry and the Humanities*, trans. T. Gora and M. Waller, 6: 33–48.

—— (1984a) 'Julia Kristeva in Conversation with Rosalind Coward', in *Desire*, London: ICA Documents.

—— (1984b) 'My Memory's Hyperbole', in D. C. Stanton (ed.), *The Female Autograph: Theory and Practice of Autobiography from the Tenth to the Twentieth Century*, trans. A. Viscusi, Chicago, Ill.: University of Chicago Press.

—— (1984c) *Revolution in Poetic Language*, trans. M. Waller, New York, NY: Columbia University Press.

—— (1986a) *About Chinese Women*, trans. A. Barrows, New York, NY: Marion Boyars Publishers.

—— (1986b) *The Kristeva Reader*, ed. T. Moi, New York, NY: Columbia University Press.

—— (1986c) 'A New Type of Intellectual: The Dissident', in *The Kristeva Reader*, ed. T. Moi, trans. S. Hand, New York, NY: Columbia University Press.

—— (1987a) *In the Beginning Was Love: Psychoanalysis and Faith*, trans. A. Goldhammer, New York, NY: Columbia University Press.

—— (1987b) *Tales of Love*, trans. L. S. Roudiez, New York, NY: Columbia University Press.

—— (1989) *Black Sun: Depression and Melancholia*, trans. L. S. Roudiez, New York, NY: Columbia University Press.

—— (1991) *Strangers to Ourselves*, trans. L. S. Roudiez, New York, NY: Columbia University Press.

—— (1993) *Nations Without Nationalism*, trans. L. S. Roudiez, New York, NY: Columbia University Press.

—— (1994) *The Old Man and the Wolves*, trans. Barbara Bray, New York, NY: Columbia University Press.

—— (1998) *Possessions*, trans. Barbara Bray, New York, NY: Columbia University Press.

—— (2000) *Crisis of the European Subject*, trans. S. Fairfield, New York, NY: Other Press.

—— and Clément, Catherine (2001) *The Feminine and the Sacred*, trans. Jane Marie Todd, New York, NY: Columbia University Press.

Kurzweil, Edith (1995) *Freudians and Feminists*, Boulder, Col.: Westview Press.

Lacan, Jacques (1966) *Écrits*, Paris: Éditions du Seuil.

—— (1968) *Speech and Language in Psychoanalysis*, trans. A. Wilden, Baltimore, Md.: Johns Hopkins University Press.

—— (1977) *Écrits: A Selection*, trans. A. Sheridan, New York, NY: W. W. Norton.

—— (1981) *The Four Fundamental Concepts of Psycho-Analysis*, ed. J.-A. Miller, trans. A. Sheridan, New York, NY: W. W. Norton.

—— (1985a) *Feminine Sexuality: Jacques Lacan and the école freudienne*, ed. J. Mitchell and J. Rose, trans. J. Rose, New York, NY: W. W. Norton.

—— (1985b) 'The Meaning of the Phallus', in *Feminine Sexuality: Jacques Lacan and the école freudienne*, ed. J. Mitchell and J. Rose, trans. J. Rose, New York, NY: W. W. Norton.

—— (1988) *The Seminar of Jacques Lacan*, Book II, *The Ego in Freud's Theory and in the Technique of Psychoanalysis (1954–55)*, ed. J.-A. Miller, trans. S. Tomaselli, New York, NY: W. W. Norton.

Lan, David (1985) *Guns and Rain*, London: James Currey; Berkeley, Calif.: University of California Press.

Lechte, John (1990) *Julia Kristeva*, London and New York, NY: Routledge.

Leder, Drew (1990) *The Absent Body*, Chicago, Ill.: University of Chicago Press.

Leland, D. (1989) 'Lacanian Psychoanalysis and French Feminism: Toward an Adequate Political Psychology', *Hypatia* 3, 3: 81–102.

Lie, S. (1999) 'Life Makes Text from My Body: A Reading of Hélène Cixous's "La Venue à l'Écriture" ', in L. A. Jacobus and R. Barreca (eds), *Hélène Cixous: Critical Impressions*, Amsterdam: Gordon & Breach.

McAfee, Noëlle (1993) 'Abject Strangers: Toward an Ethics of Respect', in Kelly Oliver (ed.) *Ethics, Politics and Difference in Julia Kristeva's Writing*, New York, NY: Routledge.

MacGillivray, Catherine A. F. (1994) 'Introduction: The Political Is – (and the) Poetical', in Hélène Cixous, *Manna: For the Mandelstams For the Mandalas*, trans. Catherine A. F. MacGillivray, Minneapolis, Minn.: University of Minnesota Press.

Magee, Penelope Margaret (1995) 'Disputing the Sacred', in Ursula King (ed.), *Religion and Gender*, London: Blackwell.

Mâle, Émile (1949) *Religious Art: From the Twelfth to the Eighteenth Century*, London: Routledge.

Marion, Jean-Luc (1991) *God Without Being: Hors-texte*, trans. T. A. Carlson, Chicago, Ill.: University of Chicago Press.

Marks, Elaine (1979) 'Review of Hélène Cixous, *Préparatifs de noces au delà de l'abîme*', *The French Review* 53: 309–10.

Marrouchi, Mustapha (1997) 'Decolonizing the Terrain of Western Theoretical Productions', *College Literature* 24: 1–34.

Martin, Alison (1995) 'Luce Irigaray and Divine Matter', in D. Knight and J. Still (eds), *Women and Representation*, Women Teaching French Occasional Papers 3, Nottingham: WIF Publications.

Maso, Carole (1993) *Ava*, Normal, Ill.: Dalkey Archive Press.

—— (2000) *Break Every Rule: Essays on Language, Longing, and Moments of Desire*, Washington, DC: Counterpoint.

Mazzoni, Cristina (1996) *Saint Hysteria: Neurosis, Mysticism, and Gender in European Culture*. Ithaca, NY: Cornell University Press.

Merchant, Carol (1980) *The Death of Nature: Women, Ecology and the Scientific Revolution*, New York, NY: Harper & Row.

Milbank, John et al. (eds) (1999) *Radical Orthodoxy: A New Theology*, London: Routledge.

Miller, Barbara Stoller (trans.) (1995) *Yoga: Discipline of Freedom, The Yoga Sutra Attributed to Patanjali*, Berkeley, Calif.: University of California Press.

Minsky, Rosalind (1998) *Psychoanalysis and Culture*, New Brunswick, NJ: Rutgers University Press.

Mortley, Raoul (1991) *French Philosophers in Conversation*, London: Routledge.

Nabar, V. (1995) *Caste as Woman*, New Delhi: Penguin Books India.

Nair, Janaki (1994) 'On the Question of Agency in Indian Feminist Historiography', *Gender and History* 6, 1: 82–100.

Narasimhan, Sakuntala (1992) *Sati: Widow Burning in India*, New York, NY: Anchor Books.

Narayan, Uma (1997) *Dislocating Cultures: Identities, Traditions and Third-World Feminisms*, New York, NY: Routledge.

Narayanan, Vasudha (1999) 'Brimming with *Bhakti*, Embodiments of *Shakti*: Devotees, Performers, Reformers, and Other Women of Power in the

Hindu Tradition', in A. Sharma and K. Young (eds), *Feminism in World Religions*, Albany, NY: State University of New York Press.

Nerval, Gérard de (1949) *Les Chimères*, Lille: Librairie Giard; Geneva: Librairie Droz.

Neumann, Erich (1963) *The Great Mother*, trans. R. Manheim, Princeton, NJ: Bollingen.

Nevins, Albert J. (1980) *Saints for Girls: A Saint for Your Name*, Huntington, Ind.: Our Sunday Visitor Inc.

The New Catholic Encyclopedia (1967) Volume II, New York, NY: McGraw-Hill.

Newman, Barbara (1998) 'Possessed by the Spirit: Devout Women, Demoniacs, and the Apostolic Life in the Thirteenth Century', *Speculum* 73: 733–70.

Niebuhr, Reinhold (1932) *Moral Man and Immoral Society*, New York, NY: Scribner & Sons.

Nikolchina, Miglena (1991) 'Parables of Exile in Julia Kristeva', *Semiotica* 86: 314.

Nygren, Anders (1982) *Agape and Eros* (Part 1, 1932; Part 2, 1938), trans. P. S. Watson, London: SPCK.

O'Grady, Kathleen (1996) 'Guardian of Language: An Interview with Hélène Cixous', *Women's Education des femmes* 12, 4: 6–10.

—— (1998) 'Dialogue with Julia Kristeva' (section), *Parallax*, special issue: *Julia Kristeva 1966–96: Aesthetics, Politics, Ethics* (July–September) 8: 8–11.

O'Hanlon, Rosalind (1988) 'Recovering the Subject: Subaltern Studies and the History of Resistance in Colonial South Asia', *Modern Asian Studies*, 22, 1: 189–224.

Oliver, Kelly (1993) *Reading Kristeva: Unraveling the Double Bind*, Bloomington and Indianapolis, Ind.: Indiana University Press.

—— (1998) *Subjectivity without Subjects*, Lanham, Md.: Rowman & Littlefield.

Outka, Gene (1972) *Agape: An Ethical Analysis*, New Haven, Conn.: Yale University Press.

Pardes, Ilana (1992) *Countertraditions in the Bible: A Feminist Approach*, Cambridge, Mass.: Harvard University Press.

Partner, Nancy (1991) 'Reading *The Book of Margery Kempe*', *Exemplaria* 3: 29–66.

—— (1996) 'Did Mystics Have Sex?', in Jacqueline Murray and Konrad Eisenbichler (eds), *Desire and Discipline: Sex and Sexuality in the Premodern West*, Toronto: University of Toronto Press.

Patai, Raphael (1967) *The Hebrew Goddess*, Detroit, Mich.: Wayne State University Press.

Pickstock, Catherine (1998) *After Writing: On the Liturgical Consummation of Philosophy*, Oxford: Blackwell.

Pintchman, Tracy (2000) 'Is the Hindu Goddess Tradition a Good Resource for Western Feminism?', in A. Hiltebeitel and K. M. Erndl (eds), *Is the Goddess a Feminist?: The Politics of South Asian Goddesses*, Sheffield: Sheffield Academic Press.

Plumwood, Val (1993) *Feminism and the Mastery of Nature*, London and New York, NY: Routledge.

Poovey, Mary (1998) *A History of the Modern Fact: Problems of Knowledge in the Sciences of Wealth and Society*, Chicago, Ill.: University of Chicago Press.

Ragland-Sullivan, Ellie (1992) 'Lacan', in E. Wright (ed.), *Feminism and Psychoanalysis: A Critical Dictionary*, Oxford: Blackwell.

Ranger, T. O. (1967) *Revolt in Southern Rhodesia, 1896–97*, Evanston, Ill.: Northwest University Press.

Raoul, Valerie (1995) 'Is Feminist Theory Anti-Feminist? (Reprise)', in Barbara Godard (ed.), *Collaboration in the Feminine: Writings on Women and Culture from Tessera*, Toronto: Second Story Press.

Reineke, Martha (1992) 'The Mother in Mimesis: Kristeva and Gerard on Violence and the Sacred', in D. Crownfield (ed.), *Body/Text in Julia Kristeva: Religion, Women, and Psychoanalysis*, Albany, NY: State University of New York Press.

—— (1997) *Sacrificed Lives: Kristeva on Women and Violence*, Bloomington and Indianapolis, Ind.: Indiana University Press.

—— (1998) 'Mimetic Violence and Nella Larsen's *Passing*: Toward a Critical Consciousness of Racism', *Contagion: Journal of Violence, Mimesis, and Culture* 5: 74–97.

Rich, Adrienne (1979) *On Lies, Secrets and Silence: Selected Prose 1966–1978*, New York, NY: Norton.

Roberts, Julian (1995) 'Melancholy Meanings: Architecture, Postmodernity and Philosophy', in N. Wheale (ed.), *The Postmodern Arts: An Introductory Reader*, London: Routledge.

Roy, Kumkum (1995) '"Where Women Are Worshipped, there the Gods Rejoice": The Mirage of the Ancestress of the Hindu Woman', in T. Sarkar and U. Butalia (eds), *Women and Right-Wing Movements: Indian Experiences*, London: Zed Books.

Roy, Marie-Andrée (ed.) (2000) 'Luce Irigaray: le féminin et la religion', *Religiologiques* 21.

Royle, Nicholas (1995) *After Derrida*, Manchester: Manchester University Press.

Ruether, Rosemary Radford (1983) *Sexism and God-Talk: Toward a Feminist Theology*, London: SCM Press.

Said, Edward (1978) *Orientalism*, New York, NY: Vintage Books.

Samupindi, Charles (1990) *Death Throes: The Trial of Mbuya Nehanda*, Harare: Mambo Press.

Sartre, Jean-Paul (1953) *Being and Nothingness: An Essay on Phenomenological Ontology*, trans. H. Barnes, New York, NY: Washington Square Press.

Sawday, Jonathan (1998) *The Body Emblazoned: Dissection and the Human Body in Renaissance Culture*, London and New York: Routledge.

Schiesari, Juliana (1992) *The Gendering of Melancholia: Feminism, Psycho-analysis, and the Symbolics of Loss in Renaissance Literature*, Ithaca, NY: Cornell University Press.

Sellers, Susan (ed.) (1988) *Writing Differences: Readings from the Workshop of Hélène Cixous*, New York, NY: St Martin's Press.

—— (1996) *Hélène Cixous: Authorship, Autobiography and Love*, Cambridge: Polity Press.

Sered, Susan Starr (1994) *Priestess, Mother, Sacred Sister*, New York, NY: Oxford University Press.

Shapin, Steven (1996) *The Scientific Revolution*, Chicago, Ill.: University of Chicago Press.

Shiach, Morag (1991) *Hélène Cixous: A Politics of Writing*, New York, NY: Routledge.

Smith, Anna (1997) *Julia Kristeva: Readings of Exile and Estrangement*, New York, NY: Palgrave MacMillan.

Sokal, Alan and Bricmont, Jean (1997) *Impostures intellectuelles*, Paris: Odile Jacob.

Sontag, Susan (1972) *Under the Sign of Saturn*, New York, NY: Farrar, Straus & Giroux.

Speake, Jennifer (1994) *The Dent Dictionary of Symbols in Christian Art*, London: Dent.

Spivak, Gayatri C. (1999) *A Critique of Postcolonial Reason*, Cambridge, Mass.: Harvard University Press.

Starbird, Margaret (1993) *Woman with the Alabaster Jar*, San Francisco, Calif.: Bear Press.

Stavrakakis, Yannis (1999) *Lacan and the Political*, London and New York: Routledge.

Stone, Merlin (1976) *When God was a Woman*, New York, NY: Harcourt, Brace, Jovanovitch.

Suleiman, Susan R. (1991) 'Writing Past the Wall or the Passion According to H. C.', in Hélène Cixous, *'Coming to Writing' and Other Essays*, trans. S. Cornell et al., Cambridge, Mass.: Harvard University Press.

Sullivan, Lawrence (1988) *Icanchu's Drum*, New York, NY: Macmillan.

Summers-Bremner, Eluned (2000) 'Reading Irigaray, Dancing', *Hypatia* 15, 1: 90–124.

Tate, Claudia (1998) *Psychoanalysis and Black Novels*, New York, NY and Oxford: Oxford University Press.

Thapar, Romila (1966) *A History of India*, Vol. 1 of 2, Baltimore, Md.: Penguin.

—— (1989) 'Imagined Religious Communities? Ancient History and the Modern Search for Hindu Identity', *Modern Asian Studies* 23, 2: 209–31.

Thurston, Herbert and Attwater, Donald (eds) (1981) *Butler's Lives of the Saints*, London: Palm Publishers.

Trinh, T. Minh-ha (1989) *Woman, Native, Other*, Bloomington and Indianapolis, Ind.: Indiana University Press.

Upton, Lee (1993) 'Coming to God: Notes on Dickinson, Bogan, Cixous', *Denver Quarterly* 27, 2: 83–94.

Varenne, Georges (1976) *Yoga and the Hindu Tradition*, Chicago, Ill.: University of Chicago Press.

Vera, Yvonne (1993) *Nehanda*, Harare: Baobab Books.

Walsh, Lisa (1999) 'Her Mother Her Self: The Ethics of the Antigone Family Romance', *Hypatia* 14, 3: 96–125.

Ward, Graham (1996) 'Divinity and Sexuality: Luce Irigaray and Christology', *Modern Theology* 12, 2: 221–37.

Weiss, Ruth (1986) *The Women of Zimbabwe*, London: Kesho Publications.

Weissman, Hope P. (1982) 'Margery Kempe in Jerusalem: *Hysterica Compassio* in the Late Middle Ages', in Mary J. Carruthers and Elizabeth D. Kirk (eds), *Acts of Interpretation: The Text in its Contexts, 700–1600*, Norman, Okla.: Pilgrim Books.

Whicher, I. (1998) *The Integrity of the Yoga Darśana: A Reconsideration of Classical Yoga*, Albany, NY: State University of New York Press.

White, Carol Wayne (2000) 'Strategic Posit/ioning/s: Poststructuralism, Feminism, and Religion', in K. Biezeveld and A.-C. Mulder (eds), *Toward a Different Transcendence*, Berne: Peter Lang AG – European Academic Publishers.

White, David Gordon (ed.) (2000) *Tantra in Practice*, Princeton Readings in Religions, Princeton, NJ: Princeton University Press.

Whitford, Margaret (1991a) 'Irigaray's Body Symbolic', *Hypatia* 6, 3: 97–110.

—— (1991b) *Luce Irigaray: Philosophy in the Feminine*, London: Routledge.

Wilden, Anthony (1968) *Speech and Language in Psychoanalysis: Jacques Lacan*, Baltimore, Md.: Johns Hopkins University Press.

Wittig, Monique (1966) *The Opoponax*, trans. H. Weaver, New York, NY: Simon & Schuster.

—— (1975) *The Lesbian Body*, trans. D. LeVay, New York, NY: William Morrow.

—— (1985) *Les Guérillères*, trans. D. LeVay, Boston, Mass.: Beacon Press.

—— (1987) *Across the Acheron*, trans. D. LeVay and M. Crosland, London: Peter Owen.

—— (1992) *'The Straight Mind' and Other Essays*, Boston, Mass.: Beacon Press.

Wittig, Monique and Zeig, Sande (1979) *Lesbian Peoples: Material for a Dictionary*, trans. M. Wittig and S. Zeig, New York, NY: Avon Books.

Wright, Elizabeth (ed.) (1992) *Feminism and Psychoanalysis: A Critical Dictionary*, Oxford: Blackwell.

Young, Iris Marion (1990) *'Throwing Like a Girl' and Other Essays in Feminist Philosophy and Social Theory*, Bloomington, Ind.: Indiana University Press.

Žižek, Slavoj (1989) *The Sublime Object of Ideology*, London: Verso.

Index